ANTI-AGEING

Let the Silvers Sparkle

Strategies • Food • Medicine

ANTI-AGEING

Let the Silvers Sparkle

Strategies • Food • Medicine

DR. R. KUMAR
MBBS, MS Ex PGI
Eye Specialist, Health Columnist and
Medical Tourism Advisor,
Chandigarh

Foreword by

RASHPAL MALHOTRA
Director-General CRRID
Chandigarh

DEEP & DEEP PUBLICATIONS PVT. LTD.
F-159, Rajouri Garden, New Delhi-110027

ANTI-AGEING

LET THE SILVERS SPARKLE

ISBN 978-81-8450-090-5

Typeset by S.S. COMPOSERS,
3190, Mohindra Park, Shakur Basti, Delhi-110034.

Printed in India at MAYUR ENTERPRISES,
WZ Plot No. 3, Gujjar Market, Tihar Village, New Delhi-110018.

Published by DEEP & DEEP PUBLICATIONS PVT. LTD.
F-159, Rajouri Garden, New Delhi-110027.
Phones: 25435369, 25440916
E-mail: ddpbooks@yahoo.co.in • ddpubs@gmail.com
Showroom:
2/13, Ansari Road, Daryaganj, New Delhi-110002 • Telefax; 23245122

Contents

Rashpal Malhotra
Director General

Phones : (0172) 2725136, 2549450
Fax : (0172) 2725215,
Gram : CRRID
EPABX : 2724010, 2725059, 2725406
(Ext. 244, 245)
E-mail : rashpalmalhotrasancharnet.in
crridchd@sancharnet.in
sscrrid@hub.nic.in
crrid_chd@dataone.in
Website : www.crrid-chd.org

Foreword

Ageing is a natural process. The normal functioning of the organs of human body leads both to a healthy mind and healthy body. It is only when malfunctioning of any organ in human body occurs in the system; the desire for learning about Anti-Ageing device becomes a must.

Dr. Ram Kumar has done a highly commendable work in going deeper into the various aspects of ageing and identifying the remedies for Anti-Ageing process. Personally, I cannot claim any knowledge as an expert, but as a normal human being having completed 71 years of my active life, free of any incurable disease or malfunctioning of any organ of my body, perhaps gives me a legitimate claim to put forward my view prefacing this valuable contribution made by Dr. Ram Kumar in his book 'Anti-Ageing'. Though he has been a well-known Eye Specialist, yet his in-depth understanding of ageing as well as Anti-Ageing is highly commendable. He seems to have worked very hard in studying all the factors which accelerate the process of ageing. The multi-disciplinary approach which he has ably displayed through his vast knowledge, should be a source of both reference and practice that one may like to adopt to ensure the prolonging of healthy and stress-free life. The multi-disciplinary approach covering the disciplines of demography, health, education, social and psychological factors have undisputedly presented this volume for use by the students, teachers and even for awareness of laymen, the capacity in which I have put my thoughts.

Rashpal Malhotra

Chandigarh

RASHPAL MALHOTRA
Director-General, CRRID

Preface

Sagging skin, graying hair, loss of muscle and increasing fat, especially around the waist, faulty memory, and slower thinking and reactions, decreased libido—these are just a few of the obvious manifestations of ageing. While it is easy to recognize an ageing person with the above manifestations, it is not be so easy to define what ageing is.

The dramatic rise in life expectancy that the world has experienced throughout the twentieth century has made the quest for a prolonged and healthy lifespan, an important topic. As a result, chronic degenerative diseases—that very few people lived long enough to experience in the past—have replaced infectious diseases as the primary cause of death. The most visible aspect of this change is the success of the Anti-Ageing industry that caters to the needs of the elderly. The Anti-Ageing market is replete with products: yoghurt cures, enema regimens, cell injections, magnetic devices, skin creams, herbal elixirs, glandular extracts, hormonal therapies, vitamin supplements, fad diets and exercise programmes.

Gerontologists (the scientists who study ageing) define ageing as a continuous, universal, progressive, intrinsic, and deleterious (CUPID) process that decreases a organism's ability to maintain homeostasis in the face of environmental stressors and therefore increases the organism's likelihood of dying early. Approach to anti-ageing is based on the early detection, prevention, and reversal of ageing-related diseases. All diseases fall into four categories; the first three—inherited genetic disease, infectious disease, and trauma—account for only 10% of the cost for treating all diseases in America. Ninety percent of all health care cost occurs on extraordinary care in the last two to three years of life. If we really want to make an impact on health care in the world, we must focus on the prevention/reversal of diseases of ageing. If we can prevent ageing, we can eliminate more than 50% of all diseases overnight. The science of anti-ageing medicine is truly multi-disciplinary. Not only represented by advances in the fields of biochemistry, biology, and physiology, the field is enhanced by contributions from mind/body medicine, sports medicine, molecular genetics, and emerging medical technologies.

Sensing the large differentials in the demography in various communities and nations and also the individuals belonging to different strata, "anti-ageing industry" has developed over recent years to exploit the human desire for relief from the unpleasant realities of human ageing. The last decade has seen a massive growth of so-called anti-ageing medicine. This might seem surprising, since there are currently no verified treatments for human ageing, yet duping the elderly by selling them bogus treatments for ageing is becoming a practice. Today, it is big business: according to the American Academy of Anti-Ageing Medicine (AAAAM OR A4M) the US anti-ageing industry alone rakes in $ 56 billion annually.

To combat ageing we must find positive models and style ourselves to new mental images of health, fitness, and appearance. Discover how thousands of people combat ageing, getting fitter, leaner, and stronger than they ever thought possible. Antioxidants, hormones and other nutritional supplements are used to modulate ageing. Although immortality and eternal youth may never be possible, achieving a healthy old age without major diseases is now a possibility. What may bring a feeling of premature ageing are:

1. Overwhelmed by stress.
2. Drinking too much alcohol.
3. Moving too little.
4. Eating too much saturated fat: meats, poultry, milk and butter and resultant obesity.
5. Smoking cigarettes.
6. Breathing polluted air.

7. Getting too much sun.
8. Getting too little sleep: obesity, diabetes, blood pressure, memory problems.
9. Being overweight: tendency to add kilos is on the rise.
10. Eating too much sugar: switch to fruits and vegetables.

Research continues to show that eating certain foods can help to keep us young by preventing degenerative changes in our bodies and can even extend our life span itself. Research in nutrition medicine over the past few decades increasingly has born out the truth "You age how you eat." The easiest move you can make is to add more fruits, vegetables, and whole grains to your daily food. Most have no fat, cholesterol, or sodium—and they're low in calories. What you get is lots of fiber, calcium, iron, magnesium, and vitamins, which all play a part in keeping you functioning at your best. Minerals from calcium-rich dairy foods and greens can strengthen your bones. Fiber from whole grains helps to keep bowel movements regular.

While low-calorie diets have been linked to a longer lifespan in both animals and humans, the reason for the association has been unclear. The researchers have evidence from studies in mice that cutting calories shields brain cells from the decline that comes with ageing. In experiments with mice, scientists used a gene chip, a new type of gene-scanning technology, to rapidly determine the activity of more than 6,000 genes in the animals' brain tissue. The researchers found that ageing boosted the activity of some genes and decreased it in others. As the mice aged, activity increased in genes responsible for inflammation and the stress response—two key factors related to cell damage. In addition, activity declined in genes involved in repairing cell damage. Inflammation in the brain is believed to be related to certain diseases such as Alzheimer's. A study in Parkinson's patients has suggested that high calorie intake contributes to the risk for the disease. "These findings," he said, "provide a link at the molecular level."

It is well known that many hormones levels go down

with age. The most well known of these is human growth hormone (HGH). It has been used as an anti-ageing treatment for a long time and some evidence suggests it has beneficial effects in elderly people. HGH might increase muscle mass, strengthen the immune system, increase libido, etc. A Surgeon of Indian-origin 55, claimed in London recently that he had discovered the secret of eternal youth to renew the human body. He asserted that he and his wife 48, have been revitalized by injections of human growth hormone (HGH) after a long treatment of one and a half years. According to him it made their skins shine and improved libido. He estimates that the treatment could cost about £12000 each for his patients. This treatment is popular in United States, though other parts of the globe are still picking up. Others warn that HGH may make you feel great but may diminish your lifespan, while shrinking your wallet.

Be cautious on accepting the treatment for ageing and while practicing anti-ageing medicine. The author has presented the aspects of anti-ageing in the following chapters: 1. Humanity is graying; let the silvers sparkle, 2. Strategies of anti-ageing; How not to become old?, 3. Advances in anti-ageing medicine: can you put the clock back?, 4. Anti-ageing foods; can you stay youthful for ever?, 5. Caloric restriction is the key; can it lead to life extension?, 6. Human Growth hormone; can it defy ageing?, 7. Mid-life crisis; Good understanding can prevent ill-health in old age, 8. Anti-ageing in women: can Gender make a difference?, 9. Ageing and skin care; is it just skin deep approach?, 10. Scourge of obesity; the older and ugly look is not the whole story, 11. Memory loss and ageing; use it or lose it approach works, 12. Futuristic technologies; years into the life or life into the years?, 13. Critiques of anti-ageing medicine; is it a myth or fact?, 14. American Academy of Anti-Ageing (AAAA) Medicine; Umbrella to many organizations in USA.

R. KUMAR

1

Humanity is Graying

Let the Silvers Sparkle

The population of India is graying in larger numbers than ever before. In fact, the proportion of the silvers is growing fast all over the world. Whereas in United States approximately one person in 8 is in the silver age group (33.4 million); in India and other Asian countries, 5 percent of the total population is aged, between 65 and 70 years. In the near future, virtually all nations will face population ageing. This situation, no doubt, raises challenges in planning and development of anti-ageing strategies.

WHAT IS AGEING?

Ageing is known as 'senescence', i.e. the state of ageing. The word itself comes from the Latin word 'senex', meaning "old man" or "old age." Senescence is the process of cellular ageing. It is the process of growing older and showing a progressive deterioration of bodily functions over a period of time. Premature ageing of your brain, circulation, heart, joints, skin, digestive tract and immune system can begin at any time of life. Various factors may cause your body to deteriorate faster including injuries, allergies, toxins, heavy metals, smoking, poor nutrition, stress and inactivity. Bad lifestyle and nutritional, chemical and hormonal imbalances (e.g. low hormone levels, impaired functioning of hormone receptors and auto-immune reactions) are the top reasons for physical and mental degeneration, leading to rapid ageing.

Genetic factors account for about 30 percent of the ageing process. Lifestyle factors like, diet, physical exercise, smoking, and alcohol consumption play a significant role for the initiation of the ageing process. Ageing can be a pain because it slows you down, makes you less resistant to illness and saps your energy. Although no one lives forever, we can now slow the ageing process and thus enjoy more of life—if we know how to take care of ourselves. But defining ageing as a disease and then trying to cure it is unscientific. Ageing just happens, accept it gracefully, but don't allow yourself to become a victim of pre-mature ageing by indulging yourself in faulty lifestyle. Take medical help wherever required.

No doubt the ageing persons tend to become frail; a condition that refers to diminished ability to withstand stresses and inability to undertake essential activities. Loss of muscle forms the main factor in causing fraility. Incorporation of amino acids can lead to rejuvenation. The stimulation of stem cells can also lead to repair of muscles. Use of testosterone and growth hormone can activate insulin growth factor and that in turn can stimulate muscle growth. Resistence exercise and supplemental vitamin D along with attention to associated diseases like diabetes can go a long way to prevent fraility. Let us distinguish ageing from other deleterious processes that can decrease one's ability to fight diseases. If you are infected with HIV, aspects of your functioning will decline, particularly your immune system function, but this is not ageing. Ageing is a progressive process. It gets worse with time. The effects of the ageing process accumulate with time. Ageing is an intrinsic process. If one were kept in an ideal environment, fed an ideal diet, exercised the right amount, and were not subjected to stressors that one could not handle, one might live longer than average. But many of the manifestations of ageing would still set in. Ageing is not benign and is not desirable.

Anti-ageing medicine physicians are often accused of fueling the fire of the cult of youth and therefore of being 'ageist.' Most organisms don't start to age until sometime just after they acquire the ability to reproduce. From conception to reproductive maturity, the organism is developing, not ageing.

Winter brings more problems for the aged

Shorter days, lack of sunshine and chilly weather conditions bring a perception of decreased well-being. This also entails reduced exercises and increased eating; adding to the health problems. Causes of winter ill-health include: immobility, respiratory infections, influenza, depression, falls and related injuries, isolation, bereavement, hypothermia, poor nutrition, etc. There could be a number of reasons for depression. Seasonal affective disorder involves lethargy, desire to hibernate, sleep till the sun shines again, eating more and feeling in low mood.

Hypothermia or low body temperature can be a silent killer in old age. The condition may develop on exposure to even mild cold. Generally the victims belong to deprived sections of society. Malnourished, Dehydration, alcohol and hypnotics predispose to the problem. The symptoms of hypothermia include shivering, cold skin, pale skin, apathy, swollen face, stiff muscles, poor co-ordination, confusion, slow and shallow breathing, drowsiness, etc. Such persons need extra care from the family and the doctor.

Bleeding from the stomach or oesophagus is more common in old age and it may be serious. A vigil on this account is required.

Theories of ageing

- The Autoimmune Theory,
- The Caloric Restriction Theory,
- The Cross-Linking Theory,
- The Death Hormone Theory (DECO),
- The DNA and Genetic Theories,
- The Errors and Repairs Theory,
- The Hayflick Limit Theory,

- The Membrane Theory of Ageing,
- The Mitochondrial Decline Theory,
- The Neuroendocrine Theory,
- The Redundant DNA Theory,
- The Telomerase Theory of Ageing,
- The Thymic-Stimulating Theory,
- The Acidification Theory of Ageing, and
- The "Wear and Tear" Theory.

Let us study a few of them

Free radical theory

Free radical theory tells us that premature ageing is merely the accumulation of bodily changes caused by the presence of oxygen-based scavengers in your body. Free radicals are groups of unstable and reactive atoms. In excess they attack your body's cells, stealing electrons from your body's delicate membranes and genetic structure, causing cell damage and malfunction. They come from your food, water, air, smoking, chemical exposure and even exercise. They cannot be avoided, so it is important to provide nutrients to combat them. You can do this by using antioxidants. An antioxidant is a substance that inhibits the above free radical damage. As free radicals continue to scavenge for electrons from your body, antioxidants intercept by offering their own electrons to the free radicals in order to stop them scavenging yours. This converts the free radicals into simple harmless molecules. Antioxidants protect your cells from the oxidative damage that leads to premature ageing and disease.

The DNA and Genetic Theories

Our DNA is the blue-print of individual life obtained from our parents. It means we are born with a unique code and a predetermined tendency to certain types of physical and mental functioning that regulate the rate at which we age. But this type of genetic clock can be greatly influenced with regard to its rate of timing. For example, DNA is easily oxidized and this damage can be accumulated from diet, lifestyle, toxins, pollution, radiation and other outside influences. Thus, we each have the ability to accelerate DNA damage or slow it down. Telomeres can be repaired by the introduction of the relevant hormone. In other words, telomeres and their subsequent processes affect each other. It may be possible, to precisely introduce the necessary hormone and aid genetic repair, as well as the hormonal balance, etc. we know that free radicals damage DNA (Free Radical Theory of Ageing) and so does glycosylation (Cross-Linking Theory of Ageing).

Immunity theory

Generally you live about as long as your immune system allows you to. When you can't defend yourself any longer, you die. Either pathogenic organisms will vanquish you or cancer will invade and have a ball inside your tissues. You won't be able to resist. Full-blown AIDS is a frightening reminder of what it would be like when your immune system crashes. AIDS patients seem to age very rapidly. Allergies are also caused by a dysfunctional immune system. They are put on detoxes, better diets, chemically and electrically safer environments, nutritional supplements, anti-Candida plans, and, last but not least, a psychological clean up.

The brain and ageing

No organ is more critical than our brain, which means the wear and tear of ageing will show up first in thought function; we begin to get slower in our movement and manners, easily muddled, more forgetful and eventually a little silly. The human brain has been described as the universe, meaning that all our thoughts, actions, perceptions, emotions, desires and dreams are contained in an organ weighing no more than 50 ounces, lodged inside the skull! There are approximately 100 billion brain cells (neurones), each making between 5,000 and 50,000 hard-wired connections. That means around 4 quadrillion connections! In fact our brain, which is only 2% of body weight, requires over 25% of our nutritional energy output. That makes the brain very vulnerable to damage and degeneration, from lack of oxygen, poor nutrition, toxic overload and chemical deposits, including drugs.

Steady decline in many cognitive processes are seen

across the lifespan, starting in one's thirties. Research has focused in particular on memory and ageing, and has found decline in many types of memory with ageing, but not in semantic memory or general knowledge such vocabulary definitions, which typically increases or remains steady. Given the physical and cognitive declines seen in ageing, a surprising finding is that emotional experience improves with age. Older adults are better at regulating their emotions and experience negative effects less frequently than younger adults and show a positivity effect in their attention and memory.

Genes and ageing

The 'non-genetic principle' asserts that there is neither a genetic cause for, nor a programme that controls the ageing process. Those genes that do influence ageing and longevity have evolved in accordance with the evolutionary history of a species, but they do not necessarily control the further progression of the organism beyond reproduction. There are positive correlations between lifespan and the ability to repair DNA, detoxify reactive oxygen molecules, respond to and counteract stress, and replace worn-out cells. We do not imply that genes have no influence on survival, longevity and ageing. These genes are involved in a wide range of biochemical pathways and agents, such as insulin metabolism, kinases and kinase receptors, transcription factors, DNA helicases, telomerase, membrane glucosidases, GTP-binding protein-coupled receptors, cholesterol metabolism, heat-shock protein genes, cell-cycle arrest pathways and others. These principles and the underlying knowledge will soon allow researchers to develop reasonable therapies that intervene in the ageing process and treat various age-related diseases and frailties.

Signs and Symptoms of ageing

Premature ageing occurs initially without any actual symptomatic signs. Over time, without much warning you may begin to notice symptoms. More often than not it takes a serious condition to develop, such as a heart attack or stroke, before you realise what is happening and what your body has been trying to tell you all these years. Generally your body sends you some kind of message to let you know it is malfunctioning. These messages can take the form of pain, inflammation, joint instability, insufficient blood supply, high blood pressure, muscle weakness, etc. More serious signs can include diseases such as diabetes, osteoporosis, thyroid malfunction, sexual hormone deficiency, other glandular deterioration, decreased hormone levels, or brain atrophy (such as in Alzheimer's disease). Aside from disease, general signs can also include deterioration in previously acceptable areas, such as:

- Poor balance,
- Reduced skin elasticity,
- Increased focal length,
- Reduced muscle mass,
- Slower reaction time,
- Loose joints,
- Joint pain, swelling or stiffness, and
- Age spots.

The signs and diseases mentioned here are all preventable and/or treatable and are by no means a 'normal' part of growing old. Premature ageing is not a requirement of life. Millions of prescriptive medicines are provided each year to patients suffering from age-related diseases and symptoms. These medications will sometimes be successful in suppressing your symptoms, but hardly ever rectify your underlying condition. It is a sad fact that thousands of people die each year from using over-the-counter drugs in an attempt to mask some of these symptoms. In addition, more than 100,000 people die from drugs 'correctly' prescribed by their doctor. Virtually all these deaths are preventable. The reality is that most prescriptive medicines are no more than 'band aids' and only delay an inevitable and serious deterioration in your quality of life. There are really no prescriptive medicines that can prevent premature ageing.

Enemies of Youthhood

1. Sugar

One of the reasons inflammation occurs is from a rapid rise in blood sugar, which causes biochemical changes in the cell. When blood sugar goes up rapidly, sugar can attach itself to collagen in a process called "glycosylation," or the Browning Reaction that increases inflexibility and inflammation. C-reactive problem (CRP) is not found in foods. However, its levels in the body are strongly influenced by diet. The body makes CRP from interleukin-6 (IL-6), a powerful inflammatory chemical. IL-6 is a key cell communication molecule, and it tells the body's immune system to go into asperity, releasing CRP and many other inflammation-causing substances.

2. Carbohydrates

Staying away from sugar and high-glycemic (simple) carbohydrates, which the body rapidly converts to sugar, is one of the best ways to decrease inflammation. C-reactive protein (CRP) is a key factor of inflammation. In a major study, published in the New England Journal of Medicine, people with elevated CRP levels were four and one-half times more likely to have a heart attack. Not only is elevated CRP more accurate than cholesterol in predicting heart attack risk, but high CRP levels have turned up in people with diabetes and pre-diabetes and in people who are overweight. A recent study by Simin Liu, M.D., Ph.D., of the Harvard Medical School found that women who ate large amounts of high-glycemic (or diabetes promoting) carbohydrates, including potatoes, breakfast cereals, white bread, muffins, and white rice, had very high CRP levels. Women who ate a lot of these foods and were also overweight had the highest and most dangerous CRP levels.

3. Saturated Fats

These are found primarily in animal products, including dairy items, such as whole milk, cream, ghee and cheese, and fatty meats like beef, lamb, pork, and ham. The fat marbling you can see in beef and pork is composed of saturated fat. Some vegetable products including coconut oil, palm kernel oil, and vegetable shortening—are also high in saturates. The liver uses saturated fats to manufacture cholesterol. Therefore, excessive dietary intake of saturated fats can significantly raise the blood cholesterol level, especially the level of low-density lipoproteins (LDLs), or "bad cholesterol." Guidelines issued by the National Cholesterol Education Program (NCEP), and widely supported by most experts, recommend that the daily intake of saturated fats be kept below 10 percent of total caloric intake. However, for people who have severe problems with high blood cholesterol, even that level may be too high.

4. *Excess Sun Exposure*

Exposure of up to 20 minutes in the sun is imperative for Vitamin D activation. It is the sun that is so important in cases of Seasonal Affective Disorder. But, excess sun exposure without a sunscreen of at least SPF of 15 can damage the skin by starting the inflammation process. Scientists agree that one of the most significant factors contributing to ageing is chronic inflammation. This inflammation process is due to an excess of free radicals which produce harmful oxidation or "oxidative stress" that can damage cell membranes and cell contents. These free radicals cause inflammation.

5. *Hypertension*

The main factor in most cases of high blood pressure is an increase in resistance to blood flow. This can occur if the diameter of your arterioles becomes smaller. Your heart has to work harder to pump the same amount of blood, and the pressure at which the blood is pumped increases. Sympathetic tone is constantly too high, arteries are constantly constricted, and blood pressure remains elevated to levels that can eventually damage the heart and arteries, kidneys, and other organs. Because the sympathetic nervous system deals with fear and uses adrenalin and nonadrenalin as its chemical messengers, it is not surprising that anxiety is a factor in essential hypertension.

6. Alcohol

Alcohol stimulates the inflammatory process within the body. Drink only in moderation, if you must—better avoid.

7. Sedentary Lifestyle

To build and maintain muscle strength and bone mass, start (or continue) a regular program of weight-bearing exercises, such as walking or weight training. A cardiovascular workout is imperative in order to maintain weight and oxygenation of red blood cells. Maintain a healthy weight for your age and sex.

8. Smoking

If you smoke, stop. Nothing you can take as a supplement can counter-act the negative effects of smoking on your health and longevity. Stopping the habit can! Tobacco, in the form of cigarettes, is the most addictive drug in the world. Nicotine is one of the strongest stimulants known, and smoking is one of the most efficient drug-delivery systems. Smoking actually puts drugs into the brain more directly than intravenous injection. It is true that one of the "benefits" of smoking is the brief relief of internal tension; unfortunately, within 20 minutes the tension is back stronger than before.

9. Excessive Stress

Stress can kill you. It is the underlying factor which can undermine any one suffering from an illness, fear, or just plain insecurity. The mind and body altercation brought on by our own self-affliction. Anxiety is a vague, uncomfortable feeling of fear, dread or danger from an unknown source. For some it may be a one time episode. Others become constantly anxious about everything.

How to manage stress?:

- Simplify your life. Rather than looking for ways to squeeze more activities or chores into the day, find a way to leave some things out. Ask yourself what really needs to be done, what can wait—and what can be dropped entirely. Learn to say no.

- Manage your time wisely. Update your to-do list every day—both at work and at home. Delegate what you can, and break large projects into manageable chunks. Tackle one task at a time.
- Be prepared. Anticipate challenges. Whether it's preparing for a project at work, planning a family gathering or handling a sick child, being prepared can help you face stressful situations with confidence. Find a way to approach each task with humor.
- Exercise regularly. Consider exercise a break from the tension of daily life. Exercise can help keep depression and anxiety at bay, too.
- Eat smart. A diet rich in fruits, vegetables and whole grains can give you more energy—plus the fuel you need to keep stress under control. Consider whether you're truly hungry before you have a snack. Don't be fooled by the jolt you may get from caffeine or sugar. It'll wear off quickly.
- Adjust your attitude. This will be tough. But we can make it work. Putting a positive spin on negative thoughts can help you work through stressful situations.
- Take a break. If you begin to feel overwhelmed, take some time to clear your mind. A few slow stretches or a quick stroll may renew your energy for the task at hand. Or take a mental vacation.
- Relax. Set aside time for yourself every day, even if it's only a few minutes. When you feel your muscles begin to tense, breathe deeply. Inhale to the count of six, pause for a second and then slowly exhale.
- Laugh. Humor is a great way to relieve stress. Laughter releases endorphins—natural substances that help you feel better and maintain a positive attitude.
- Let go. Take responsibility for your tasks, but don't worry about things you can't control.

10. High Cholesterol

Too much cholesterol in the blood is what creates a problem. A risk factor for both heart attack and stroke, high blood cholesterol increases the chance of plaque or blockages developing in arteries. Lowering blood cholesterol can slow or stop the buildup of plaque. While your risk of cardiovascular disease depends on many factors, from genetics to lifestyle habits, keeping your blood cholesterol levels within ideal ranges can greatly lower your risk.

What the World Health Organization (WHO) says?

Ageing affects every aspect of the body and mind, from your organs and bones to your muscles and joints. But that doesn't mean your physical/mental health has to nosedive as you age. Keeping a positive attitude, cheerful mood, taking responsibility, involvement in decision-making and participation in actual work of household or society and being inquisitive about something new and happening around, will keep you away from the feeling of old age. Keep a record of your appointments and carry them out diligently and responsibly. Remain interested in yourself and others and may be in the world as a whole. On the other hand, do not be a glutton, do not be greedy. This will be the secret of your good mood, independence, confidence, good health and longevity. An active lifestyle can help you maintain strength, flexibility, endurance and balance. Strength training is especially important for maintaining bone density peaks that declines sharply with age. The exercise boosts metabolism so you burn more calories at rest. That's good news for avoiding the age-related weight creep. The effects of extra abdominal girth show up not only in the mirror but also in the form of increased risk of heart disease, diabetes, blood pressure, and many other illnesses. Filling up the body with junk foods or "empty calories" like refined carbohydrates taxes your body's systems and saps your energy reserves. Eating plenty of whole grains, lean proteins, and fresh fruits and vegetables will help shore up your health. Don't forget to safeguard your health by getting an annual health examination. Your check-up should include a full blood workup to measure total cholesterol, levels of good and bad cholesterol, and triglycerides. Depending on your age, a pap smear, mammogram, bone-density examination or thyroid test may also be warranted. Blood Tests.

When it comes to assessing hormone status, the use of standard reference ranges has failed ageing people because reference ranges are adjusted to reflect a person's age. Since it is normal for an ageing person to have imbalances of critical hormones, standard laboratory reference ranges are not flagging dangerously high levels of estrogen and insulin or deficient levels of testosterone, thyroid, and DHEA.

The recommended "Male Panel" consists of a complete blood count (CBC)/chemistry test, homocysteine, free testosterone, estradiol, prostate-specific antigen (PSA), and DHEA.

The recommended "Female Panel" consists of the complete CBC/chemistry test, estradiol, progesterone, free testosterone, DHEA, and homocysteine.

In addition to these special male and female panels, the following tests are especially important for men and women over 40: Fasting Insulin, Ferritin, Cortisol, Fibrinogen, Thyroid Stimulating Hormone (TSH), and Free triiodothyroxine (T3). If a serious abnormality is detected—such as elevated homocysteine, hormone imbalance, high PSA—testing should be repeated more often to determine the benefits of whatever therapy you are using to correct the potentially life-shortening abnormality.

WHO has advised the following to combat/reverse the problems associated with ageing:

1. Address factors that contribute to the onset of disease and disabilities like poverty, low literacy levels and lack of education.
2. Control tobacco use and alcohol abuse throughout the life.
3. Ensure appropriate nutrition and healthy eating starting at an early age.
4. Promote physical activity at all ages.
5. Create ageing friendly environments by making walking safe.

6. Increase affordable access to healthcare and devices like eyeglasses or walkers.
7. Promote mental health.
8. Reduce avoidable hearing impairment and blindness.
9. Provide a continuum of care and support of care-givers.

The rules of anti-ageing medicine are:

A. Early Detection

Early detection offers opportunities to prevent or effectively intervene in disease:

- screening whole body computed tomography (CT) scans; and
- metabolic profiles and cancer antigens (blood testing).

B. Stay Slim

- Obesity is the second leading cause of preventable deaths:
  - o Annually:
    - > Causes at least 300,000 excess deaths in the US.
    - > Costs the country more than $ 100 billion.
  - o Medical risks associated with obesity:
    - > Type 2 diabetes.
    - > Gout.
    - > Hypertension.
    - > Osteoarthritis.
    - > Cardiovascular disease.
    - > Sleep apnea.
    - > High cholesterol.
    - > Cancers.
    - > Gallbladder disease.
    - > Impaired respiratory function.
    - > In women—increased incidence of varicose veins, asthma, and hemorrhoids.

C. Avoid Trauma

- Trauma kills more people between the ages of and 44 than any other disease or illness:
  - o Nearly 100,000 people of all ages in the United States die from trauma each year, roughly half of them in automobile crashes.
  - o According to the National Center for Heath Statistics, trauma (unintentional injuries + homicides) causes 62% of all deaths in ages 15 to 24.
- Trauma can strike at any time of the day. Each year in the US:
  - o 8 to 9 million individuals suffer disabling injuries.
  - o more than 3 million people suffer permanent disabilities.

D. Don't Smoke

- Tobacco use, particularly cigarette smoking, is the single most preventable cause of death.
- Cigarette smoking is ...
  - o The most significant cause of lung cancer and the leading cause of lung cancer death in both men and women.
  - o Responsible for most cancers of the larynx, oral cavity, and esophagus.
  - o Highly associated with the development of, and deaths from, bladder, kidney, pancreatic, and cervical cancers.
- Environmental tobacco smoke ...
  - o Is responsible for lung cancers in several thousand nonsmokers each year [US Environmental Protection Agency].
  - o Contributes to coronary heart disease [California Environmental Protection Agency].

E. Regular Exercise: Wide-Ranging Benefits

- Reduces the risk of heart disease by improving blood circulation throughout the body.
- Keeps weight under control.
- Improves blood cholesterol levels.
- Prevents and manages high blood pressure.
- Prevents bone loss.
- Boosts energy level.
- Helps manage stress.
- Releases tension.
- Improves the ability to fall asleep quickly and sleep well.
- Improves self-image.
- Counters anxiety and depression and increases enthusiasm and optimism.
- Increases muscle strength.
- Provides a way to share an activity with family and friends.
- In older people, helps delay or prevent chronic illnesses and diseases associated with ageing and maintains quality of life and independence longer.

F. Be Social

- 38% less risk of dementia in the population of study group with highest leisure/social activity.
- More than physical activity, social interaction leads to more satisfaction with life: Any pursuit that brought people together proved beneficial for promoting positive self-image and personal fulfillment.

G. Active Sex Life

Men who had sex 3 or more times a week looked an average of 12 years younger than they actually were: Having sex helps the body produce growth hormones that produce lean muscle tissue and decrease body fat, which can make you look younger. Age is no barrier to having an active sex life.

H. Mental Stimulation

The brain must be exercised in order to stay in peak form. Challenge yourself with activities such as hobbies, adult education, and volunteering.

I. Stress Reduction Tips

- Reduce responsibilities.
- Reduce expectations.
- Meditate.
- Visualize.
- Take one thing at a time.
- Exercise.
- Hobbies.
- Healthy lifestyle.
- Share your feelings.
- Avoid arguments ... Be flexible!
- Go easy with giving and receiving criticism.

J. Restful Sleep

- Sleep is Necessary for survival, Necessary for proper nervous systems function. Deep sleep Coincides with the release of growth hormone in children and young adults.

K. Good Dietary Choices

A notably low incidence of chronic diseases and high life-expectancy rates is present in populations living along the Mediterranean Sea: diet features grains, fruits, vegetables, legumes, nuts, good fats—olive oil and omega-3 fatty acids (fish). Okinawan Diet provides world's longest life expectancy and the world's longest health expectancy: low caloric intake, high vegetables/fruits consumption, higher intake of good fats—omega-3s, monounsaturated fat, high fiber in diet, high flavonoid intake.

Some people say: Dark beer contains large amounts of disease-fighting antioxidants. Beer prevents the oxidation of low-density lipoprotein (LDL) and very-low-density lipoprotein (VLDL). Antioxidants (Vitamin A, C, E, and selenium) protect cells by neutralizing free radicals and beneficially altering the risk of disease.

L. Maintain Immunity

Infectious diseases are responsible for 1/4 to 1/3 of the 54 million deaths globally each year. Twenty well-known diseases—including tuberculosis, malaria, and cholera—have re-emerged. At least 30 previously unknown disease agents have been identified—including HIV, ebola, and hepatitis C—and there is no known cure for these.

M. Enhance Water intake

Replenish lost fluids with an intake of 8 to 12 8-ounce glasses of water every day. We drink water from municipal water supplies containing potentially dangerous levels of chloro- and fluoro-chemicals, lead, fecal bacteria, as well as pesticides and other impurities associated with cancer and metabolic dysfunction. Sterile water is best.

What you can do?

To begin the process of treatment your doctor needs to determine your health status. He/she may carry out tests for antioxidant status, digestive analysis, immune system function, hormone status and circulatory condition. Your lifestyle will also be discussed for any contributory factors that may require attention. An electrocardiogram (testing heart function), electroencephalogram (testing the brain) or electroretinography (testing vision) may be employed. X-rays and ultrasound may also be used. Prevention, or at least early diagnosis and treatment of disease, is the key to successful health. However, general practitioners are 'interventionists' not 'protectionists', i.e. they are taught how to intervene with disease and stop the furthering of symptoms, but not in how to prevent the body from reaching that state in the first place.

Another point to grasp is that your brain thrives on activity! It is a use it or lose it thing. This brings us to the point that smiles and laughter produce endorphins which help raise our mood. Smile at yourself in front of a mirror! It's amazing how gratifying and cheering the sight of yourself grinning with delight can be. Try on all kinds of happy facial expressions, until one makes you smile for real. Daily exercise is also important. It stimulates and tones up both body and mind. Exercise releases endorphins, increases circulation and therefore oxygen supply to the brain. Endorphins are natural fell-good substances in our bodies. Walking is very good and non-stressful. Dancing is even better, since it has the added joy element, which reminds us we are young at heart and that life after all is great! Balancing your hormones can return brain function to more youthful levels.

Foods to Feed Your Brain

Oily fish, flax seeds (linseeds) are rich in Omega 3 fats which nourish nerve fibres. Eat oily fish at least twice weekly. Linseeds can be sprinkled over cereals, into desserts or blended with fresh juices. Eat plenty of fresh fruits and vegetables which are high in anti-oxidants that protect the brain from degeneration.

Dark blue foods, such as blackberries, blueberries and bilberries, are rich in particularly powerful antioxidants called anthocyanins. Eating half a cup of fresh blueberries daily helps to reverse brain ageing thanks to their high anti-oxidant activity. Green tea is also high in anti-oxidants but black tea also has plenty of catechins, which work as antioxidants. Recent studies have shown it has anti-cancer properties, too.

Combating Brain fatigue

Some experts advise a short-term (10-day) diet consisting only of fruit, vegetables, fish, herb teas and spring water, but avoid completely grains and flour (bread, cakes, biscuits, pastry, pasta, etc.), dairy produce (milk, cheese, cream, butter, yoghourt), stimulant drinks (no tea, coffee or alcohol and absolutely no manufactured foods of any kind, no packets, tins or jars of anything). No sugar is allowed. You can work the rest out be imagining what a cavemen would have eaten and sticking only to that.

In addition, a chemical-free environment is desirable. This is impossible to achieve fully but you must make sure you are not exposed to house gas, petrol fumes, pesticides, strong cleaning agents, paints, cosmetics and all other artificial chemicals in the home and at work. Try to avoid as many drugs and medicines as possible. You will need to talk this over with your doctor but it is important to realize that much of the pollution we face is medicinal in nature, from pills and potions, to antiseptics, creams, patch and inhalers.

Hormonal and other approaches to Anti-Ageing?

Some approaches include supplementation with hormones, including the growth hormone, dehydroepiandrosterone (DHEA), melatonin and oestrogen, and nutritional supplements that contain synthetic and natural antioxidants in purified form or in plant extracts. Although some of these therapies have demonstrated various clinical benefits in the treatment of the elderly, none really modulate the ageing process itself. Paradoxically, studies performed on nematodes, insects and rodents have shown that lifespan extension is almost always associated with a reduction in the levels and activities of several hormones and hormone signalling pathways, including insulin, growth hormone and sex steroids. Increasing the levels of various hormones through supplementation may therefore actually shorten lifespan. Similarly, therapies that use high doses of vitamins and antioxidants due to their supposed Anti-Ageing and life-prolonging effects are backed by very little scientific evidence.

Cosmetic treatments of ageing are at best only superficial and temporary, and cosmetics are not legally allowed to affect or modulate underlying cellular and biochemical processes.

War on Anti-Ageing Medicine?

Anti-ageing medicine has emerged in recent times as a promising approach to increased longevity with improved quality of life. Anti-ageing physicians believe that most illnesses associated with ageing can be prevented, or at least slowed, through optimal cellular health. Their techniques are nutrition, physical fitness and a range of complementary therapies. They frequently prescribe nutritional supplements, including vitamins, minerals, botanical medicines and natural hormones.

However, the history of anti-ageing research is replete

with fraud, pseudoscience, quackery and charlatanism, which together have given it a bad name. Another, more rational, approach involves targeting specific age-related diseases. Although this is usually effective in curing or halting a specific disease, it does not address ageing itself. Cancer therapy, for instance, will ideally eliminate cancerous cells and restore the affected organ or tissue to its original disease-free state. Nevertheless, although it reduces the risk of dying from cancer, it does not address other age-related diseases and disorders such as Parkinson's or Alzheimer's diseases, dementia, progressive organ failure or cardiovascular diseases. It also means that a 'cure for ageing' will most likely not succeed.

Some gerontologists have launched a war on anti-ageing medicine since they regard it as the pseudoscience of practitioners that purvey hormone injections, special mineral waters and other services and products purported to combat the effects of ageing. One of their prime targets is the American Academy of Anti-Ageing Medicine (A4M), which board-certifies practitioners and claims 11,000 members in 65 nations. Those who would study ageing in order to retard or halt the process have been considered on the fringe of biomedical research, looking for the fountain of youth . . . a marginal area . . . with so little backing from the scientific community.

2

Strategies of Anti-Ageing Medicine

How not to become Old?

Some of the strategies given below help to live longer and feel and look younger. The two things are outstanding: maintenance of physical activity throughout life, and maintenance of social and intellectual connections.

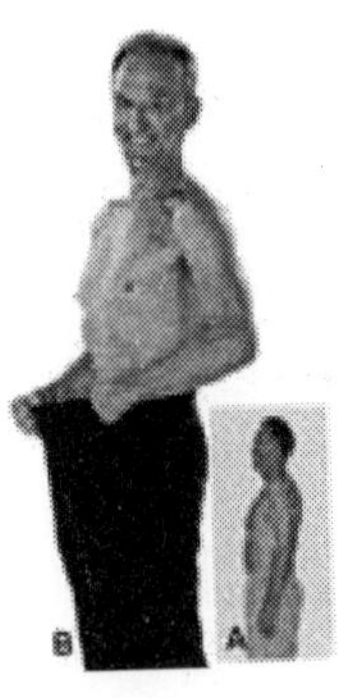

Strategy 1: Exercise regularly

The details about the exercises is given in Chapter 11. Some of the exercises are: 1. Aerobics, 2. Mind Quietening,

3. Breathing, 4. Weight Bearing, 5. Yoga, 6. Stretching, 7. Power Walking, 8. Swimming, 9. Tai Chi, Qi Gong, Aikido (Asian art forms), and 10. Elastic Bands.

Strategy 2: Calorie restriction

Calorie restriction is considered the gold standard. Calorie-restricted diets have about 30 percent fewer calories, but they're rich in fruits and vegetables. Restricting your diet to the point that you aren't getting enough nutrients can be dangerous.

Strategy 3: Sharpen your mind

Doing mental aerobics can improve memory and lower your risk for Alzheimer's disease. Try different approaches to expanding your mental horizons, whether it's traveling to new destinations, learning a musical instrument, taking up ballroom dancing or going back to school. Stay mentally active through puzzles, games, reading and other stimulating hobbies, but be sure to train and not strain your brain. With a sharp mind, we're more inclined to stay fit, have good relationships, eat well and live a healthy lifestyle.

Strategy 4: Cultivate relationships

Socially connected people have longer life expectancies than isolated individuals. Cultivate intimacy with your partner since good sex makes for a longer life; it lowers blood pressure, reduces pain, promotes restful sleep and boosts the immune system so we are better able to fight-off infections.

Empathy; our ability to understand another person's emotional viewpoint and to express that understanding—is the social glue that keeps us together. Ask your mate or friend to talk about a feeling or issue important to him and just listen without interrupting or interpreting. Maintain eye contact and stay focused.

Strategy 5: Reduce stress

Stress is the trigger of most diseases. When your brain is stressed and anxious, you have trembling, twitching, palpitations, irritable bowel syndrome, loss of sex drive, chronic fatigue. These are the warning signs of the worn-out brain. Regulation of breathing is the most powerful technique for neutralizing anxiety and helping the body deal with stress, and it's free. Also stress is the major player in cancer.

Strategy 6: Think positive

Optimists have a greater life expectancy than pessimists. Make an effort to see the cup half full. Recent studies show that we can learn optimism when we set our minds to it. Take care of your needs. Satisfied people are twice as likely to survive compared with dissatisfied individuals. Attending a house of worship once a week is associated with a seven-year-longer survival compared with never attending one.

Strategy 7: Manage your environment

The environment has a big influence on how we feel and how long we live. Whether it's traffic, noise, smog or other aspects of the environment, or more personal issues such as aesthetics or bedroom temperature. Bear in mind function and aesthetics when designing your home and work space. Control clutter and noise and arrange the bedroom in a way that enhances sleep and restfulness. Minimize your exposure to sun, smoke, mold, smog and other toxins. Stay safe on the road—let someone else drive if you can't handle it. Make your workplace safe and comfortable.

Strategy 8: Choose your foods wisely

A recent study found that persons who ate large amounts of high-glycemic (or diabetes promoting) carbohydrates, including potatoes, breakfast cereals, white bread, muffins, and white rice, had very high CRP levels. Women who ate a lot of these foods and were also overweight had the highest and most dangerous CRP levels. Good (complexed) carbohydrates, which are low on the glycemic index include: apples, apsaragus, beans, broccoli, blackberries, blueberries, cabbage, cantaloupe, citrus fruits, green beans, honeydew melon, kiwi, leafy greens, peaches, pears, plums, raspberries, spinach, and strawberries. Bad (simple) carbohydrates, which are high on the glycemic index include: bananas, breads, carrots, cereals processed with added sugar, corn, French fries, French toast, fruit juices, mangos, pancakes, papaya, pasta, peas, popcorn, white potatoes, white rice, sugar, waffles.

Strategy 9: Supplements and antioxidants

Use of comprehensive antioxidants, supplements with vitamins, minerals, antioxidants, amino acids and other important nutrients may help. A list of some micronutrients is given below:

- B vitamins* 25-50 milligrams (mg)
- [mcg] of folic acid. 400 micrograms
- Vitamin E 400 international units (IU)
- The natural form of Vitamin E, d-alpha-tocopherol, is preferred
- Vitamin C (with rosehips) 2,000-4,000 mg (in divided doses)
- Vitamin A (beta carotene) 5,000-10,000 IU
- Calcium 1,500 mg (in divided doses, 1000 mg in am, 500mg in pm)
- Vitamin D 400 IU (divided doses with calcium and magnesium)
- Magnesium 500 mg (divided doses with calcium and Vitamin D, 250 mg in am, 250 mg in pm)
- Iron 8 mg. The recommendation for iron for women is 18 mg.
- Iodine 150 mcg
- Zinc 10-15 mg
- Selenium 100-400 mcg
- Copper 2 mg
- Manganese 10 mg
- Chromium 200 mcg
- Molybdenum 25 mcg
- Potassium 90 mg
- Boron 50-100 mcg

- Lycopene 5-10 mg
- Lutein 25-50 mg
- Polyphenols (green tea) 10-100 mg
- Proanthocyanidins (grape seed, pine bark) 25-100 mg
- Alpha-lipoic acid 200-1,500 mg
- N-acetyl-cysteine 500-2,000 mg
- Coenzyme Q 50-300 mg
- Soy isoflavones 20-100 mg
- L-Carnitine (500 mg)
- Acetyl-L-Carnitine (250 mg)
- Coenzyme Q-10 (50 mg)
- Grape Seed Extract (50 mg)
- Turmeric (400 mg)
- L-glutamine (500 mg)
- Essential Oils (Fulfils daily Omega-3, 6, 9 requirements)
- DMAE (100 mg)
- other Supplements such as coral calcium, ginseng and Echinacea
- Aspirin has an effect on blood platelets, making them less likely to clump together and making blood flow smoothly, thus preventing heart attacks and brain strokes.

Antioxidants

The antioxidants can be classified as follows:

- AMINO ACIDS
  cysteine, glutathione, methionine, taurine.
- BIOFLAVINOIDS
  anthocyanins (blue-black fruits), citrus bioflavinoids (lemon, orange, grapefruit, etc.), oligometric proanthocyanidins (OPC) in pycnogenol.
- CAROTENOIDS
  alpha and beta carotene (red, yellow and orange fruits and vegetables), lycopene (red fruits and vegetables).

- HERBS
  Gingko, green tea, milk thistle, sage
- MINERALS
  Copper, zinc, manganese, selenium
- VITAMINS AND CO-FACTORS
  A, B2, C, E and coenzyme Q10, NADH (nicotinamide adenine dinucleotide)
- ENZYMES
  catalase, glutathione peroxidase, superoxide dismutase
- HORMONES
  Glutathione , HGH, Testosterone, estrogen, etc.

It is advisable to eat plenty of fresh fruit and vegetables, which all contain anti-oxidants. Antioxidant supplements are being widely recommended as anti-ageing agents. There's no proof that antioxidants in pill form can improve your general health or extend your life, say others. Some antioxidants are:

- Vitamin A
- Vitamin B-6
- Vitamin B-12
- Vitamin C
- Vitamin E
- Beta carotene
- Folic acid
- Selenium

Carotenoids; precursors of Vitamin A

Beta-carotenes are the most popular, and are found in many fruits and vegetables, animals, plants and microorganisms. The body converts beta carotene into Vitamin A. Vitamin A is a fat-soluble vitamin essential for vision, growth, cell division, reproduction and immunity. Among the 600 or more carotenoids in foods, beta-carotene, lycopene, and lutein are well-known leaders in the fight to reduce the damage from free radicals. Some studies have shown that beta-carotene may be an effective ally against prostate cancer. A recent study found men with the lowest level of beta-carotene in their blood were at the greatest risk of developing this cancer.

Lycopene

It is a carotenoid found in tomatoes, and is one of the most powerful antioxidants. Lycopene is the most predominant carotenoid in human plasma. Lycopene presents naturally in greater amounts than beta-carotene and other dietary carotenoids. Lycopene levels are affected by several biological and lifestyle factors. Because of its lipophilic nature, lycopene concentrates in low-density lipoprotein portions of the serum. Lycopene is also found in the adrenal, liver, testes, and prostate. However, unlike other carotenoids, lycopene levels in serum or tissues do not correlate with overall intake of fruits and vegetables. Research shows that lycopene can be absorbed more efficiently by the body after it has been processed into juice, sauce, paste, or ketchup. In fresh fruit, lycopene is enclosed in the fruit tissue. Therefore, only a portion of the lycopene that is present in fresh fruit is absorbed. Lycopene appears to protect against many diseases, including cancers of the mouth, pharynx, esophagus, stomach, colon, and rectum. Another study showed that women with the highest levels of lycopene in their blood were five times less likely to develop precancerous signs of cervical cancer than women with the lowest levels.

Lutein

It is another carotenoid found in vegetables and fruits. Lutein acts as an antioxidant, protecting cells against the damaging effects of free radicals. The central area of the retina in humans and primates is called the macula and contains lutein as the primary carotenoid. Lutein acts to filter and shield harmful blue light from the eye and may decrease the risk of developing macular degeneration, the eye disease that afflicts one in three people over age 65. Smokers who consumed the most beta-carotene and flavonoids from food, also appeared to cut their Alzheimer's risk. Yet, smokers who take excessive beta carotene supplements may increase their risk of lung cancer.

Vitamin A

A recent study has also shown the risk of osteoporosis with excessive Vitamin A. Retinol is the direct form of vitamin A found in most multivitamins, cod liver oil, liver, fortified foods, and whole milk products. Dietary retinol is associated with fractures, beta carotene is not. Beta carotene, which is converted to Vitamin A by the body, is not associated with any increased risk of fracture. This study has shown that intake of vitamin A or beta carotene, can be best obtained by eating more red and yellow vegetables than taking supplements. The recommended safe upper limit of retinol is 3000 mcg (9900 IU) per day. This includes all sources of retinol, including foods such as liver, dietary supplements such as cod liver oil and vitamin A supplements, fortified foods such as cereals, and multivitamins. Foods high in carotenoids include red, orange, deep-yellow, and some dark-green leafy vegetables, such as tomatoes, carrots, cantaloupe, pumpkin, sweet potatoes, winter squash, brussel sprouts, spinach, kale and broccoli.

Vitamin B5 (Pantothenic Acid)

Pantothenic acid (PA), a B-complex vitamin, is essential for humans and animals for growth, reproduction, and normal physiological functions. It is a precursor of the coenzymes, CoA and acyl carrier protein of fatty acid synthase, which are involved in more than 100 different metabolic pathways including energy metabolism of carbohydrates, proteins and lipids, and the synthesis of lipids, neurotransmitters, steroid hormones, porphyrins and hemoglobin.

Vitamin B6 (Pyridoxine)

Vitamin B6, also known as pyridoxine is part of the B group vitamins and is water-soluble and is required for both mental and physical health.

Folic Acid, Vitamin B12

Cardiovascular disease, the number-one killer of men and women, claims the lives of almost 40% of the more than 2.4 million Americans who die each year. Today, about 64 million Americans have some form of cardiovascular disease. Homocysteine a non-essential, sulfur-containing amino acid, is an independent marker of risk for the development of cardiovascular disease. Some researchers consider homocysteine as important a cardiovascular risk factor as low-density lipoprotein (LDL). Homocysteine can make blood clot more easily than normal, increasing the risk of both heart attack and death by heart attack. Inadequate levels of folic acid and vitamins B6 and B12 can lead to increased homocysteine levels.

Vitamin C

The most abundant, water-soluble antioxidant in the body is Vitamin C. Vitamin C acts primarily in cellular fluid. Vitamin C scavenges free radicals and cleans up waste products. In addition to its anti-oxidative activities, vitamin C benefits many other body functions. Vitamin C is necessary for the synthesis of collagen, which is an important component in the structural make up of blood vessels, tendons, ligaments, and bone. Vitamin C also plays an important role in the synthesis of the neurotransmitters and nor-epinephrine. Neurotransmitters are critical to brain function and are known to affect mood. Vitamin C, even in small amounts, can protect molecules in the body, such as proteins, lipids, carbohydrates, and nucleic acids from damage by free radicals. Vitamin C helps in the fight against free-radical formation caused by pollution and cigarette smoke and also helps return vitamin E to its active form. Vitamin C may lower the risk of developing cataracts and other eye diseases. In some studies, Vitamin C has helped lower blood pressure and cholesterol and has been shown to help prevent stroke and heart attacks. Researchers have found that people who suffer from asthma, arthritis, cancer, diabetes, heart disease and muscle injury after exercise have lower levels of vitamin C in their blood than non-sufferers.

Vitamin E

Vitamin E is the most abundant fat-soluble antioxidant in the body. Vitamin E primarily defends against oxidation and lipid peroxidation, which is the creation of unstable molecules containing more oxygen than is usual. Vitamin E may affect ageing, infertility, heart disease, Alzheimers, and diabetes. Vitamin E works together with other antioxidants, such as vitamin C, to offer protection from some chronic diseases. Evidence exists that vitamin E can help prevent atherosclerosis by interfering with the oxidation of low-density lipoproteins (LDL), a factor associated with increased risk of heart disease.

Another component of Vitamin E is tocotrienols. in addition to their antioxidant activity, tocotrienols have other important functions, especially in maintaining a healthy cardiovascular system. Test tube and animal studies indicate a possible role for tocotrienols in protecting against breast cancer and skin cancer. It may offer protection against atherosclerosis by preventing oxidative damage to LDL cholesterol. Vitamin E is found in vegetable oils, salad dressings, margarine, wheat germ, whole-grain products, sunflower seeds, cashew nuts, spinach, green peas, sweet potatoes, bean sprouts black eyed peas, almonds and peanut butter. Recommended doses of Vitamin E is 400 IU before age 40 and 800 IU from age 40 onward.

Some other products categorized as Anti-oxidants are mentioned below.

Acetyl-L-Carnitine (ALC)

The amino acid acetyl-L-carnitine boosts mitochondrial energy production through its ability to facilitate fatty acid transport and oxidation in the cell. Studies show that it stimulates the growth of new neurites by an astounding 19.5%. It acts together with acetyl-l-carnitine to increase neurite outgrowth. ALC occurs in many common foods, including milk. Studies have shown that ALC may help protect the brain by nourishing NMDA-sensitive glutamate receptors, which normally decline with age. ALC has also been shown to help prevent the formation of lipofuscin, a potassium age pigment, and to increase cerebral blood flow. ALC has become one of the premiere "anti-ageing" compounds under scientific investigation, especially in relation to brain and nervous system deterioration. It helps to enhance cognition. It is involved in the metabolism of food into energy. Mild mental impairment in the elderly showed a significant improvement of several performances during and after ALC treatments. ALC has been given in the doses from 500 to 2500 mg daily in divided doses. Younger, healthy adults would probably want to take 500-1000 mg daily. ALC may cause symptoms of over stimulation or headache in some sensitive individuals.

Alpha-Lipoic Acid

Alpha-Lipoic Acid, also known as lipoic acid, is a highly potent antioxidant that counteracts reactive free radicals in the mitochondria, the power plants of cells where energy for all cellular activities is generated. Some scientists believe that mitochondrial free radicals play an important role in human ageing, and have theorized that extra amounts of free-radical inhibiting compounds such as alpha lipoic acid may be able to slow ageing. Alpha-Lipoic Acid is also effective in recycling other antioxidants such as Vitamin E back into their original form after they detoxify free radicals. There also is evidence that alpha lipoic acid can reduce glycation damage due to excess glucose in the blood, which may be involved in ageing, and that it can improve patients with diabetes, which has been described as an accelerated form of ageing.

Alpha Lipoic Acid is both water and fat soluble, which allows it to enter all parts of the cell to neutralize free radicals. Alpha Lipoic Acid contributes to and is important for the production of energy inside the cell by utilizing sugar to produce energy contributing to mental and physical stamina, reducing muscle fatigue and neutralizes free radicals. Because it's the only antioxidant that can easily get into the brain, it could be useful in preventing oxidative stress and damage from a stroke. This also makes it important for regulating aspects of the immune system, in particular, T-lymphocytes. It may help reduce the effects of inflammatory diseases such a rheumatoid arthritis and psoriasis. Suggested dosage for Alpha Lipoic Acid is 100-200 mg in divided doses daily. Side effects can include: Skin rash and the potential of hypoglycemia in diabetic patients.

ALT-711

ALT-711 is one of the latest anti-ageing compounds to receive worldwide attention. It acts by catalytically breaking AGE crosslinks: Advanced Glycosylation End-product crosslinks occur when glucose is attached to a protein, like it can happen in arteries. For this, ALT-711 seems to be useful against heart disease by reducing pulse pressure and improving arterial elasticity. The full effects and side-effects of this drug are still unknown but it seems like a promising intervention to ameliorate ageing effects, though it probably does not delay ageing as a whole.

Selenium

There has never been a study to test the effects on lifespan of the trace mineral selenium, but an early study, which examined the toxicity of selenium found, by accident, that it extended the lifespan of laboratory mice. There have been dozens of studies showing that dietary selenium can help to prevent a wide variety of cancers, and that it may be useful in the treatment of cancer. Anyone taking selenium on a daily basis for anti-ageing purpose should be careful to keep their doses low to avoid the possibility of toxic side effects.

CoQ10 (Coenzyme Q10)

It is a vitamin-like compound also called "ubiquinone". Coenzyme Q10 acts as an antioxidant, much like vitamins C and E, helping to neutralize the cell-damaging molecules known as free radicals. The primary function of CoQ10 is as a catalyst for metabolism. Acting in conjunction with enzymes, the compound speeds up the vital metabolic process, providing the energy that the cells need to digest food, heal wounds, maintain healthy muscles, and perform other bodily functions. CoQ10 may play a role in preventing cancer, heart attacks, and other diseases linked to free-radical damage. It's also used as a general energy enhancer and anti-ageing supplement. Because levels of the compound diminish with age, some doctors recommend daily supplementation beginning about age 40. CoQ10 has generated much excitement as a possible therapy for heart disease, especially congestive heart failure or a weakened heart. In some studies, patients with a poorly functioning heart have been found to improve greatly after adding the supplement to their conventional drugs and therapies. Further research suggest that CoQ10 may protect against blood clots, lower high blood pressure, diminish irregular heartbeats, treat mitral valve prolapse, lessen symptoms of Raynaud's disease and relieve chest pains (angina). CoQ10 also appears to aid healing and reduce pain and bleeding in those with gum disease, and speed recovery following oral surgery. CoQ10 shows some promise against Parkinson's and Alzheimer's Diseases and fibromyalgia. For daily supplementation, the dosage range is from 30-100 mg, with the most common dosage at 30 mg. It takes up to eight weeks to see results with CoQ10.

Idebenone

Idebenone is an analogue of Coenzyme Q10. In most respects, Idebenone shares its traits with Coenzyme Q10. Like Coenzyme Q10 is might be useful for ageing. It differs from it in some important ways, which may make it more useful. Under certain circumstances, Coenzyme Q10 (CoQ10) may become a pro-oxidant. These circumstances are conditions in which hypoxia or lack of oxygen occurs. In cases of shock, heart attack, stroke, or poor circulation, CoQ10 auto-oxidizes and unleashes massive amounts of various free radicals that damage delicate tissues and because CoQ10 is necessary for electron transport and ATP (chemical energy) production, cellular death may ensue. Idebenone, on the other hand, suppresses free radicals and continues ATP production in hypoxic situations. This may make it a useful supplement for individuals at risk for those conditions.

Carnosine

Carnosine is a multifunctional dipeptide made up of a chemical combination of the amino acids beta-alanine and L-histidine. It is found both in food and in the human body. Long-lived cells such as nerve cells (neurons) and muscle cells (myocytes) contain high levels of carnosine. Muscle levels of carnosine correlate with the maximum life spans of animals. Carnosine levels decline with age. Muscle levels decline 63% from age 10 to age 70, which may account for the normal age-related decline in muscle mass and function. Since carnosine acts as a pH buffer, it can keep on protecting muscle cell membranes from oxidation under the acidic conditions of muscular exertion. Carnosine enables the heart muscle to contract more efficiently through enhancement of calcium response in heart myocytes. Ageing causes irreversible damage to the body's proteins. The underlying mechanism behind this damage is glycation. A simple definition of glycation is the cross-linking of proteins and sugars to form non-functioning structures in the body. The process of glycation can be superficially seen as unsightly wrinkled skin. Glycation is also an underlying cause of age-related catastrophes including the neurologic, vascular, and eye disorders. Carnosine is a unique dipeptide that interferes with the glycation process.

Green Tea Extract/Herbal Teas

Herbal teas are the easiest form of herbal remedy for long term use. The herb's powerful ingredients are either "infused" or "decocted" in water when made into teas. These herbal teas are made from the freshest herbs, organically grown. Loose tea is more aromatic and contains all the parts of the medicinal portions of an herb, unlike tea bags, which, for the most part, contain only the left over portions of the herb. Green tea extract helps maintain cellular DNA and membrane structural integrity. The active constituents in green tea are powerful antioxidants called polyphenols (catechins) and flavonols. Several catechins are present in green tea and account for the bulk of favourable research reports. Epigallocatechin gallate (EGCG) is the most powerful of these catechins. EGCG functions as an antioxidant that is about 25-100 times more potent than vitamins C and E. One cup of green tea may provide 10-40 mg of polyphenols and has antioxidant effects that are greater than a serving of broccoli, spinach, carrots, or strawberries.

Fish Oil/Super Omega-3 Alaska Deep Sea Fish Oil

Super Omega 3 Alaska Deep Sea Fish Oil is known for being rich in unsaturated fatty acids and provides rich

Omega-3 fatty acids, (Pure EPA 360 mg/DHA 240 mg). It is made from natural marine lipid concentrate and may help reduce or inhibit risk factors involved in cardiovascular disease, as well as inflammatory and immune disorders. Long term use of Fish Oil help prevent ageing skin, menopausal symptoms, promote better circulation, lower cholesterol, prevent blood clots, reduce heart related risk, and the pain of arthritis. Omega-3 and polyunsaturated fatty acids found in fish Oil help to protect against heart and blood vessel disease.

There are several mechanisms attributed to fish oil's beneficial effects. One is triglyceride-lowering effect of fish oil on reducing heart and blood vessel disorders. Another beneficial mechanism of fish oil is to protect healthy blood flow in arteries.

Nexrutine and 5-Loxin

Nexrutine and 5-Loxin are natural plant-based substances which can help inhibit the destructive actions of inflammation-inducing enzymes COX-2 and 5-LOX. Research indicates that these two substances are best taken together for maximum effectiveness.

L-Alpha-glycerylphosphorylcholine (GPC)

L-alpha glycerylphosphoryl-choline (GPC); a byproduct of phosphatidylcholine helps to boost acetylcholine. It aids in the synthesis of several brain phospholipids, which increases the availability of acetylcholine in various brain tissues. The GPC form of choline has been shown to help protect against cognitive decline normally seen in ageing.

Glutathione

The star nutrient is the antioxidant glutathione, a naturally occurring amino acid within the body. It is a powerful brain and liver food, which helps those organs detoxify and take care of themselves. But as we age glutathione levels fall, and toxins such as heavy metals and pesticides reduce levels even further. Glutathione is manufactured in our cells from a number of precursors such as Alpha Lipoic Acid (ALA); Acetyl-L ñ Carnitine and N Acetyl Cysteine (NAC). After the age of 50 we suggest you take 200mg of ALA, and 500 mg of either NAC or Acetyl L Carnitine on a daily basis.

Reishi Mushroom Capsules

As an anti-inflammatory agent, the extract is effective in substantially alleviating the problems and pain related to migraine, rheumatism or osteoarthritis and gout. In treating hypertension or hypotension the extract has been shown to be highly effective. The extract has been found effective in reducing and in some cases eliminating asthma attack. The extract is effective in reducing blood sugar levels and the amounts of insulin required for diabetic patients. The extract is effective in regaining stamina and energy or debility due to prolonged illness especially for cancer patients after undergoing radio and/or chemotherapy. The extract is effective in clearing up a large variety of skin allergic conditions either due to food or airborne allergens. The extract has been found to be useful in detoxifying the kidneys and improving its overall function. Patients receiving hemodialysis should find that the duration and frequency of the treatment could be reduced. The extract has been shown effective in reducing or eliminating excessive menstrual pain and irregularities. It has been found effective in addressing a variety of cardiovascular problems. This is an organic product. 600 mg capsules.

Vinpocetine

This substance is an extract of the wonder plant Vinca minor (periwinkle); from the same source we also get two anti-cancer chemo-therapeutic agents (vinblastine and vincristine). In humans vinpocetine has been shown to: dilate brain arteries, reduce the tendency of blood to clot, speed up brain metabolism, act as an antioxidant, aid recovery after stroke. Vinpocetine protects against dementia and improves those who already have it. Never forget to add a multi- vitamin/mineral formula that contains at least 500 mg of vitamin C, 25 mg of B6, and 25 mg of B1 and 100 mcg of B12.

Magnesium

Magnesium helps prevent osteoporosis, protects against

heart disease, lowers blood pressure and acts as an antioxidant. The mineral also may help prevent diabetes and can ease symptoms of premenstrual syndrome. People who do not regularly eat magnesium-rich foods (such as whole grains, nuts, seeds and legumes) should supplement each day. Magnesium oxide should be avoided in most cases, as most people do not tolerate it well. Better choices for magnesium supplementation are magnesium chloride, magnesium Aspartate, magnesium gluconate and magnesium lactate. Most people can tolerate as much as 500 mg of magnesium daily, if they have normal kidney function. Anyone with kidney problems, heart failure, or a history of heart attacks, should consult a physician before considering magnesium supplements.

Magnesium is known as Nature's Tranquillizer. A deficiency of magnesium has a detrimental effect on a huge array of enzyme reactions which take place in our bodies, many of them related to the energy-building cycle of metabolism that takes place in the mitochondria. The brain is one of the first organs to feel the lack. Magnesium also helps prevent conditions you would recognize simply as a catalogue of ageing! Magnesium is regarded by many as the number one mineral supplement. Women are especially vulnerable to magnesium lack. Dose: 300 mg daily.

Fibre

Dietary fiber is an important ingredient for better health and as an anti-ageing food. Here's a look at the fiber content of some common foods. Recommended fiber intake for women is 21 to 25 grams a day and for men is 30 to 38 grams a day.

Pollution control

Pollution overload is one of the reasons for our immune systems not functioning properly. If you want to help your immune system, you must reduce at least some of the chemical exposure you face. At least eliminate the bulk of cleaners, deodorants, pesticides, air-fresheners, gardening chemicals and the like.

Fruits	*Serving size*	*Total fiber (grams)*
Pear	1 medium	5.1
Figs, dried	2 medium	3.7
Blueberries	1 cup	3.5
Apple, with skin	1 medium	3.3
Strawberries	1 cup	3.3
Peaches, dried	3 halves	3.2
Orange	1 medium	3.1
Apricots, dried	10 halves	2.6
Raisins	1.5-ounce box	1.6

Grains, cereal and pasta	*Serving size*	*Total fiber (grams)*
Spaghetti, whole-wheat	1 cup	6.3
Bran flakes	3/4 cup	5.1
Oatmeal	1 cup	4.0
Bread, rye	1 slice	1.9
Bread, whole-wheat	1 slice	1.9
Bread, mixed-grain	1 slice	1.7
Bread, cracked-wheat	1 slice	1.4

Legumes, nuts and seeds	*Serving size*	*Total fiber (grams)*
Lentils	1 cup	15.6
Black beans	1 cup	15.0
Lima beans	1 cup	13.2
Baked beans, canned	1 cup	10.4
Almonds	24 nuts	3.3
Pistachio nuts	47 nuts	2.9
Peanuts	28 nuts	2.3
Cashews	18 nuts	0.9

Vegetables	*Serving size*	*Total fiber (grams)*
Peas	1 cup	8.8
Artichoke, cooked	1 medium	6.5
Brussels sprouts	1 cup	6.4
Turnip greens, boiled	1 cup	5.0
Potato, baked with skin	1 medium	4.4
Corn	1 cup	4.2
Popcorn, air-popped	3 cups	3.6
Tomato paste	1/4 cup	3.0
Carrot	1 medium	2.0

Some useful elements that can help in brain health are:

Eldepryl, Selegiline and Deprenyl

These work to help prevent premature brain cell death by inhibiting an enzyme that breaks down dopamine, thereby elevating dopamine levels in the brain and central nervous system. Possible side effects of these medications include abdominal or stomach pain, dizziness or feeling faint, dryness of mouth, nausea, trouble in sleeping and vomiting.

Centrophenoxine

This is used widely to increase brain energy through glucose uptake. It is used in the treatment of brain damage, injury caused by chemicals and drugs, and excess alcohol. Possible side effects include headaches, nausea and muscle stiffness.

Isoprinosine (Imunovir)

An immunomodulator and synthetic derivative with antiviral properties used in chemotherapy. It is used to restore immune responses for the treatment or management of secondary viral infections. Side effects include dizziness, problems with digestion (for example, slight stomach pain and feeling full after you ate only a small amount of food) and itching.

KH3

KH3 contains the world famous "youth" drug procaine, along with a compound called hematoporphyrin to enhance the activity of procaine. It slows down some aspects of ageing and is used to improve alertness, concentration, memory, physical coordination, and blood circulation in the brain. Possible side effects of KH3 include dizziness, restlessness (delirium/confusion), disorders of stomach and bowels (nausea, gastric distress, vomiting and diarrhea. Allergic reactions and occasional menstruation during menopause can occur.

Nimodipine

This is a calcium channel blocker specific to the central

nervous system. It prevents movement of calcium into the cells of blood vessels, thereby relaxing the vessels and increasing the supply of blood and oxygen. Potential side effects include breathing difficulty, coughing, or wheezing; irregular or fast, pounding heartbeat; skin rash; swelling of ankles, feet, or lower legs.

Ribavirin

Ribavirin has antiviral activity against both RNA and DNA viruses. It exerts its antiviral effect by acting as an analogue of Inosine Monophosphate (IMP) or Guanosine Monophosphate (GMP). Adverse Reactions: anemia, headache, drowsiness and cramp.

Other ingredients consist of a wide range of amino acids, antioxidants, bioflavanoids, neuronutrients, herbal extracts, enzymes and specialized trace elements. They must be combined in specific dosages to enable them to enhance one another's effectiveness.

Standardized herbal extracts:

Bilberry
Black cumin
Cranberry
Ginger
Gingko biloba
Gotu kola
Green tea
Hawthorne berry
Mahonia grape
Myrrh (Guggulipid)
Olive-leaf
Red clover
Turmeric

Vitamins (used in combination as on their own they do not produce a noticeable effect nor produce sufficient action):

Vitamin B1 (Thiamine)
Vitamin B2 (Riboflavin)
Vitamin B3 (Niacinamide)
Vitamin B5 (D-Pantothenate)
Vitamin B6 (Pyridoxine HCL)
Vitamin B12 (Cyanocobalamin)
Vitamin C (Ascorbic acid)
Vitamin D3 (Cholecalciferol)
Vitamin E (Succinate)

Vitamin co-factors:

ATP precursors
Beta carotene
Biotin
Folic acid
Hesperidin
Inositol hexaphosphate
Lutein
Naringin
PABA (Para-aminobenzoic acid)
Phosphatidyl choline
Piperine
Rutin
Tocotrienols
Zeaxanthin

Essential minerals:

Boron
Calcium
Copper
Magnesium
Manganese
Potassium
Zinc
Sulfur (as MSM).

Trace elements (to ensure pure bioavailability):

Chromium
Indium
Iodine
Lithium
Molybdenum
Rubidium
Selenium
Strontium
Tungsten

Active enzymes:

Betaine HCL
Isolase Pro
Lipase
Papain.

Amino acids and other natural supplements:

Acetyl L-Carnitine
Alpha Lipoic Acid
DIM, 3, 3 (Diindolylmethane)
DMAE
DMG (Di methyl glycine)
L-Arginine HCL
L-Methionine
L-Proline
L-Tyrosine
Myricetin
N-Acetyl L-Cysteine
Policosanol

L-Carnosine
L-Glutathione
L-Lysine
Quercitin
Resveratrol
Ribonucleic acid (RNA).

Plus:

Aloe vera
Beta glucan
Tea polysaccharides, and

Omega 3/DHA fish oil esters

Here we look at some notable anti-ageing treatments, what they might do, and evidence for or against their effectiveness.

Treatment	*What is it and what is it claimed to do?*	*Evidence for or against?*
Vitamins	Vitamins A, C, and E are part of the body's antioxidant defences. By boosting their levels, it is claimed, oxidative damage would be reduced and ageing slowed.	Vitamin supplements can help to keep you healthy, but there is no evidence they slow human ageing. In mice, studies indicate that antioxidants do not slow ageing although they may slightly increase lifespan.
Synthetic antioxidant enzymes	The body has enzymes (such as superoxide dismutase and catalase) that clean up free radicals. Drugs that work as synthetic enzymes—called mimetics—could boost this antioxidant proces.	In one study, nematode worms given synthetic superoxide dismutase/catalase enzymes lived, on average, 44 per cent longer. These findings have been disputed and their relevance to humans remains unclear.

Growth hormone	Influences the growth of cells, bones, muscles and organs throughout the body. Levels peak at adolescence, then decline. Companies selling growth hormone claim this decline is linked to ageing.	No evidence that taking growth hormone slows ageing; in fact, some data suggest that taking it advances ageing.
Melatonin	Hormone that seems to affect circadian rhythms, our sleep-wake clock. Its production declines with age.	No evidence that it can combat ageing in humans, and it may have harmful side effects.
DHEA	Dehydroepiandosterone (DHEA) is a steroid hormone produced by the adrenal glands. It plays a role in the production of other hormones, notably oestrogen and testosterone. Levels fall with age, dramatically in women.	No evidence it can affect ageing, although in theory DHEA supplementation could have beneficial effects.
Royal jelly	Fed to young bee larvae and to queen bees. The spectacular fertility and long lifespan of the queens have led people to believe that royal jelly pro-	Little evidence, although in one study, the average lifespan of mice fed royal jelly increased by a quarter (their maximum lifespan was unaffected), perhaps by decreasing oxidative damage.

	duces similar effects in humans.	
Ginkgo biloba	A popular herbal medicine derived from the leaves of the ginkgo biloba tree. Used in Chinese medicine for thousands of years. Claimed to boost circulation, improve mental function, and protect nerve cells against the effects of ageing.	Ginkgo may help combat age-related memory loss, but there is no evidence that it slows ageing itself.
ALT-711	A drug that acts by breaking crosslinks between sugars and proteins, such as happens in arteries.	Seems to help against heart disease by reducing pulse pressure and improving arterial elasticity. Full effects and side effects are still unknown, but it seems a promising way to ameliorate the effects of ageing.
Resveratrol/ red wine	A compound found largely in the skins of red grapes, resveratrol is touted as an antioxidant and an anti-cancer agent.	In yeast, resveratrol activates the Sir2 enzyme and extends lifespan. In human cells, resveratrol reduces the activity of the p53 protein. This may be a good thing, giving the cell more time to try to repair DNA damage, or a bad thing—a key role of p53 is to kill.

Green tea	In the East associated with long life for centuries. Claimed to have numerous health benefits, including anti-ageing and anti-carcinogenic properties related to the presence of powerful antioxidants called catechins.	Certainly seems to be good for you, although teasing apart its complex and numerous effects on humans has proved difficult.

Cosmetic ingredients

Aged skin often feels dry to the touch, its dryness worsening in cold climates. Moisturizers are recommended as a means to relieve feelings of dryness and itching. They should be applied on a daily basis to ensure maximum benefit. Successful treatment of dry skin with appropriate moisturizer leads to smoother, softer and firmer skin. Moisturizing Pearl Cream is made from well selected pure precious pearls, which are reduced into very fine powder. The pearl powder is then blended with rich moisturizing lotion, cooling Aloe Vera and soothing Vitamin E to give the skin a smooth layer of protection for the elements as well as the appropriate balance of both nutrients and moisture. Pearls are an excellent source of minerals, aminoacids and calcium carbonate, the most absorbable form of calcium. Pearl Cream is recommended to speed the skin's natural metabolism in order to tone and rejuvenate complexion. It has been used to heal blemishes, minimize large pores and reduce redness. Pearl Cream and Pearl Powder are one of the best natural products for scar reduction!

3

Advances in Anti-Ageing Medicine

Can you put the Clock Back?

The ageing process isn't well understood and they have yet to find a "magic bullet" that can reverse the effects of ageing. They have not found a sure way to free you of wrinkles and loss of youthful energy. Many say that new remedies like human growth hormone (HGH) can empty out your wallet and possibly harm your body. It's unlikely that a product, pill or potion could cure all of the ills, age can bring. Many believe that medical treatment can keep them feeling young and vigorous, well into old age. The science has made certain advances in the understanding of the ageing processes. 'Our future health and our personal life expectancy are potentially under our individual control to a far larger level than is usually realized', opine some scientists.

You have to look after your health

You can extend the likely years you will live, by prudent attention to diet, exercise and lifestyle. You can also turn the years you have in store, with more pleasure and

more energy. All it takes is a little intelligent care now, to reap the advantages later. It would be a tragedy to have to endure a forlorn aching old age, with your body ruined, yet be unable to depart this life quietly and so have to continue to suffer it. Logically, you can see that if we eliminate diseases, then fewer people will be dying and the expected age span will rise even more. Don't be startled to know that Cancer and heart disease are preventable conditions. Don't be confused by the trigger factors, such as tobacco smoking and lung cancer. Other factors include nutrition, moderate lifestyle, a cleaner environment and personal health care.

We have seen how free radicals are produced due to oxygen metabolism and how these free radicals cause damage to your health. You can prevent the damage and delay ageing. Ozone is another reactive oxygen species which is highly destructive to living cells. However, it is little found at sea level, remaining largely in the upper atmosphere, where it shields us from harmful UV radiation. Unfortunately, urban pollution, notably with traffic emissions, in the presence of sunlight, creates dangerous levels of ozone, which we may breathe. It causes lung damage. Oxidation stress, leading to tissue damage, has now been implicated in a wide variety of disease complaints, including arthritis, heart disease, cancer, dementias and other degenerative illnesses. Environmental pollution and overburdened lifestyles unquestionably potentiate the ageing process. Smoking and excess alcohol increase oxidative damage, too.

Do you know . . . what the wise said?

- You can add approximately 40-50 years to your lifespan using periodic fasting and caloric restriction.
- Anti-ageing supplements can add 20-30 years to your lifespan.
- It's likely to add 15-25 years to your life if you eat

a nutritionally sound, individually tailored diet.

- High-tech bio-medicine such as ethical stem cell therapy may add 15-25 years or more to your lifespan.
- Quality of life (prosperity, relaxation, regular holidays) can add 15-25 years to your lifespan.
- Regular exercise and moderate physical activity can add 10-20 years to your lifespan.

These approaches taken together can add 60-80 years or more to your lifespan, if you start young (say at age 20). But even if you only start later (say at 45-50), you can still gain 30-40 years. The substances which protect us from this occurrence have assumed steadily greater significance. We call these, anti-oxidants. Common Anti-oxidants have been described in the earlier chapter. Some other substances that may help us to delay ageing are described here.

Let us look at the advances in the field of anti-ageing medicine.

(a) Super hormones

Whatever your span of years, one can add life to years. One of the greatest advances in recent years has been the emergence of what we sometimes call super hormones. It is wrong to accept the hormone levels as normal (if it is subnormal) because the patient is older that would be considered a disease in a younger person. As the levels of these hormones decline, so do our health. The loss of these hormones saps our energy and vitality. They say that while restoring these hormones to their youthful levels, it is possible to restore our youthful zeal and energy. One such super hormone is DHEA, also called "mother hormone", since it precedes testosterone, oestrogen and progesterone. Low levels of DHEA lead to fatigue, depression, loss of vitality and decreased libido. Yet this important substance begins to decline in our bodies from the 20s onwards; by 40 we feel the effects of the loss, by 80 our DHEA could be as low as 15% of its "youth level". Another common and important marker is thyroid hormone; the decline of which depresses your metabolism. Human Growth Hormone (HGH) has been shown to actually turn back the clock. In 1990 a study was published in the prestigious New England Journal of Medicine, that showed that, in real terms, six months of adequate supplementation of HGH was capable of reversing the ageing process by as much as 10-20 years; skin wrinkling was reduced significantly, lean muscle mass returned and excess fat melted away, resulting in weight loss even without dieting. The super hormone promise applies equally to men and women. More details on HGH and some other hormones is given in a subsequent chapter.

(b) Chelation

The word chelation is derived from the Greek word chele that means claw (like that of a scorpion or crab). The concept of chelation is based on the observation that when a certain aminoacid complex called EDTA (ethylene-diamine-tetra-aceticacid) comes in contact with certain positively charged metals and other substances such as lead, iron, copper, calcium, magnesium, zinc, plutonium and manganese, it grabs them (hence the chele or claw), and removes them. Chelation therapy is the process of removing from the body the undesirable and toxic metals. Metals are among the most poisonous substances in our environment; almost none of them belong there and certainly not in the kind of quantities encountered in industrial society. Certain metals are known to cause cancer. Aluminium and mercury have been implicated in Alzheimers.

Chelation therapy is known to increase blood flow where hardening of the arteries has resulted in years of organ deterioration. It cleans and increases blood flow throughout the body and at the same time limits free radical activity by clawing misplaced toxic substances from sites where they have accumulated. By adding brain-booster glutathione to the IV formula, we can make these important benefits into a powerful restorative package that can reverse brain ageing, DNA cross-linkages and tissue decay. Renewed nutrient and oxygen supply for the tissues, especially the brain, can result in feeling years younger. Sexual organs can be revitalized, with obvious benefits. Sometimes it can lead to miraculous outcomes, in which Parkinsonës patients can walk again, motor neurone disease and MS are treated, and poor brain performance is reversed.

(c) Non-hormonal anti-ageing factors

Kinetin

Plant hormone KINETIN delays the onset of many cellular and biochemical characteristics associated with cellular ageing of cultured human cells . . . Natural sources of kinetin related cytokinins are: very high levels in coconut milk; all germinating seeds and growing tips, etc. Some of the main effects of kinetin are: maintaining the youthful morphology for much longer period, reversing senescent morphology, maintaining youthful cytoskeletal organization, maintaining youthful pattern of DNA, RNA and protein synthesis, slowing down the rate of accumulation of age-pigment like things. These effects can be best seen as "preventive" effects instead of reversion of ageing.

DIM (Diindolylmethane)

It is a plant compound called an indole, and has been shown to help regulate and promote a more efficient metabolism of estrogen, and an optimal ratio of estrogen metabolites. DIM balances estrogen levels, promoting health and well-being. This powerful phytonutrient is found in broccoli, cauliflower, cabbage and brussels sprouts, unlike other phytonutrients like soy isoflavones, has no hormonal properties in itself.

Studies show it works indirectly by increasing the activity of enzymes that control estrogen production. DIM boosts levels of "good" estrogens called 2-hydroxy estrogens and reduces levels of "bad" estrogens which are 16-hydroxy and 4-hydroxy estrones. Both forms of "bad" estrogen are carcinogens, and studies show that women with elevated levels of 16-hydroxy estrone have a high rate of breast cancer. Men can also benefit from DIM supplementation. There's evidence that benign prostate enlargement and some types of prostate cancer may be related to a buildup of estrogen in that gland, not testosterone. In overweight men because fat cells convert DHEA and testosterone to estrogen, DIM supplementation can be especially helpful.

Dietary supplementation with diindolylmethane (DIM) from cruciferous vegetables has established an important and effective nutritional approach to increasing the safety of estrogen. The availability of dietary supplements containing DIM provide an important new alternative in preventive nutrition and offer a source of support for the hormonal systems of men and women. To be effective, phytochemical supplements containing highly insoluble substances like DIM require absorption enhancing formulations. DIM supplementation can be combined with reduced alcohol intake to provide a dietary means of reducing the risk of breast and uterine cancer associated with HRT. The supplemental use of DIM allows women to promote and maintain a safer metabolism of estrogen. This expands the opportunities for women to derive the full preventive health benefits from long-term hormonal replacement. DIM also increases the safety of exposure to estrogen derived from DHEA. This supports the rationale for long term supplementation with DHEA by both men and women. Documented, ageing-related changes in men support their need for an improved metabolism of estrogen. DIM use by men provides a promising dietary means to minimize the impact of increased estrogen on atherosclerosis and prostate disorders characteristic of andropause. These important benefits for successful ageing in men and women all relate to an optimal and safer "estrogen balance".

DMAE (Dimethylaminoethanol)

It is a chemical; naturally produced in the human brain. It is thought to be used by the body in converting the precursor choline to the neurotransmitter, acetylcholine. Lipofuscin is a cellular pigment consisting of aggregated molecular waste. It tends to occur in the cells of people over 40 years old. It is thought that lipofuscin is not simply a byproduct of ageing but may also contribute to the ageing process. Neurons, heart and skin of older people usually contain particularly large amounts of lipofiscin. DMAE has shown that it reduces the accumulation of lipofuscin deposits inside cells. DMAE was found helpful in patients with age related cognitive decline. In a study, DMAE was given in a dosage of 600 mg a day for four weeks to fourteen older patients. Ten patients improved and four were unchanged. The patients on DMAE had reduced depression, less anxiety, and increased motivation, but they had no improvement in memory. The researchers suggest that although DMAE may not improve memory, it may produce positive behavioral changes in some dementia patients. A recent study shows DMAE cream is able to increase firmness of skin. Most people notice being more alert and focused within a couple of hours after taking DMAE orally. The effects can last most of the day. It is best to take DMAE early part of the day. DMAE is available in dosages ranging from 100 to 400 mg. It is best to start with a low dose, such as 50 to 150 mg since high doses can cause anxiety, restlessness, and muscle tension in the neck and shoulders. DMAE taken late in the day may cause insomnia. Clinical studies of DMAE have used up to 1,600 mg per day with no reports of side effects. DMAE is believed to be relatively nontoxic. DMAE can be found in cold water fish such as sardines and salmon.

(d) Stevia

This plant's extract are approximately 300 times sweeter than sugar, unless diluted. The plant is native to Brazil. Since pre-Columbian times the Guarani Indians in Paraguay have used the Stevia leaves to sweeten medicines and drinks. It can be found in most health food stores and comes as a white powder or in tincture (liquid) form. Stevia has zero calories and it even helps prevent cavities by reducing plaque build-up. It does not affect blood sugar levels like sugar does and is recommended for diabetics. Stevia is heat stable at 392 degrees Fahrenheit, so, unlike some artificial sweeteners, you can cook with it. It is non-toxic and has been extensively tested in animals and extensively used by humans with no adverse effects. Stevia in a glycerine base compound, seems to have the best taste of all.

All American grapes; muscadines

Muscadines naturally contain an extra set of chromosomes that other grapes don't have. These extra chromosomes contain genes that help create a phytochemical profile with a broader range of health-supporting potential than other grapes. And many of these phytochemicals are antioxidants. These are available in capsule forms as well. The seeds of these grapes are loaded with resveratrol! . . . Resveratrol is different from nearly all antioxidants because it can cross your blood-brain barrier to help protect brain cells. The biomedical literature is filled with studies detailing the potential health-promoting benefits of numerous natural substances found in muscadines. Flavonoids are particularly beneficial to your health (and found in abundance in muscadine grape seed). In particular, muscadine compounds such as flavanol, anthocyanidin, OPC, catechin, quercetin and tannins inhibit LDL oxidation 5, 6. That they stop LDLs (commonly called "bad cholesterol") from oxidizing is significant, as this promotes arterial health.

5-HTP or 5-hydroxy-tryptophan

This is the precise precursor of serotonin. 5HTP may help in serotonin deficiency related conditions such as severe depression, epilepsy, anxiety, insomnia, weight loss and addiction. Also studied for PMS, migraine and chronic tension headaches. 5-HTP comes from an extract of Griffonia simplicifolia. Used traditionally in African medicine to inhibit diarrhea, vomiting and constipation, and as an aphrodisiac. The extraction process uses alcohol and produces an oily solid. The oily extract is then purified into a dry solid. 5-HTP can also be made synthetically in the laboratory. The final product is the same as the one made by the body.

Tryptophan is an essential amino acid that must be taken in through protein containing foods since the body can not synthesize it. Of the eight essential aminoacids, tryptophan is the least common, accounting for only about one percent of protein content, and it is used up rapidly by the body. About ninety-percent is used in protein synthesis. The rest is divided between serotonin production and niacin production, which requires 60 mg for every 1 mg of niacin produced. However, 5-HTP is only used in serotonin production. 5- hydroxytryptophan is also able to pass through the blood-brain barrier easily, unlike tryptophan, which can only pass through the barrier by using the same transport molecule that carries leucine, isoleucine, and valine.

Serotonin production increases with light, meaning the darker the day is, it is not utilizing seratonin into action. Some symptoms include depression, marathon napping, low self-esteem, obsessive ness over little things, irritability, shyness, and panic attacks.

Symptoms can range from mild to severe, and people generally recover completely around April or May—once the days become longer. However, there are things you can do yourself that can help boost serotonin levels: bright indoor light, Exercise, Eat wisely (salad and fruits). Protein should be eaten three times a day. Another good rule is to eat four cups of brightly coloured veggies a day. Vegetables are carbs, but the kind that work into your system slowly. Vitamin B-6 helps convert 5-hydroxy-tryptophan (5HTP) into the mood chemical serotonin, and it also helps in making dopamine. Aim for roughly 2 to 10 milligrams a day if you supplement. B-6-rich foods include bell peppers, cranberries, turnip greens, cauliflower, garlic, tuna, mustard greens, and kale. 5HTP standard dosage ranges between 50-100 mg.

(e) Supplements

The following supplements can be considered for a scientifically-based anti-ageing regime.

Trimethyl glycine (TMG)

TMG protects the youthful methylation process in our metabolism. TMG can lower dangerous plasma homocysteine levels, thus reducing the risk of heart disease and stroke. It helps the integrity of nerve fibres and so may improve Alzheimer's and Parkinson's disease. It protects against liver damage from alcohol and other dangers. Finally, it protects DNA and so may slow cell ageing. DOSE: 500-2,000 mg daily. It works better with co-factors B6, B12 and folic acid.

Gingko biloba

Extract of the tree Gingko biloba have been used by the Chinese for 2800 years. It is now well recognized as an important brain food and anti-oxidant and improves mental function in people of all ages. It quenches free radicals and improves neurotransmission, thus protecting circulation and enhancing memory. Protects against Parkinsonism, Alzheimer's and other dementia. DOSE: 50-100 mg.

S-ADENOSYL METHIONINE

A derivative of important methionine; widely distributed in the tissues of young healthy adults. But with ageing and sickness, it is depleted. It is needed for the body to metabolize efficiently, for neuronal regeneration and the synthesis of energy through ATP, the basic energy molecule. It may help prevent or reverse liver damage. Additionally, it may be the safest, fastest acting anti-depressant available and is widely prescribed in Europe for that purpose. DOSE: 200-800 mg daily. Best taken on an empty stomach, with water.

ESSENTIAL FATTY ACIDS

Essential fatty acids are vital for tip top body and mind function. So-called omega 3s and omega 6s have different effects. You need both. Plant sources provide omega-6s and fish oils provide omega-3s. Studies show that eating lots of fish reduces inflammatory chemicals and leads to better health and more mental clarity, with less chance of Alzheimers. Didn't your mother tell you eating fish is good for the brain? DOSE: 500-2,000 mg. Food sources—fish, star flower, and flax seeds.

(f) Hormonal anti-ageing factors

Dehydroepiandrosterone (DHEA): It is a natural steroid hormone, one of the hormones produced by the adrenal glands. After being secreted by the adrenal glands, it circulates in the bloodstream as DHEA-sulfate (DHEAS) and is converted as needed into other hormones. DHEA is chemically similar to testosterone and estrogen and is easily converted into those hormones. DHEA production peaks in early adulthood and declines in production with age in both men and women. Increasing DHEA may increase testosterone, which in men may lead to prostate enlargement and in women may lead to facial hair. Some experts believe that daily intakes of 5-15 mg of DHEA for women and 10-30 mg for men are appropriate amounts for people with deficient blood levels of DHEA. See more details on DHEA in another chapter.

MELATONIN

Melatonin is secreted by the pineal gland located near the bottom of the brain and regulates the body's sleeping pattern. Again as we grow older, the pincea gland calcifies and the secretion of Melatonin declines, causing the sleeplessness so often suffered by the elderly. Melatonin also helps in stress and helps the immune system repair itself. It is helpful for migraine and has been shown to slow down the growth of cancerous cells in certain types of cancer. Its role in anti-ageing is that melatonin is the regulator of other hormones released from the brain and diminised secretation may be responsible for ageing. Melatonin helps against degenerative diseases, such as cardiovascular disease, osteoporosis, age-associated immune impairment, Alzheimers and Parkinsonism. It slows multiplication of cancer cells and appears to aid regression of certain tumours. Melatonin may be the most effective anti-ageing miracle of all. Yet it is safe and relatively cheap. Dose: 3-9 mg daily. Don't take melatonin if you weigh less than 85 lbs, could become pregnant or you are operating machinery.

Pregnenolone

Pregnenolone like DHEA, Melatonin, Estrogen, Progesterone, Testosterone and Human Growth Hormone is a hormone that declines with increasing age. Recent studies demonstrated that Pregnenolone has a remarkable capability to increase memory function at very low doses. Pregnenolone is also known as the "mother hormone" because it is the precursor of number of hormones including DHEA, testosterone and estrogen. See more on this hoemone in another chapter.

TESTOSTERONE

The hormonal stimulus for sex drive in both men and

women is Testosterone, which declines with advancing age in both sexes. Testosterone also plays an important role in maintaining muscle mass and strength and bone density. The hormone is often administered to ageing men and women as a topical cream, but also is available in oral and injectable forms.

Testosterone is responsible for libido and sperm production. But it is not only a sex hormone, it also increases protein synthesis in the cells, and keeps up aerobic metabolism thus reducing the risk of cancer as cancer cells use anaerobic metabolism. Aerobic metabolism is also important to regulate cholesterol, supply sufficient oxygen to vital organs like the heart and the pancreas thus helping to prevent heart disease and diabetes. At any age aerobic exercise can increase the production of testosterone. Testosterone has fibrinolytic properties, this means it helps to prevent blood clots that would lead to thrombosis. Testosterone has anabolic properties and is counteracted by cortisol and adrenalin. Constant stress increases cortisol and adrenalin and ageing decreases testosterone secretion. This leads to a catabolic state, where muscle mass is lost.

Women in their forties/fifties enter menopause, caused by a rapid decline of sex hormones—particularly progesterone. Until recently it was only suspected that men go through a change like menopause. New evidence confirms this supspicion. The decline of the male sex hormone testosterone is much slower than in women making the symptoms develop more slowly and hardly noticeable. Testosterone therapy should be done under the supervision of a specialized physician. Only natural testosterone should be used such as Testosterone cream or patches. Most other forms are synthetic and not identical to the bodys' own testosterone.

Estrogen and Progesterone

The "female" steroid hormones estrogen and progesterone play important roles in maintaining bone density and strength, sexual function, mental function and, in women, in countering the effects of the menopause. Recent studies indicate that estrogen may be an effective treatment for age-associated memory problems. Both estrogen and progesterone are available in a variety of forms—natural or synthetic, oral or topical. There is considerable interest in the use of plant-derived phytoestrogens, which have weak (but safe) estrogenic activity as a possible replacement for drug forms of estrogen. One product, Natural Estrogen, has been specially designed for this purpose.

(g) Newer Therapies

Magnetic Therapy

Once considered an ancient mystery, magnetic therapy is now recognized as fact by scientists across the world. The Aztec Indians of South America and their counterparts in Ancient Greece, Egypt, India, China constantly used magnetic therapy, both for pain relief and to promote good health.

Ozone Therapy

This is an old technology with a new beginning; especially, in the field of alternative health medicine. It is a natural alternative that could bring new life to everyone. Medical ozone therapy is recognized in several countries. Physicians in these states can legally use it and other safe effective non-conventional treatments as an alternative treatment in their practice without being persecuted.

Acarbose

Acarbose is used to treat type 2 (noninsulin-dependent) diabetes. Acarbose works by slowing the action of certain chemicals that break down food to release glucose (sugar) into your blood. Slowing food digestion helps keep blood glucose from rising very high after meals.

Adrafinil

Adrafinil acts to stimulate brain activity only when stimulation is required. Modafinil is the latest, more potent analogue of Adrafinil. Both drugs act on brain Alpha 1 post synaptic receptors and make them more susceptible to norepinephrine, thus increasing alertness and concentration. They do not appear to affect other brain functions.

Aminoguanidine

Aminoguanidine may have the potential to slow the ageing process by protecting the proteins that make up the human body. Proteins such as the skin proteins (collagen and elastin), eye lens protein, nerve protein and kidney proteins. All the body's proteins deteriorate with advancing age and more so in diabetes (diabetics have 2-3 times the number of cross-linked proteins when compared to non-diabetics and this has lead credence to the fact that diabetes can be viewed as a form of accelerated ageing).

Aniracetam

Aniracetam acts on the central nervous system (CNS), stimulating the learning process and the memory. Pharmacological studies have shown that Aniracetam stimulates the functions of certain neuronal receptors by means of glutamic acid, bringing about memorization processes (AMPA receptors) and protection of nerve cells (metabotrophic receptors). Clinical studies have shown specific therapeutic activity in elderly patients affected by alterations of the cognitive functions. Both long- and short-term memory improvement have seen in addition to learning, attention span, alertness, concentration, reasoning and absent mindedness.

Centrophenoxine

Centrophenoxine removes lipofuscin, potassium age pigment from the brain, heart and skin. Appearances of lipofuscin in the skin are referred to as liver, or age spots. Lipofuscin occurs in much higher levels in Alzheimer's patients than in their counterparts, and some theories relate brain and memory function to the ability of potassium to enter and exit brain cells. As we age, this ability is reduced and potassium levels rise. Centrophenoxine can also increase production of brain RNA and aid in a patient's oxygen consumption and carbon dioxide production.

Chromium Picolinate

Chromium picolinate is a nutritional supplement that works to increase the efficiency of insulin to optimal levels.

Gaining increased popularity in the United States, this supplement has been touted a miracle mineral, one advertised to have myriad effects including weight loss, mood enhancement, energy promotion, increase in life span, and even the prevention of acne (Krzanowski, 1996).

Conjunctisan A

A product specifically designed to treat ageing eye disorders such as cataracts, Conjunctisan A contains natural lysates, which purport to improve eye conditions by stimulating the natural healing and repair processes. Regular, longer use of conjunctisan A may improve eyesight in cataract sufferers, as well as myopia.

Deprenyl

Deprenyl is a drug that has been widely used to treat Parkinson's disease. In Parkinson's disease, dopamine, a major nerve transmitter, decreases due to the action of two enzymes, nonoamine oxidases (MAOS). MAO B occurs in the brain; MAO A occurs outside the brain and breaks up some amino acids present in food, thus serving a necessary purpose. Deprenyl inhibits only MAO B, and thus in combination with L-Dopa may be used to treat Parkinson's. Deprenyl may also act against several toxic chemicals produced when MAO B destroys dopamine and may act as an antidepressant.

Dilantin (Phenytoin)

In 1980, Russian scientists reported that the drugs Dilantin (phenytoin) and Phenformin had extended animal lifespan by 25% and 23% respectively in a strain of mice prone to autoimmune disease. Dilantin is an FDA-approved drug commonly prescribed to normalize electrical activity in epilepsy patients. Studies around the world have shown that Dilantin is useful for a wide variety of conditions including depression, headache, and neurologic disorders. Phenformin is a prescription antidiabetic drug, which lowers blood sugar in patients suffering from this disease, which suggests that it might have antiglycosylation effects. Both drugs have serious side effects, which makes them relatively poor candidates for long-term use.

DMAE (Dimethylaminoethanol)

DMAE (Dimethylaminoethanol) is a chemical naturally produced in the human brain. It is thought to be used by the body in converting the precursor choline to the neurotransmitter, acetylcholine. This is the basis for the reasoning behind the theory that supplementing with DMAE will enhance brain activity.

Ginkgo

Ginkgo, derived from the leaves of the ginkgo tree, stimulates brain activity by increasing levels of dopamine and improves the flow of blood to the brain and all other organs by dilating, or relaxing the arteries and veins. Rich in flavonoids, antioxidants that protect the body against free radicals, ginkgo has also been shown to prevent blood clots by inhibiting blood cells from sticking together. Ginkgo has been used in Oriental medicine for thousands of years. European researchers have recognized its properties since the 1970s and today ginkgo is widely prescribed in Europe for maladies ranging from headaches to hemorrhoids. Studies have shown ginkgo may have significant anti-ageing benefits: improving mental performance and circulation, as well as inhibiting free radicals, thus preventing heart disease, cancer and arthritis. There are no known side effects, or contraindications.

Ginkgo is available without a prescription in natural food stores and most drug stores. The recommended dosage is one 60 mg capsule, or tablet, three times daily, as the effects only last a few hours at a time.

Garlic

Odorless Garlic is extracted from Allum sativum and is a specially made Japanese product. Garlic has been the subject of numerous studies in the past decade and has been endorsed by celebrities and athletes alike.

Ginseng

This plant extract contains many good things to feed the brain. Special glycosides improve cerebral blood flow and work as stimulants of certain neurotransmitters, chemical messengers the brain uses to send out signals. Ginseng helps regulate blood sugar and so is of benefit in reducing the insulin resistance-diabetes progression. It also has benefits for the thymus gland and spleen, thus making it a great all-round anti-ageing substance. Ginseng is taken as teas, powders and capsules.

For 5000 years, the Chinese have revered this herb as a cure-all and antidote to the ravages of ageing. Ginseng is primarily a stimulant and some researchers speculate that it may indirectly stimulate the production of stress hormones that can increase stamina. Ginseng also contains choline, a chemical found in the brain that is essential for learning and memory retention. Studies have found that people taking ginseng make fewer mistakes and complete tasks more quickly than those who do not.

Researchers at Japan's Kanazawa University found that compounds called unpurified saponins found in ginseng inhibited the growth of cancer cells and even converted diseased cells into normal cells. In addition, ginseng contains antioxidants, known to prevent cellular damage due to free radicals.

Other anti-ageing benefits of ginseng are that it helps to raise levels of beneficial high-density lipoprotein or "good" cholesterol. In addition, ginseng may help to control some of the side effects of menopause, such as hot flashes.

Hydergine

An important anti-ageing drug, hydergine may help protect the brain from free radical damage and oxygen starvation. Hydergine maintains the brain's optimal metabolism of oxygen. Oxygen is a free radical scavenger and generator. Free radicals cause age-associated damage, and at optimal levels, oxygen will neutralize more free radicals than it generates. Hydergine may also stimulate the growth of dendrite nerve fibers, which may have a possible link to intelligence. Also, recent studies suggest that hydergine may reduce Senescent Cell Antigen (SCA), a destructive auto-antibody appearing more frequently in elderly cells. SCA damages cells and finally destroys them.

The body's ability to absorb nutrients can be inhibited by many factors, including previous medicine and antibiotic use, yeast, or bacterial overgrowth, as well as prevailing nutritional deficiencies. To ensure absorption of nutrients, intravenous vitamins and minerals are given. By receiving the necessary nutrients intravenously, a person's body is able to utilize them and receive their benefits immediately. Intravenous vitamins and minerals have been used in treatment of various chronic conditions, including cancer, fatigue and immune dysfunction.

Metformin

Metformin may improve insulin use and help prevent diabetes. It may increase the sensitivity of muscles to the effects of insulin, restoring the effects of glucose and insulin to younger physiological levels. Metformin may also be a useful dieting aid as it acts to stabilize sugar levels, thus preventing sugar highs and lows and sugar cravings. Metformin's anti-ageing benefits may also include decreasing risk of age-related adult-onset diabetes, prevention of sugar cravings, improved body composition with improved insulin use, stabilization of sugar levels and slowing of the effects of diabetes. Use of Metformin is contraindicated when combined with Thiazide, Cimetidine, diuretics, or other anti-hypertensive products, which could cause renal malfunctioning. Also contraindicated in individuals with ketonuria, serious hepatic and renal disorders, serious cardiovascular problems, serious respiratory problems, suprarenal insufficiency, chronic alcoholism, serious dystrophic illness, acute hemorrhaging, gangrene, diabetes with previous episodes of lactic acidosis, or hypersensitivity to Metformin.

Side Effects in healthy ageing individuals are rare, but may include nausea, loss of appetite, and very rarely, vomiting, stomach pain and diarrhea.

NADH (Nicotinamide Adenine Dinucleotide)

NADH, is a coenzyme made from vitamin B2, or niacin. It's present in all living cells. As a coenzyme, NADH serves an important role in helping enzymes to function as they should. (An enzyme is a protein that works like a catalyst in the body to prompt chemical changes in other substances; breaking down food into energy is an example.)

Picamilon

Sometimes also spelled Pikamilon or Pikamilone, this is a Russian developed nootropic. It is in essence Niacin (vitamin B3) bonded to GABA. Studies have shown that it rapidly crosses the blood-brain barrier, however its effects are much greater and broader than just taking a GABA and Niacin supplement.

Piracetam

The world's best-selling nootropic drug, Piracetam, is purported to prevent and correct memory loss due to old age, sharpening memory and improving clarity and attention to detail. It is used to treat senile dementia and Down's syndrome. A derivative of the amino acid GABA, Piracetam helps to restore levels of the neurotransmitter Acetylcholine. It also increases the sensitivity of muscuarinic receptors, which decreases with age. It brings about important metabolic modifications in nerve cells, which results in greater receptiveness and increased use of chemical energy by these cells.

Prolotherapy

A ligament is a band of fibrous tissue that holds bones together. Just like a rubber band, a ligament can become "overstretched". The resulting laxity can cause severe pain as bones rub together, or muscles are overworked as they tighten in an attempt to stabilize the bones. Prolotherapy is a treatment where a proliferate solution of natural substances is injected directly into the site where the weakened ligament attaches to the bone. Injections trigger the body's own immune system to grow new and healthy tissue, which then properly stabilizes the bones and joints, relieving musculoskeletal pain and stiffness. Prolotherapy is one of the treatments of choice for chronic pain.

Pyritinol

Recent evidence suggests that a European medication called Pyritinol may be an effective treatment for Alzheimer's disease. When compared with Hydergine and placebo, Pyritinol produced continuous improvement in cognitive function, which was more pronounced than in the Hydergine group. Pyritinol is used in Europe for the treatment of a wide variety of neurologic disorders.

RN13

RN13 is designed specifically to treat premature ageing and geriatric complaints. It acts on cell respiration and metabolism in organs which are particularly affected by ageing. RN13 contains 13 different animal source RNAs, as well as vitamins, amino acids, procaine and glutamic acid and biolecithin to improve cerebral activity. In the body, RNAs are responsible for protein biosynthesis help repair and regenerate body tissues and organs, and RN13 purports to work on the principle that animal source RNAs from specific organs may stimulate the same organs in humans. RN13 has been shown to make ageing individuals more alert and vital and to improve weak concentration, defective memory, anxiety, troubled sleep and lack of appetite.

RN13's anti-ageing benefits may include prevention and treatment of premature ageing and all types of age-related disorders, lifting of apathy and potential increase in life span. In severe cases, RN13 is administered by injection and supplemented by ampules, or capsules. In less severe cases, 2 ml ampules and 0.5 ml liquid capsules are available. VitOrgan of Germany manufactures RN13 under the trade name NeyGeront.

Sodium Oxybate (SO)

Sodium Oxybate (SO) is one of the controversial anti-ageing drugs available today. Normally referred to as GHB, its effects are varied and wide. Low to medium doses have been used to treat alcohol withdrawal and as a mild general anesthetic. Medium doses may act as a relaxant. At high doses, SO may be a potent stimulator of human growth hormone, as well as a very powerful sleep agent. It has been noted to double concentrations of dopamine in the brain and appears to inhibit the release of dopamine from nerve endings without preventing the manufacture of dopamine. Although it has not been sufficiently studied clinically, SO is reported to have a significant effect on the libido in both men and women. SO's anti-ageing benefits may include reduced fat levels, improved muscle mass and condition, deep REM sleep, treatment of insomnia and narcolepsy, improved libido and sexual performance and the ability to act as a general relaxant and soothing agent.

Side effects may include sudden sleep, dizziness, nausea, vomiting and headaches. At higher doses, side effects may include a moderate slowing of the heart, small changes in blood pressure and cardiac and respiratory depression and also, in a few cases, muscle spasms, or twitches as the patient enters SO-induced sleep. Patients suffering from Cushing's disease, convulsions, bradycardia, severe cardiovascular problems, severe hypertension, hyperprolactinemia, epilepsy, narcotic drug dependence, individual hypersensitivity, or who are using depressants, should avoid SO. It should not be used with alcohol. SO is available in liquid form in vials of 10 ml, 50 mg, 100 mg, 30 ml and 140 ml under the trade names Alcover, Gamma-oh and Somsanit.

Thym-Uvocal

Thym-Uvocal contains a standardized combination of thymus peptides, which may, in a natural manner, replace the decrease of thymic secretion associated with increasing age. The thymus gland undergoes an age related decrease in production of its various peptides. As thymus factors have been correlated with the strength of the immune system, Thym-Uvocal may help increase the strength of the immune system. It appears to have a favourable action on the T-4 cell ratio, and thus a stimulating and modulating action on the cellular immune system. Thym-Uvocal increases levels of antibodies and phacytosis, increases interleukin-1 production, and activates macrophages and enhances their cell destruction action.

Thym-Uvocal's anti-ageing benefits may include improved strength of immune system, an increase in the thymic peptide blood count, prevention and treatment of infection, treatment of cancer, treatment of rheumatic disease, treatment of dermatology disorders such as neurodermatitis, aphtosis and psoriasis, treatment of skin allergic reaction and states of exhaustion, and management of AIDS.

Thymic proteins are produced by the thymus gland, which plays an important role in the immune system. Thymic proteins program T-lymphocytes, the "shock troops" of the immune system., T-4 (helper) cells are central to the functioning of the immune system, and are activated by a certain thymic protein. This protein has been reported to strengthen the immune system, fight viral infections, and stimulate the bone marrow to produce more white and red blood cells, and fights against future illness. Thymic protein's anti-ageing benefits may include an increase in total white blood cell count, increased T-4 and T-8 levels, increase in total red blood cells and an increased potential life span. This thymus protein should be avoided in patients taking large doses of steroid hormones. The standard dosage for healthy people is 2 micrograms per day.

Trimethylglycine

Trimethylglycine is a methyl donor supplement that assists in methylation and may help protect cellular DNA from mutation. As humans age, methyl groups can decrease. Mildly elevated levels of homocysteine, an aminoacid, have been found in 21 percent of patients with coronary artery disease and 24 percent of patients with cerebrovascular disease. Trimethylglycine aids in the conversion of homocysteine to methionine.

Vasopressin

Vasopressin is a hormone secreted by the posterior portion of the pituitary gland. While it may help prevent frequent urination, vasopressin's main use is to treat memory deficits due to old age, senile dementia, drug toxicity and amnesia. Whenever a memory is deposited in the brain, vasopressin regulates the process. It helps select bits of information from the stream of consciousness and forms this information into an image, or concept, which is eventually transformed from an electrochemical impulse into a chemically encoded long-term memory. Vasopressin's benefits may include enhanced clarity, increased attention to detail, improved short-term memory and improved memory imprinting. Vasopressin's anti-ageing benefits may include treatment and prevention of age-related mental decline, prevention and treatment of senile dementia, improved short-term memory, attention and clarity, enhanced memory imprinting, and treatment of diabetes insidious.

Side effects include rhinorrhoea and nasal itchiness, headaches, conjunctivitis, sore throat, nausea, abdominal pain and the urgent need to defecate as a result of increased peristalsis. Vasopressin is contraindicated for patients suffering from coronary insufficiency, or using halothane, or cyclopropane anesthetics. It should be administered with caution in cases of hypertension, epilepsy, advanced arteriosclerosis, or any case where increased blood pressure is to be avoided.

Vinpocetine

Vinpocetine improves brain energy and blood supply and has been used as a preventative and as a treatment for stroke and other brain injury. It acts as a cerebral metabolic activator, which may improve cerebral circulation and enhance oxygen and glucose utilization in the brain. Vinpocetine may diminish, or reduce, disturbances due to hypoxia, or to deficient cerebral metabolism. It has been noted to improve oxygen and glucose utilization by brain cells and increase their resistance to damage by hypoxia.

Yohimbine

Yohimbine is a pharmaceutical preparation derived from the bark of a tree, called the Corynanthe Yohimbine, which has been useful in the treatment of impotence. Furthermore, Yohimbine increases blood levels of the neurotramsmitter norepinephrine, one of the body's own prosexual chemicals affecting the hypothalamus. Yomhimbine may also increase levels of acetylcholine, a neurotransmitter that has an effect on male erection response. The anti-ageing benefits of Yohimbine are purported to be the improvement of strength, duration and response of male erection, libido enhancement and improved sexual performance. Yohimbine is likely to be more sensitive in the elderly, where it can lead to over stimulation to the point of nervousness and anxiety. Other side effects may include nausea, vomiting, increased blood pressure, tremors, dizziness and headaches. Patients with inflammatory disease of the urogenital tract, known or suspected prostate or mammary cancer, hypercalciuria, ischemic heart disease, untreated congestive heart failure, glaucoma, extrapyramidal disorders and hyperexcitable states should avoid Yohimbine. Yohimbe is available in 1 mg, 2.5 mg, 5 mg and 10 mg tablets under the trade names Aphrodyne, Dayto Himbin, Plain Prowess, Yocon and Yohimes.

GABA (Gamma-aminobutyric acid)

It is one of the most potent stimulators of HGH-release from the pituitary. Proper medical supervision by a knowledgeable physician is required in supplementing these compounds, since the glutamine-arginine-lysine stack may release insulin as well as growth hormone. We now know that raised insulin levels can be damaging and definitely shortens life, so beware. Generally when HGH levels are rising, insulin levels are falling. However, if it is possible to raise insulin levels at the same time as growth hormone, it has a very high anabolic effect. That is to say the body builds up muscle and tissue, and carries out cell repair essential to reverse ageing.

Anti-Ageing Foods

Can you Stay Youthful Forever?

The antioxidants from fruits and vegetables help to prevent cancer, by fighting off free radicals, the byproducts of the body's everyday processes that damage DNA, cells, and tissues. A study revealed that less than a third of American adults eat the amount of fruits and vegetables the government recommends. That's "well below" the government's goal of getting 75 percent of Americans to eat two servings of fruits and having half of the population consume three servings of vegetables each day. It indicates the country is only about halfway toward meeting its healthy eating goal three years from now. Specifically the survey showed that 27 percent of adults ate vegetables three times a day, and about 33 percent ate fruit twice a day. A serving size is a half-cup for most fruits and vegetables, one cup for leafy greens. Though, no such figures are available for India, one can estimate that it would be much lower than that of USA.

Senior citizens were more likely than others to follow Mom's advice to eat more veggies, with slightly more than a third of that group eating three or more servings each day. Younger adults, age 18 to 24, ate the fewest vegetables. Nearly four-fifths of that age category scraped the veggies to the side of their plates—if they had vegetables on the plate at all. Likewise, seniors also ate the most fruit, with nearly 46 percent eating two or more servings of fruit daily. People age 35 to 44 ate fruit the least, with fewer than 28 percent eating the recommended amount of fruit each day. A researcher said people are eating more refined sugars or choosing proteins instead of fruits and vegetables. The situation in India is much worse.

Not only are fruits and vegetables low in calories, they also have minerals and fiber that help guard against chronic diseases and cancers.

Consider these facts:

- The number of calories you consume profoundly affects your level of free radical production and the types of food from which you derive these calories determine the range and amounts of antioxidants available to neutralize these free radicals. Restricting the calories of a laboratory mouse by 30% can increase its lifespan by 50%.
- The types of fats you eat can change the balance between inflammatory and anti-inflammatory molecules circulating in your blood. This can affect such conditions as PMS, arthritis, cardiovascular disease and cancer risk.
- The timing of meals and the rapidity with which the carbohydrates in them are absorbed can change the metabolism of fats and the production of hormones such as insulin and growth hormone. Avoid sugars and observe discipline in diet schedule. Over eating is always harmful.

Eat to Stay Young

Don't just live to eat. In a study published in the April 26, 2000, issue of the Journal of the American Medical Association, researchers reported finding that women who ate diets high in fruits, vegetables, grains were 30% less likely to die of any cause than women who didn't eat such a diet during the study. What is clear is that heart attacks, osteoporosis, and other signs of ageing take years to develop. Eating healthy foods slows that development, helping you to live better and longer.

1. Apples

"An apple a day could very well keep the doctor away," is an old saying. Apples contain naturally-occurring chemical compounds known as phytochemicals, polyphenols, or flavonoids, some of which have been proven to have antioxidant activity that inhibits, or scavenges, the activity of free radicals in the body. Cell damage from free radicals can be a factor in certain cancers, heart disease, strokes, and other conditions. The major antioxidant components in apples are polyphenols contained mainly in the skin known as quercetin glycoside, phloretin glycoside, chlorogenic acid, and epicatechin. The names are complex, but their health value is clear: Quercetin has been reported to reduce carcinogenic activity, inhibit enzymatic activities associated with several types of tumor cells, enhance the antiproliferative activity of anticancer agents, and inhibit the growth of transformed tumorigenic cells.

2. Blackberries, Blueberries, Raspberries, Strawberries

Antioxidant compounds found in blueberries, sweet cherries, strawberries and blackberries may fight arterial disease by preventing the oxidation of LDL ("bad") cholesterol, according to a team of researchers at the University of California, Davis. In studies conducted at the University, Dr. I. Marina Heinonen, a visiting scientist from the University of Helsinki in Finland, and colleagues extracted antioxidant compounds from blackberries, red raspberries, sweet cherries, blueberries and strawberries. In a series of experiments in laboratory culture dishes, they found that blackberries and Blueberries are of particular interest because of their high antioxidant capacity. They had the most antioxidant activity in one experiment and sweet cherries in another.

3. Bitter Melon, Cantaloupe, Honeydew Melon, Kiwi

Melons are widely available and grown in many parts of the world. In ancient Egypt, watermelons were traditionally offered to thirsty travelers, and they are still important today in times of drought or water pollution. Aromatic melon varieties were prized from early times in the Middle East. Melons are related to cucumbers, pumpkin, squash, and gourds, growing as they all do on long, trailing vines. These fruits which are full of antioxidants are often served for breakfast, as an appetizer, dessert, or snack. Larger melons are sliced in serving-size portions; smaller melons are typically cut in half and the pulp and seeds are scooped out before serving. Depending on their size, melons can be served in their skins, halved or cut in wedges, or peeled for used in salads or appetizers. The flesh can also be cut into cubes or scooped into balls with a melon-baller.

4. Citrus Fruits

Hundreds of studies have been conducted on the nutrients found in citrus fruit, including orange juice, and the role these nutrients play in reducing the risk of such diseases as cancer and heart disease, when part of a low fat diet rich in fruits and vegetables. Citrus fruit, which contain essential vitamins and minerals, are an important part of a healthy diet for all men, women and children. In fresh and juice form, citrus—including oranges, grapefruit and specialty varieties such a temple oranges, tangerines and tangelos—have many important nutritional benefits.

5. Oranges and Grapefruit

These fruits contain dietary fiber, including soluble fiber. Fiber helps in digestion and elimination, and, when part of a low fat diet rich in fruits and vegetables, may help reduce the risk of some cancers. Folate, a B vitamin commonly found in orange juice and green leafy vegetables, has been shown to help reduce the risk of certain types of birth defects. An eight-ounce glass of orange juice supplies 100 percent or more of the Daily Value for vitamin C. Citrus juices like orange juice are natural sources of potassium, and all citrus fruits are sodium and cholesterol-free.

6. Peaches, Pears, Plums

Peaches contain phytochemicals—chemical compounds produced by plants—that are important for healthy skin. Phytochemicals act as antioxidants that are critical to maintaining healthy skin. Peaches are also good sources of powerful antioxidants that, according to experts, may hold the secret to long life and vitality. Pears are a good source of fiber. Just one medium pear has 16% of the fiber our bodies need everyday for good health. Fiber helps our bodies with digestion and adds bulk to our diet. Plums are high in carbohydrates and are an excellent source of vitamin A, calcium, magnesium, iron, potassium and fiber and stimulate the bowel movement. Plums contain a substantial amount of vitamin C. Dried plums contain iron, potassium, vitamin A, magnesium and fiber. They are also high in antioxidants which help neutralize the damaging effects of oxidation on the ageing process, protect against certain cancers, heart and lung diseases and cataract formation.

7. Asparagus

Asparagus is spring's most luxurious vegetable. It was once cultivated for medicinal purposes as a natural remedy for blood cleansing and diuretic properties. Asparagus is rich in immunity-enhancing antioxidants and vitamins. Asparagus can be processed into juice and other products to increase total utilization and increase net value. Asparagus juice contains antioxidants, such as rutin, ferulic acid and ascorbic acid. When buying asparagus look for compact tips and smooth green stems that are uniform in colour down the length of the stem. Check the cut stem end for drying and avoid withered spears. Asparagus is low in calories and provides substantial amounts of antioxidants—Vitamins A and C. It truly shines as a source of folate and has a goodly amount of fiber.

8. Beans

People who pay attention to the colours of the foods they cook and serve are enhancing not only visual and gustatory pleasure, but nutritional punch as well. Enjoy your platter of rainbow coloured fruit and vegetables. These foods contain coloured pigments with nutritious cancer- and heart-disease-fighting compounds called flavonoids. Agricultural Research Service food quality geneticist and plant breeder George L. Hosfield has found these flavonoids in bean seed coats, which is where bean colours are also found. Certainly beans come in a mosaic of colours that can rival those of fruits and vegetables—from the plain white great northern and navy beans, to the mottled brownish pink pintos, to the cranberry bean's cream colour with red streaks and flecks, the light and dark reds of kidney beans, the maroon-red adzuki, delicious green beans all the way to the black bean. The seed coat, which is 10 percent of the bean, is not only high in antioxidants for some beans, but is also where the high fiber content of beans comes into play.

9. Broccoli

Broccoli is known as the "Crown Jewel of Nutrition" for its vitamin-rich, high in fiber, and low in calorie properties. Not only does broccoli give you the best vegetable nutrition available, it also gives you many ways to lead a healthier, longer life. Heart disease is the number one cause of death in the United States with cancer as the second, and broccoli gives you many ways to help fight and prevent these and other diseases. Broccoli has multiple cancer-fighting properties including vitamin C, beta carotene, and fiber. It is also rich of phytochemicals which appear to offer us protection against certain cancers and heart disease. Indole carbinol and sulforaphane are two different phytochemicals that are found in broccoli. Broccoli and tomatoes, (both of which have been found to help fight cancer), have been found to be even more effective against prostate cancer when eaten together as part of a daily diet. Researchers fed rats who had been implanted with prostate cancer cells a diet containing 10 percent broccoli powder and 10 percent tomato powder for a period of 22 weeks. The combination of vegetables may be more effective than either one alone because different compounds in each food work on different anti-cancer pathways.

10. Cauliflower

Nutritionally and medicinally, the cauliflower is similar to the cabbage. Of course, the lower sulphur content is obvious. Cabbage and cauliflower are rich in antioxidants, which help prevent cancer, and prevent heart disease caused by oxidative damage to blood vessels. It is especially rich in Vitamin C—one cup of chopped flowerets or laces of cabbage meets a whole day's requirement of this vitamin. A deficiency of Vitamin C causes scurvy because it interferes with collagen synthesis. Collagen is one of the structural frameworks of normal tissues. Other anti-cancer molecules present in significant amounts included the phytochemicals sulforaphane and indole-3-carbinol.

11. Leafy Greens, Spinach

Leaf lettuce, beet greens, and spinach are just the tip of the iceberg when it comes to these salad vegetables. Greens actually come in a wide variety of colours, textures, shapes, and flavors. They may be green to yellow-white, or red to purple, soft to crisp, curly to flat, and peppery to bitter to mild. Mix and match them and you've created an exciting salad! Greens are an excellent source of vitamin A and a good source of vitamin C. For a bigger boost of vitamin A, buy greens that are medium to dark green (the darker the leaves, the more vitamin A). Many greens, such as spinach, kale, and collards are known for their mineral content, especially iron, calcium, magnesium—as well as the vitamins folate, riboflavin (B2) and vitamin K. Leaves are very rich in antioxidants—the carotenoids and beta-carotene, the tocopherols (vitamin E) and of course, vitamin C.

12. Black and Green Tea

For years, studies have indicated that the antioxidants in green tea offer protection against diseases, including cancer, and even fight dental cavities. One of the most beneficial of these antioxidants is called epigallocatechin gallate (EGCG). According to the University of California Wellness Letter, Mar 2002, regular black tea is turning out to be just as healthful as green tea. The evidence for tea's health effects comes mainly from lab studies, though some human studies point to possible benefits in preventing heart disease and cancer. EGCG, inhibited an enzyme that cancer cells need in order to grow. The cancer cells that couldn't grow big enough to divide self-destructed. It would take about 4-10 cups of green tea a day to get the blood levels of EGCG that inhibited cancer in the study. Black tea also contains EGCG, but at lower concentrations.

13. Vitamin Therapy

They are broadly divided into two categories, namely, fat-soluble and water-soluble. Vitamins A, D, E and K are all soluble in fat and are therefore, known as fat-soluble. They are not easily lost by ordinary cooking methods and they can be stored in the body to some extent, mostly in the liver. They are measured in international units. Vitamin B Complex and C are water soluble. They are dissolved easily in cooking water. A portion of these vitamins may actually be destroyed by heating. They cannot be stored in body and therefore, they have to be taken daily in foods. Any extra quantity taken in any one day is eliminated as waste. Their values are given in milligrams and micrograms, whichever is appropriate. Vitamins, used therapeutically, can be of immense help in fighting disease and speeding recovery. Latest research indicates that many vitamins taken in large doses far above the actual nutritional needs can have a healing effect in a wide range of common complaints and illnesses.

Here are some of the effective anti-ageing food groups:

Dark Coloured Fruits

Red or purple fruits such as black grapes, blueberries, bilberries, black cherries and blackberries are rich sources of flavanoids and vitamin C. Both flavanoids and vitamin C keep the walls of our blood vessels strong, which encourages good blood circulation.

Whole grains

Once your liver has processed toxins which could stress your body and prematurely age it, they are sent to your intestines. To prevent them from being re-absorbed into your blood, it is important to keep your bowels working well and the fiber in whole grains such as brown rice, whole meal bread and porridge is especially helpful. Whole grains are also rich in the free-radical fighter, vitamin E and B vitamins, which are needed to keep your nervous system healthy and to combat heart disease and Alzheimer's. Brown rice is rich in methionine, which is needed to make free-radical fighting enzymes.

Water

All cells need the right amount of water to stay healthy. Research suggests that dehydration, is a common problem. Long-term dehydration can lead to problems such as kidney damage and cell and joint deterioration over time, so it is really important to drink eight glasses of water a day and build this into your regular daily routine.

The Cabbage Family

Members of the cabbage family—especially broccoli, Brussels, sprouts and greens—contain natural chemicals which help your liver to break down cancer-causing toxins and pollutants which are known to cause many age related problems such as Parkinson's, Alzheimer's and motor neuron disease. A further bonus of these cabbage family super foods is their ability to help prevent osteoporosis by providing an excellent source of vitamin K, which is needed for bone formation and repair.

Soya

Key ingredients in soya products, including genistein and daidzein, can help prevent breast cancer and prostrate cancer and are a natural form of hormone-replacement therapy for the menopause. They are a type of flavanoid which happens to be a good oestrogen balancer. The best soya products are tofu, soya yoghurt, soya flour and soya milk.

Brazil Nuts

Brazil nuts are one of the very good sources of selenium. The body needs selenium to make an enzyme called gluthathione peroxidase, which helps prevent free-radical damage to your cells. Studies show that people who eat selenium rich food have a greatly reduced risk of developing cancer and heart disease and that increasing selenium intake can help the kidneys to clear toxins from the body better.

Oily Fish

Since it was discovered that heart attacks are rare amongst Eskimos/Japanese, who eat a lot of fish, studies have been done on the effects of fish consumption on our blood and arteries. It was found that omega 3 oils found only in oily fish (mackerel, herrings and sardines) may prevent our red blood cells from clumping and blocking our blood vessels. Oily fish are also rich in zinc, which helps prevent prostrate cancer in older men. Eating fish provides far more omega 3 oils than any supplements.

Celery Juice

Osteoarthritis is often caused by acidity due to consumption of meat and a build-up of acid forming toxins. Celery juice can help reduce acidity levels. Drink one or two glasses a day as a preventative.

Sesame Seeds

Bones need a lot more than just calcium to keep them strong and healthy well into later life. Seasame seeds are an ideal food as they are rich in the osteoporosis fighting nutrients magnesium and zinc as well as calcium. Eat them ground up and mixed with other foods or use seasame seed paste, instead of butter.

Liver

Liver is rich in many anti-ageing nutrients: vitamin A and zinc, which help to prevent hormone deficiencies; folic acid and other B vitamins, which may prevent heart attacks and Alzheimer's; and chromium which helps keep blood sugar levels down. Vegetarians should eat a varied, whole food diet and take vitamin A (10,000 iu) and mineral supplements.

Let us look at some the anti-ageing approaches in foods that we consume.

1. Balanced diet

A healthy, balanced diet will help you maintain a healthy body composition and weight and provide you with the nutrients for optimal health and functioning. Ensure your diet is 60 to 65 per cent complex carbohydrate content—that is, fruits, vegetables, whole-grain breads, pastas and rice. Complement this with a diet that is 20 to 30 per cent fat content, and finally balance off your diet with 15 per cent protein content—that is, meats, soy and dairy products. Too much protein can promote bone loss. So it is imperative to get the correct amount of protein and avoid eating protein in excess. The older should try to get the recommended 20 to 35 grams of fiber each day by consuming a minimum of two servings of fruit, three servings of vegetables and four servings of whole-grains. Beware, too much fiber can exacerbate existing impairment of the gastrointestinal tract.

Adequate water

Water is our life force. Common complaints like headaches, lack of energy, tired and lethargic sensations, injuries, hot flashes and achy joints and muscles have seen to be associated with dehydration. If most women would commit to drinking eight glasses of water every day they would notice a great improvement in their overall health and energy. Degeneration associated with ageing will occur at a quicker rate if you are dehydrated. And you can't use thirst to help you determine when you should be drinking water, because as you age your thirst mechanism does not function as well as it should.

Five small meals

Those who do not eat breakfast and consume only a very light lunch are tricked into believing that they are reducing their caloric intake when, in fact, they are setting themselves up for a snacking binge in the late afternoon, followed by an overload at dinner. The result is just the opposite. Total calories consumed during the day will end up being higher rather than lower! Your metabolism, the rate at which you burn calories for internal functions, is like an engine—the more often you give it fuel, the better it works. When you deprive your body of food, a slowed metabolism occurs that makes it much more difficult to lose weight and much easier to gain weight. A diet that is not consistent in calorie and nutrient intake will also lead to a more rapid loss of muscle tissue that is avoidable. The rule should be that you do not go any longer than four hours during the daytime without eating something. You will probably have to change the mindset that dinner should be the largest meal.

Reduce fat Intake

Your body needs fat to function properly. Besides being an energy source, fat is a nutrient used in the production of cell membranes, as well as in several hormone-like compounds called eicosanoids. These compounds help regulate blood pressure, heart rate, blood vessel constriction, blood clotting and the nervous system. In addition, dietary fat carries fat-soluble vitamins—vitamins A, D, E and K—from your food into your body. Fat also helps maintain healthy hair and skin, protects vital organs, keeps your body insulated, and provides a sense of satisfaction after meals.

Eating large amounts of high-fat foods adds excess calories, which can lead to weight gain and obesity. Obesity is a risk factor for several diseases, including diabetes, heart disease, cancer, gallstones, sleep apnea and osteoarthritis.

When choosing fats, your best options are unsaturated fats: monounsaturated and polyunsaturated fats. These fats, if used in place of others, can lower your risk of heart disease by reducing the total and low-density lipoprotein (LDL) cholesterol levels in your blood. One type of polyunsaturated fat, omega-3 fatty acids, may be especially beneficial to your heart. Omega-3s appear to decrease the risk of coronary artery disease. They may also protect against irregular heartbeats and help lower blood pressure levels.

Here are the differences as well as the best food sources of these healthy fats:

- Monounsaturated fat remains liquid at room

temperature but may start to solidify in the refrigerator. Foods high in monounsaturated fat include olive, peanut and canola oils. most nuts also have high amounts of monounsaturated fat.

- Polyunsaturated fat liquid at room temperature. Foods high in polyunsaturated fats include vegetable oils, such as safflower, corn, sunflower, soy and cottonseed oils.
- Omega-3 fatty acids are polyunsaturated fats found mostly in seafood. Good sources of omega-3s include fatty, cold-water fish, such as salmon, mackerel and herring. Flaxseeds, flax oil and walnuts also contain omega-3 fatty acids, and small amounts are found in soybean and canola oils.

Saturated and trans-fats can increase your risk of heart disease by increasing your total and LDL ("bad") cholesterol. Intake of dietary cholesterol increases blood cholesterol levels, but not as much as saturated and trans fats do.

- Saturated fat. Usually solid or waxy at room temperature, saturated fat is most often found in animal products—such as red meat, poultry, butter and whole milk. Other foods high in saturated fat include coconut, palm and other tropical oils.
- Trans fat. Hydrogenated fat is a common ingredient in commercial baked goods—such as crackers, cookies and cakes—and in fried foods, such as doughnuts and french fries. Shortenings and some margarines also are high in trans fat.
- Dietary cholesterol. Your body naturally manufactures all of the cholesterol it needs, but you also get cholesterol from animal products, such as meat, poultry, seafood, eggs, dairy products, lard and butter.

Elderly persons who have lost weight due to reduced appetite need to consume a moderate amount of dietary fat to maintain a healthy weight. Avoid saturated fats that are

Type of fat	*Recommendation*
Saturated fat	Less than 10 percent of your total daily calories
Dietary cholesterol	Less than 300 milligrams a day

found in animal products such as beef, butter, dairy products and lard. Do not consume excess of coconut or palm oils; these are vegetable oils, but they contain some saturated fat.

Balance the pH

Human blood pH should be slightly alkaline (7.35-7.45). A pH of 7.0 is neutral. A pH below 7.0 is acidic. A pH above 7.0 is alkaline. An acidic pH can occur from, an acid forming diet, emotional stress, toxic overload, and/or immune reactions or any process that deprives the cells of oxygen and other nutrients. The body will try to compensate for acidic pH by using alkaline minerals. If the diet does not contain enough minerals to compensate, a build up of acids in the cells will occur.

An acidic balance will: decrease the body's ability to absorb minerals and other nutrients, decrease the energy production in the cells, decrease it's ability to repair damaged cells, decrease it's ability to detoxify heavy metals, make tumor cells thrive, and make it more susceptible to fatigue and illness.

The reason acidosis is more common in our society is mostly due to the typical diet, which is far too high in acid producing animal products like meat, eggs and dairy, and far too low in alkaline producing foods like fresh vegetables. Additionally, we eat acid producing processed foods like white flour and sugar and drink acid producing beverages like coffee and soft drinks. We use too many drugs, which are acid forming; and we use artificial chemical sweeteners like NutraSweet, Spoonful, Sweet 'N Low, Equal, or Aspartame, which are poison and extremely acid forming. One of the best things we can do to correct an overly acid body is to clean up the diet and lifestyle.

To maintain health, the diet should consist of 60% alkaline forming foods and 40% acid forming foods. To restore health, the diet should consist of 80% alkaline forming foods and 20% acid forming foods. Generally, alkaline forming foods include: most fruits, green vegetables, peas, beans, lentils, spices, herbs and seasonings, and seeds and nuts. Generally, acid forming foods include: meat, fish, poultry, eggs, grains, and legumes.

Highly Alkaline Forming Foods

Baking soda, sea salt, mineral water, pumpkin seed, lentils, seaweed, onion, taro root, sea vegetables, lotus root, sweet potato, lime, lemons, nectarine, persimmon, raspberry, watermelon, tangerine, and pineapple.

Moderately Alkaline Forming Foods

Apricots, spices, kambucha, unsulfured molasses, soy sauce, cashews, chestnuts, pepper, kohlrabi, parsnip, garlic, asparagus, kale, parsley, endive, arugula, mustard green, ginger root, broccoli, grapefruit, cantaloupe, honeydew, citrus, olive, dewberry, carrots, loganberry, and mango.

Low Alkaline Forming Foods

Most herbs, green tea, mu tea, rice syrup, apple cider vinegar, sake, quail eggs, primrose oil, sesame seed, cod liver oil, almonds, sprouts, potato, bell pepper, mushrooms, cauliflower, cabbage, rutabaga, ginseng, eggplant, pumpkin, collard green, pear, avocado, apples (sour), blackberry, cherry, peach, and papaya.

Very Low Alkaline Forming Foods

Ginger tea, umeboshi vinegar, ghee, duck eggs, oats, grain coffee, quinoa, japonica rice, wild rice, avocado oil, most seeds, coconut oil, olive oil, flax oil, brussel sprout, beet, chive, cilantro, celery, okra, cucumber, turnip greens, squashes, lettuces, orange, banana, blueberry, raisin, currant, grape, and strawberry.

Very Low Acid Forming Foods

Curry, Koma coffee, honey, maple syrup, vinegar,

cream, butter, goat/sheep cheese, chicken, gelatin, organs, venison, fish, wild duck, triticale, millet, kasha, amaranth, brown rice, pumpkin seed oil, grape seed oil, sunflower oil, pine nuts, canola oil, spinach, fava beans, black-eyed peas, string beans, wax beans, zucchini, chutney, rhubarb, coconut, guava, dry fruit, figs, and dates.

Low Acid Forming Foods

Vanilla, alcohol, black tea, balsamic vinegar, cow milk, aged cheese, soy cheese, goat milk, game meat, lamb, mutton, boar, elk, shell fish, mollusks, goose, turkey, buckwheat, wheat, spelt, teff, kamut, farina, semolina, white rice, almond oil, sesame oil, safflower oil, tapioca, seitan, tofu, pinto beans, white beans, navy beans, red beans, aduki beans, lima beans, chard, plum, prune and tomatoes.

Moderately Acid Forming Foods

Nutmeg, coffee, casein, milk protein, cottage cheese, soy milk, pork, veal, bear, mussels, squid, chicken, maize, barley groats, corn, rye, oat bran, pistachio seeds, chestnut oil, lard, pecans, palm kernel oil, green peas, peanuts, snow peas, other legumes, garbanzo beans, cranberry, and pomegranate.

Highly Acid Forming Foods

Tabletop sweeteners like (NutraSweet, Spoonful, Sweet 'N Low, Equal or Aspartame), pudding, jam, jelly, table salt, beer, yeast, hops, malt, sugar, cocoa, white vinegar, processed cheese, ice cream, beef, lobster, pheasant, barley, cottonseed oil, hazelnuts, walnuts, brazil nuts, fried foods, soybean, and soft drinks, especially the cola type. To neutralize a glass of cola with a pH of 2.5, it would take 32 glasses of alkaline water with a pH of 10.

Alkaline: Meditation, Prayer, Peace, Kindness and Love

Extremely Alkaline Forming Foods—pH 8.5 to 9.0

9.0 Lemons 1, Watermelon 2.

8.5 Agar Agar 3, Cantaloupe, Cayenne (Capsicum) 4, Dried dates and figs, Kelp, Karengo, Kudzu root, Limes

Acid Forming Foods

FATS and OILS

- Avocado Oil
- Canola Oil
- Corn Oil
- Hemp Seed Oil
- Flax Oil
- Lard Olive Oil
- Safflower Oil
- Sesame Oil
- Sunflower Oil

FRUITS

- Cranberries

GRAINS

- Rice Cakes
- Wheat Cakes
- Amaranth
- Barley
- Buckwheat
- Corn
- Oats (rolled)
- Quinoi Rice (all)
- Rye
- Spelt
- Kamut
- Wheat
- Hemp Seed Flour

DAIRY

- Cheese, Cow
- Cheese, Goat
- Cheese, Processed
- Cheese, Sheep
- Milk
- Butter

NUTS and BUTTERS

- Cashews
- Brazil Nuts
- Peanuts
- Peanut Butter
- Pecans
- Tahini
- Walnuts

ANIMAL PROTEIN

- Beef
- Carp
- Clams
- Fish
- Lamb
- Lobster
- Mussels
- Oyster
- Pork
- Rabbit
- Salmon
- Shrimp
- Scallops
- Tuna
- Turkey
- Venison

PASTA (WHITE)

- Noodles
- Macaroni
- Spaghetti

OTHER

- Distilled Vinegar
- Wheat Germ
- Potatoes

DRUGS and CHEMICALS

- Aspartame
- Chemicals
- Drugs, Medicinal
- Drugs, Psychedelic
- Pesticides
- Herbicides

ALCOHOL

- Beer
- Spirits
- Hard Liquor
- Wine

BEANS and LEGUMES

- Black Beans
- Chick Peas
- Green Peas
- Kidney Beans
- Lentils
- Lima Beans
- Pinto Beans
- Red Beans
- Soy Beans
- Soy Milk
- White Beans
- Rice Milk
- Almond Milk

Alkaline Forming Foods

VEGETABLES

- Garlic
- Asparagus
- Fermented Veggies
- Watercress
- Beets
- Broccoli
- Brussel sprouts
- Cabbage
- Carrot
- Cauliflower
- Celery
- Chard
- Chlorella
- Collard Greens
- Cucumber
- Eggplant
- Kale
- Kohlrabi
- Lettuce
- Mushrooms
- Mustard Greens
- Dulce
- Dandelions
- Edible Flowers
- Onions
- Parsnips (high glycemic)
- Peas
- Peppers
- Pumpkin
- Rutabaga
- Sea Veggies
- Spirulina
- Squashes
- Alfalfa
- Barley Grass
- Wheat Grass
- Wild Greens
- Nightshade Veggies

FRUITS

- Apple
- Apricot
- Avocado
- Banana (high glycemic)
- Cantaloupe
- Cherries
- Currants
- Dates/Figs
- Grapes
- Grapefruit
- Lime
- Honeydew Melon
- Nectarine
- Orange
- Lemon
- Peach
- Pear
- Pineapple
- All Berries
- Tangerine
- Tomato
- Tropical Fruits
- Watermelon

PROTEIN

- Eggs (poached)
- Whey Protein
- Powder Cottage
- Cheese
- Chicken Breast
- Yogurt
- Almonds
- Chestnuts Tofu (fermented)
- Flax Seeds
- Pumpkin Seeds
- Tempeh (fermented)
- Squash Seeds
- Sunflower Seeds

OTHER

- Apple Cider Vinegar
- Bee Pollen
- Lecithin Granules
- Probiotic Cultures
- Green Juices
- Veggies Juices
- Fresh Fruit Juice
- Organic Milk (unpasteurized)
- Mineral Water
- Alkaline Antioxidant
- Water
- Green Tea
- Herbal Tea
- Dandelion Tea
- Ginseng Tea
- Banchi Tea
- Kombucha

SWEETENERS

- Stevia
- Ki Sweet

SPICES/SEASONINGS

- Cinnamon
- Curry
- Ginger
- Mustard
- Chili Pepper
- Sea Salt
- Miso
- Tamari
- All Herbs

ORIENTAL VEGETABLES

- Maitake

- Millet
- Sprouted Seeds
- Nuts

- Daikon
- Dandelion Root
- Shitake
- Kombu
- Reishi
- Nori
- Umeboshi
- Wakame
- Sea Veggies

Mango, Melons, Papaya, Parsley 5, Seedless grapes (sweet), Watercress, Seaweeds.

Asparagus 6, Endive, Kiwifruit, Fruit juices 7, Grapes (sweet), Passion fruit, Pears (sweet), Pineapple, Raisins, Umeboshi plum, Vegetable juices 8.

Moderate Alkaline—pH 7.5 to 8.0

8.0 Apples (sweet), Apricots, Alfalfa sprouts 9, Arrowroot, flour 10, Avocados, Bananas (ripe), Berries, Carrots, Celery, Currants, Dates and figs (fresh), Garlic 11, Gooseberry, Grapes (less sweet), Grapefruit, Guavas, Herbs (leafy green), Lettuce (leafy green), Nectarine, Peaches (sweet), Pears (less sweet), Peas (fresh sweet), Persimmon, Pumpkin (sweet), Sea salt (vegetable) 12, Spinach.

7.5 Apples (sour), Bamboo shoots, Beans (fresh green), Beets, Bell Pepper, Broccoli, Cabbage; Cauli, Carob 13, Daikon, Ginger (fresh), Grapes (sour), Kale, Kohlrabi, Lettuce (pale green), Oranges, Parsnip, Peaches (less sweet), Peas (less sweet), Potatoes and skin, Pumpkin (less sweet), Raspberry, Sapote, Strawberry, Squash 14, Sweet corn (fresh), Tamari 15, Turnip, Vinegar (apple cider) 16.

Slightly Alkaline to Neutral pH 7.0

7.0 Almonds 17, Artichokes (Jerusalem), Barley-Malt (sweetener-Bronner), Brown Rice Syrup, Brussel Sprouts, Cherries, Coconut (fresh), Cucumbers, Egg plant, Honey (raw), Leeks, Miso, Mushrooms, Okra, Olives ripe 18, Onions, Pickles 19, (home made), Radish, Sea salt 20, Spices 21, Taro, Tomatoes (sweet), Vinegar (sweet brown rice), Water Chestnut.

Amaranth, Artichoke (globe), Chestnuts (dry roasted), Egg yolks (soft cooked), Essene bread 22, Goat's milk and whey (raw) 23, Horseradish, Mayonnaise (home made), Millet, Olive oil, Quinoa, Rhubarb, Sesame seeds (whole) 24, Soy beans (dry), Soy cheese, Soy milk, Sprouted grains 25, Tempeh, Tofu, Tomatoes (less sweet), Yeast (nutritional flakes).

Acid: Overwork, Anger, Fear, Jealousy and Stress

Extremely Acid Forming Foods—pH 5.0 to 5.5

5.0 Artificial sweeteners 5.5 Beef, Carbonated soft drinks and fizzy drinks 38, Cigarettes (tailor made), Drugs, Flour (white wheat) 39, Goat, Lamb, Pastries and cakes from white flour, Pork, Sugar (white) 40.

Beer 34, Brown sugar 35, Chicken, Deer, Chocolate, Coffee 36, Custard with white sugar, Jams, Jellies, Liquor 37, Pasta (white), Rabbit, Semolina, Table salt refined and iodized, Tea black, Turkey, Wheat bread, White rice, White vinegar (processed).

Moderate Acid—pH 6.0 to 6.5

6.0 Cigarette tobacco (roll your own), Cream of Wheat (unrefined), Fish, Fruit juices with sugar, Maple syrup (processed), Molasses (sulphured), Pickles (commercial), Breads (refined) of corn, oats, rice and rye, Cereals (refined) eg. weetbix, corn flakes, Shellfish, Wheat germ, Whole Wheat foods 32, Wine 33, Yogurt (sweetened).

6.5 Bananas (green), Buckwheat, Cheeses (sharp), Corn and rice breads, Egg whole (cooked hard), Ketchup, Mayonnaise, Oats, Pasta (whole grain), Pastry (wholegrain and honey), Peanuts, Potatoes (with no skins), Popcorn (with salt and butter), Rice (basmati),

Rice (brown), Soy sauce (commercial), Tapioca, Wheat bread (sprouted organic).

Slightly Acid to Neutral pH 7.0

7.0 Barley malt syrup, Barley, Bran, Cashews, Cereals (unrefined with honey-fruit-maple syrup), Cornmeal, Cranberries 30, Fructose, Honey (pasteurized), Lentils, Macadamias, Maple syrup (unprocessed), Milk (homogenized) and most processed dairy products, Molasses (unsulphered organic 31, Nutmeg, Mustard, Pistachios, Popcorn and butter (plain), Rice or wheat crackers (unrefined), Rye (grain), Rye bread (organic sprouted), Seeds (pumpkin and sunflower), Walnuts
Blueberries, Brazil nuts, Butter (salted), Cheeses (mild and crumbly) 28, Crackers (unrefined rye), Dried beans (mung, adzuki, pinto, kidney, garbanzo) 29, Dry coconut, Egg whites, Goats milk (homogenized), Olives (pickled), Pecans, Plums 30, Prunes 30, Spelt.

Neutral pH 7.0

Healthy Body Saliva pH Range is between 6.4 to 6.8 (on your pH test strips).

Butter (fresh unsalted), Cream (fresh and raw), Margarine 26, Milk (raw cow's) 27, Oils (except olive).

Whey (cow's), Yogurt (plain).

NOTE: Match with the numbers above.

1. Excellent for EMERGENCY SUPPORT for colds, coughs, sore throats, heartburn, and gastro upsets.
2. Good for a yearly fast. For several days eat whole melon, chew pips well and eat also. Super alkalizing food.
3. Substitute for gelatin, more nourishing.
4. Stimulating, non-irritating body healer. Good for endocrine system.
5. Purifies kidneys.

6. Powerful acid reducer detoxing to produce acid urine temporarily . . . causing alkalinity for the long-term.
7. Natural sugars give alkalinity. Added sugar causes juice to become acid-forming.
8. Depends on veggie's content and sweetness.
9. Enzyme rich, superior digestibility.
10. High calcium content. Corn flour substitute.
11. Elevates acid food 5.0 in alkaline direction.
12. Vegetable content raises alkalinity.
13. Substitute for coca; mineral rich.
14. Winter squash rates 7.5. Butternut and sweeter squash rates 8.0.
15. Genuine fermented for 1½ years otherwise 6.0.
16. Raw unpasteurized is a digestive aid to increase HCL in the stomach. 1 tablespoon, plus honey and water before meals.
17. Soak 12 hours, peel skin to eat.
18. Sun dried, tree ripened, otherwise 6.0.
19. Using sea-salt and apple cider vinegar.
20. Contains sea minerals. Dried at low temperatures.
21. Range from 7.0 to 8.0.
22. Sprouted grains are more alkaline. Grains chewed well become more alkaline.
23. High sodium to aid digestion.
24. High levels of utilizable calcium. Grind before eating.
25. Alkalinity and digestibility higher.
26. Heating causes fats to harden and become indigestible.
27. High mucous production.
28. Mucous forming and hard to digest.
29. When sprouted dry beans rate 7.0.
30. Contain acid-forming benzoic and quinic acids.
31. Full of iron.
32. Unrefined wheat is more alkaline.
33. High quality red wine, no more than 4 oz. daily to build blood.
34. Good quality, well brewed-up to 5.5. Fast brewed beers drop to 5.0.

35. Most are white sugars with golden syrup added.
36. Organic, fresh ground-up to 5.5.
37. Cheaper brands drop to 5.0, as does over-indulgence.
38. Leaches minerals.
39. Bleached- has no goodness.
40. Poison! Avoid it.
41. Potential cancer agent. Over-indulgence may cause partial blindness.

5

Caloric Restriction is the Key

Can it Lead to Life Extension?

The only known method that might be able to delay human ageing is caloric restriction (CR). CR, as the name implies, consists of diminishing caloric-intake while maintaining a normal diet regarding other nutrients such as vitamins and minerals. There are different implementations of CR and variants such as protein restriction, dietary restriction and food restriction, but since the reduction of energy-intake seems to be the cause of the effects we witness in CR, the term caloric restriction is preferred. Studies in animals demonstrate that CR can delay the rate of ageing. CR can delay the entire ageing phenotype, reducing the frequency of age-related diseases and decelerating ageing. CR animals look younger and some tests suggest that they are physiologically younger than their age-matched controls. There are also ongoing studies in rhesus monkeys but the final results will not be known very soon. So far, it appears that CR monkeys are shorter, smaller, have lower body temperatures, a normal intelligence, a decreased sexual appetite, and a lower mortality rate. In one group studied—so far—for 25 years, CR monkeys lived on average 32 years while controls lived 25 years, which suggests a life-extension slightly over 20% and hence lower than that witnessed in rodents.

In humans, there are no conclusive studies but some data suggests that CR might be beneficial. One study found that CR has a protective effect against atherosclerosis in people. High-calories diet is unhealthy, increasing your change of developing age-related diseases like atherosclerosis and type 2 diabetes. Perhaps CR does not delay ageing but instead an ad-libitum diet—i.e., one in which you eat everything you want, which is the diet used for the control rodents and monkeys used in CR studies—is harmful. One study recently compared the high calories diet of Japanese wrestlers, who live about 56 years, with that of male Okinawans, who have a low-calorie diet, though are not calorie-restricted, and live about 77 years. By extrapolating from the male Okinawa's to CR, the study estimated that the life-extension provided by CR for an individual with an already balanced nutrition would be less than 10%. Others too have argued that CR would not significantly extend human lifespan in people who already live a healthy life.

First of all, there is the mental stress for being hungry all the time. Then, if you undergo CR, exercise may become impossible, even though studies in mice indicate that exercise while on CR has only mild negative effects on longevity. CR also makes people feel less energetic, less alive. And finally there are the sexual problems: diminished libido is common and annoying side-effect in people under CR. Still, one can say CR might add some years to your life but it will not be a life worth-living. One final problem reported in mice is that CR may hinder their ability to fight infection.

Some say that the diminished energy intake forces an optimization of the metabolism. Since CR also delays development in mice, others say it slows down the entire genetic program, indirectly affecting ageing.

Even though the mechanisms of CR are largely unknown, several scientists have been trying to develop products that mimic the effects of CR without the side-effects. Medicines; that mimic CR have for long been an objective, but so far this search has eluded researchers. Potential targets have included inhibitors of glycolysis (e.g., 2-deoxy-D-glucose), an anti-diabetic drug called metformin, and a group of molecules called sirtuin-activating compounds (STACs) that include plant polyphenols such as resveratrol and fisetin. Although, for instance, metformin treatment has been shown to increase the average lifespan of tumor-prone mice by 8%, none of these molecules has been shown to delay ageing in mammals. Even though it is possible these compounds are healthy, just like vegetables are healthy, or may have a positive effect on certain age-related diseases like diabetes, there is no evidence they can delay, even if slightly, human ageing.

The Benefits of Caloric Restriction

While low-calorie diets have been linked to a longer lifespan in both animals and humans, the reason for the association has been unclear. The researchers have evidence from studies in mice that cutting calories shields brain cells from the decline that comes with ageing. In experiments with mice, scientists used a gene chip, a new type of gene-scanning technology, to rapidly determine the activity of more than 6,000 genes in the animals' brain tissue. The researchers found that ageing boosted the activity of some genes and decreased it in others. As the mice aged, activity increased in genes responsible for inflammation and the stress response—two key factors related to cell damage. In addition, activity declined in genes involved in repairing cell damage. Inflammation in the brain is believed to be related to certain diseases such as Alzheimer's. A study in Parkinson's patients has suggested that high calorie intake contributes to the risk for the disease. "These findings," he said, "provide a link at the molecular level."

Scientists first recognized the value of the CR practice more than 60 years ago, when they found that rats fed a low-calorie diet lived longer on average than free-feeding rats and had a reduced incidence of conditions that become increasingly common in old age. What is more, some of the treated animals survived longer than the oldest-living animals in the control group, which means that the maximum life span (the oldest attainable age), not merely the average life span, increased. Various interventions, such as infection-fighting drugs, can increase a population's average survival time, but only approaches that slow the body's rate of ageing will increase the maximum life span.

The animals on CR also look better on indicators of risk for age-related diseases. For example, they have lower blood pressure and triglyceride levels (signifying a decreased likelihood of heart disease), and they have more normal blood glucose levels (pointing to a reduced risk for diabetes, which is marked by unusually high blood glucose levels). Further, we have recently shown that rhesus monkeys kept on caloric restriction for an extended time (nearly 15 years) have less chronic disease, just as the risk data suggested.

The Journey Starts

By 1995 the scientists wanted to know how the many physiological and biochemical changes induced by caloric restriction led to delaying ageing in mammals. For a number of reasons, we suspected that changes in cellular metabolism would be the key. By "metabolism" we mean the uptake of nutrients from the blood and their conversion to energy usable for cellular activities. They focused on metabolism in part because the benefits of caloric restriction clearly depend on reducing the overall amount of fuel coming into the body for processing. Also, caloric restriction affects the ageing of a wide variety of tissues, which implies that it alters biological processes carried out by all cells. Few processes are more fundamental than metabolism. We specifically wondered whether changes related to metabolism of the sugar glucose would account for the benefits of caloric restriction. Glucose, which forms when the body digests carbohydrates, is the primary source of energy in the body—that is, it is the main material used by cells for making ATP, or adenosine triphosphate, the molecule that directly powers most cellular activities. We also wanted to know whether alterations in the secretion and activity of insulin, which influences glucose use by cells, would be important. Insulin is secreted as glucose levels in the blood rise after a meal, and it serves as the key that opens cell "doors" to the sugar. We concentrated on glucose and insulin because reductions in their levels and increases in cellular sensitivity to insulin are among the most consistent hallmarks of caloric restriction in both rodents and primates, occurring very soon after restriction is begun.

Shortly after they decided to test the hypothesis that

caloric restriction retards ageing by altering metabolism, others began publishing data showing that metabolic processes involving glucose and insulin influence life span. Such findings encouraged our belief that we were on the right track. For instance, a number of investigations achieved remarkable extensions of life span in nematode worms by mutating genes similar to those involved in molecular responses to insulin in mammals. More recently researchers have found that lowered intake of glucose or disruption of glucose processing can extend life span in yeast. And in fruit flies, genes involved in metabolism, such as INDY (I'm Not Dead Yet), have been implicated in life-span control.

An "Aha!" Moment

Around the time the nematode work came out, they began to scour the scientific literature for ways to manipulate insulin secretion and sensitivity without causing diabetes or its opposite, hypoglycemia. Their search turned up studies from the 1940s and 1950s mentioning a compound called 2-deoxy-D-glucose (2DG) that was being tested in rodents for treating cancer but that also reportedly lowered insulin levels in the blood. The compound apparently reproduced many classic responses to caloric restriction—among them reduced tumor growth (a response only slightly less robust than the well-known extension of life span), lowered temperature, elevated levels of glucocorticoid hormones and reduced numbers of reproductive cycles. If 2DG really could mimic many aspects of caloric restriction in animals, we thought, perhaps it would do the same for people.

While they were planning their first studies of 2DG, they scanned the literature for details of how it works at the molecular level, learning that it disrupts the functioning of a key enzyme involved in processing glucose in cells. The compound structurally resembles glucose, so it enters cells readily. It is also altered by an enzyme that usually acts on glucose itself. But the enzyme that completes the next of several steps involved in glucose processing essentially chokes on the intermediate produced from 2DG. When it tries to act on this intermediate, it fails; in addition, its ability to act on the normal glucose intermediate becomes impaired.

The net result is that cells make smaller amounts of glucose's by-products, just as occurs when caloric restriction limits the amount of glucose going into cells. Certain of these products serve as the raw material for the ATP-making machinery, which is composed of a series of protein complexes located in intracellular compartments called mitochondria. Deprived of this raw material, the machinery makes less ATP. In essence, 2DG tricks the cell into a metabolic state similar to that seen during caloric restriction, even though the body is taking in normal amounts of food. As long as the amount of ATP made meets the minimum requirements of cells, this diminished operation of the ATP-making machinery is apparently beneficial.

Why reduced functioning of the ATP-producing machinery help combat ageing? We can't say with certainty, but we have some ideas. A long-standing theory of ageing blames the production of molecules called free radicals. The lion's share of free radicals in the body is emitted as the ATP-making machinery operates. Over time these highly reactive molecules are thought to cause permanent damage to various parts of cells, including the protein complexes responsible for generating ATP. Perhaps by reducing the rate of ATP production, 2DG and caloric restriction slow the rate at which free radicals form and disrupt The lack of glucose's by-products might retard ageing in another way as well. Certain of those substances help to induce cells in the pancreas to secrete insulin after an organism eats. Reductions in the amount of those by-products would presumably limit insulin secretion and thereby minimize insulin's unwanted actions in the body. Aside from indirectly promoting excessive operation of the ATP-making machinery and thus boosting free-radical production, insulin can contribute to heart disease and to undesirable cell proliferation.

They also suspect that cells interpret reduced levels of raw materials for the ATP-making machinery as a signal that food supplies are scarce. Cells may well respond to that message by switching to a self-protective mode, inhibiting activities not needed for cell maintenance and repair—such as reproduction—and pouring most of their energy into preserving the integrity of their parts. If that idea is correct, it could explain why caloric restriction has been shown to increase production of substances that protect cells from excess heat and other stresses.

This adoption of a self-preservation mode would mirror changes that have been proposed to occur on an organismic level in times of food scarcity. In the generally accepted "disposable soma" theory of ageing, Thomas Kirkwood of the University of Newcastle in England has proposed that organisms balance the need to procreate against the need to maintain the body, or soma. When resources are plentiful, organisms can afford both to maintain them and to grow and reproduce. But when food is limited, the body invokes processes that inhibit growth and reproduction and takes extra care to preserve the soma.

Testing Begins

In their first experiments devoted to examining 2DG's effectiveness, they delivered low doses to rats by adding it to their feed for six months. The treatment moderately reduced fasting blood glucose levels (levels measured after food was removed for 12 hours), body weight and temperature, and robustly reduced fasting insulin levels—findings consistent with the actions of caloric restriction itself. Interestingly, after an initial adjustment to the novel diet, the 2DG group did not eat significantly less food than the controls. Thus, these exciting preliminary analyses revealed that it was possible to mimic at least some squeal of caloric restriction without reducing food intake.

Shortly after they published these results, in 1998, other groups began identifying more ways that 2DG imitates caloric restriction. For example, Mark P. Mattson, then at the University of Kentucky, and his colleagues had reported earlier that caloric restriction could attenuate damage to nerve cells and limit behavioral deficits in rodents treated with compounds toxic to brain cells. When they then treated rodents with 2DG instead of caloric restriction, they observed the same neuronal protection.

At this writing, they are in the midst of conducting long-term rodent trials of 2DG. Results from the first year of this endeavor confirm our previous findings that 2DG slightly reduces blood glucose and body temperature. They are also examining whether 2DG reduces the incidence of cancer and increases life span when fed to animals at low doses from the time they are weaned until they die.

The work so far clearly provides a "proof of concept" that inhibiting glucose metabolism can re-create many effects of caloric restriction. Regrettably, however, 2DG has a fatal flaw preventing it from being the "magic pill" we were hoping for. Though safe at certain low levels, it apparently becomes toxic for some animals when the amount delivered is raised just a bit or given over long periods. The narrowness of the safety zone separating helpful and toxic doses would bar it from human use. We hope this is not a general feature of CR mimetics.

Moving On

Assuming their long-term studies confirm that inhibiting metabolism can retard ageing, the task becomes finding other substances that yield 2DG's benefits but are safer over a broader range of doses and delivery schedules. Several candidates seem promising in early studies, including iodoacetate, being investigated by Mattson's group, now at the NIA's Laboratory of Neurosciences. In animals this agent appears to protect brain cells from assaults by toxic substances, just as 2DG and caloric restriction do. Treatment with antidiabetic medications that enhance cellular sensitivity to insulin might be helpful as well, as long as the amounts given do not cause blood glucose levels to fall too low.

A great deal of research implicates glucose metabolism in regulating life span, yet other aspects of metabolism can also change in reaction to caloric restriction. When the body cannot extract enough energy from glucose in food, it can switch to obtaining energy in alternative ways. For example, it may shift to breaking down protein and fat. Pharmaceuticals that targeted these processes might serve as CR mimetics, either alone or in combination with drugs that intervene in glucose metabolism. Some compounds that act in those pathways have already been identified, although researchers have not yet assessed their potential as CR mimetics. Drugs that replicate only selected effects of caloric restriction could have a role to play as well. In theory, antioxidant vitamins might fit that bill. Research conducted to date, however, indicates that this particular intervention probably will not extend longevity.

Unlike the multitude of elixirs being touted as the latest anti-ageing cure, CR mimetics would alter fundamental processes that underlie ageing. They aim to develop compounds that fool cells into activating maintenance and repair activities that lead to greater health and longevity of the organism. That job is difficult but no longer seems impossible. If scientists can develop agents that offer the benefits of 2DG without its drawbacks, they will finally enable people to have their cake—a longer, healthier life.

6

Human Growth Hormone

Can it Defy Ageing?

Human growth hormone (HGH) has been used as an anti-ageing treatment for a long time and some evidence suggests it has beneficial effects in elderly people. HGH might increase muscle mass, strengthen the immune system, increase libido, etc. A Surgeon of Indian-origin 55, claimed in London recently that he had discovered the secret of eternal youth to renew the human body. He asserted that he and his wife 48, have been revitalized by injections of human growth hormone (HGH) after a long treatment of one and a half years. According to him it made their skins shine and improved libido. He estimates that the treatment could cost about £12000 each for his patients. This treatment is popular in United States, though other parts of the globe are still picking up. Others warn that HGH may make you feel great but may diminish your lifespan, while shrinking your wallet.

Studies indicate that your body produces about 15% less of the hormone with each successive decade. As you get older, and your body begins to produce less of the human growth hormone, you start to notice that you look and feel older. By the age of 60, HGH levels decrease by an astonishing 80% from adolescent levels. Depletion is marked by the familiar signs of ageing, such as facial wrinkles, increased body fat, lack of vitality, decreased muscle mass, and poor general health.

Until 1996 it was authorized in the treatment of children with HGH deficiencies only (stunted growth). Now HGH can be administered (on prescription) to hormone-deficient adults also. This hormone decreases with age and it's replenishment can improve memory, muscle mass, decrease in body fat, healthier heart, lungs, kidneys, increased bone density, elevation of mood, energy and libido. HGH stimulates virtually all the systems in the body. The hormone increases your metabolism helping to break down fat, build proteins, and create lean muscle. It is often referred to as the "fountain of youth hormone". The results of a study described it as "too good to be true" by a section of medical community.

Magic Prick is here?

It is the most effective anti-obesity drug ever discovered, reviving up the metabolism to youthful levels, resculpting the body by selectively reducing the fat in the waist, abdomen, hips, and thighs, and at the same time increasing muscle mass. It may be the most powerful aphrodisiac, reviving flagging sexual potency in older men. It is cosmetic surgery in a bottle, smoothing out facial wrinkles; restoring the elasticity, thickness, and contours of youthful skin; reversing the loss of extra-cellular water. It has healing powers that close ulcerated wounds and regrow burned skin. It is the secret ingredient in the age-defying bodies of weight lifters and it enhances exercise performance, allowing them to do higher-intensity workouts of longer duration. It reverses the insomnia of later life, restoring the deepest level of sleep. It is a mood elevator, lifting the spirits along with the body; bringing back zest for life, many people thought was lost forever. The latest research shows that it holds promise for intractable and terrifying disease of ageing—Alzheimer's.

There are many doctors who are of the opinion that the treatment may prove harmful in the long-run and may lead to the development of hypertension, carpal tunnel syndrome, fluid retention and diabetes. The most serious side effect is cancer. Although HGH is not mutagenic, it makes cancer grow, which means that if you have a cancer and take HGH, the cancer will spread faster. Other side-effects might include weight gain.

What the literature says about HGH?

- New England Journal of Medicine: "Diminished secretion of growth hormone is responsible in part for the decrease of lean body mass, the expansion of adipose-tissue mass, and the thinning of the skin that occur in old age." (*N Engl J Med,* 1990; 323:1-6.)
- Colourado State University: "Frailty, muscle atrophy, relative obesity, increased frequency of fractures and disordered sleep. These clinical signs of ageing are, without doubt, the manifestation of a very complex set of changes which involve, at least in part, the HGH."
- Edward M. Lichten, M.D., P.C. "One of HGH's most dramatic effects is on the connective tissue, muscle, and healing potential of the skeletal system." The positive effect HGH has on bone mass is documented by bone scan.
- Growth hormone factors could maintain memory with ageing
- The Food and Drug Administration has OK'd the use of growth hormone for children who are healthy but abnormally short and who hope to gain height.

There are essentially 3 types of HGH products:

1. HGH Injections: Consider the following problems:
   (i) Injecting yourself 2 to 3 times everyday for the rest of your life. The pain and chore will put off most people,
   (ii) Spending at least \$ 1,200 to \$ 2,000 per month on these injections, and

(iii) Disrupting the body's natural ability to produce HGH by these artificial injections, even pituitary shut down could occur.

2. Homeopathic HGH; should be used under supervision of a homeopathic physician
3. HGH precursors (essential aminoacids that are known to stimulate the pituitary gland in our brain to produce more natural HGH) are NOT hormones but releasers or precursors. This tends to be a safer, more natural way to help our body produce more HGH hormones. The protagonists claim the following:

   (i) They are painless unlike injections,
   (ii) They are affordable and effective,
   (iii) They are natural in that they stimulate the pituitary to produce larger amount of HGH naturally. GenF20 in tablet form is manufactured in a FDA approved facility. GHR100 is yet another HGH releaser, which is available as injections,
   (iv) Improve the look and feel of your skin,
   v) Increase your bone density and reverse osteoporosis,
   (vi) Power up your brain and maintain your memory even as you age,
   (vii) Boost your sex drive,
   (viii) Tonify and improve your overall physical and mental well being,
   (ix) Helps you sleep better, and
   (x) Improve your mood, and banish depression and fatigue.

What is Growth Hormone?

Human Growth Hormone, or HGH, is produced by the pituitary gland in your brain. After the age of 20, the hormone release rate greatly decreases, and by the age of 30 most people start to notice acceleration in the ageing process. HGH is one of many hormones, like estrogen, progesterone, testosterone, melatonin and DHEA that decline in production with age. Some enthusiasts believe that HGH may turn back the clock by several years, if replenished. HGH, also known as somatotropin, is the most abundant hormone secreted by the pituitary gland. It is produced at a rate that peaks during adolescence when accelerated growth occurs. Growth hormone is primarily released in pulses that take place during the beginning phases of sleep, then it is quickly converted to the liver to its powerful growth promoting metabolite, Insulin-like Growth factor type 1 (IGF1), also known as somatomedin C. IGF1 elicits most of the effects associated with growth hormone and is measured in the blood to determine the level of growth hormone secretion.

Restoring HGH

Dr. Daniel Rudman, an endocrinologist from Madison, Wisconsin, pioneered the original research on HGH in humans. He hypothesized that the changes in body composition which become apparent around age 35 had to do with declining hormone levels. Despite the fact that he did not alter their diet, exercise, or smoking habits, the men who were given HGH gained an average of 8.8% in lean muscle while losing 14% of their body fat. They experienced localized increase in bone density and their skin became thicker and firmer. According to Rudman, the subjects of this study reversed these parameters of ageing by 10-20 years. This study, published in *The New England Journal of Medicine*, represented the biggest breakthrough in anti-ageing medicine.

HGH side effects range from the minor joint pain and some fluid retention to the more serious high blood pressure and abnormal bone and cartilage growth. The side effects from this type of use tend to be fluid retention, joint pain, a reversible insulin resistance, and some joint swelling. It can lead to long-term complications such as high blood pressure, more serious fluid retention, chronic joint pain and swelling, and some facial bone growth. Long-term abuse, as seen in athletic use, can lead to more pronounced, and sometimes deadly, side effects such as irregular heart rhythms, increased risk of diabetes, joint and facial deformities, and a shut down of the pituitary glands. Your liver has to work harder to process this externally introduced HGH. This could lead to liver damage. HGH side effects can be reduced by limiting the length of time the hormone is used. Lowering the dosage of human growth hormone can also reduce the number and severity of these reactions.

Potential side effects of HGH injections:

- High blood pressure
- Soft tissue swelling
- Thickening of the skin and abnormal hair growth
- Glucose intolerance
- Muscle weakness
- Arthritis
- Impotence
- Breathing problems
- Skin problems, rash or itchy or swollen skin
- Premature ageing and death!

HGH Precursors/HGH Enhancers

The challenge in restoring youthful levels of HGH for most of is not increasing our production or injecting the hormone itself, but releasing it from its sequestered state. HGH enhancers are used by people who are seeking to regain their youth, lose that stubborn belly fat, compete at the top of their game, or simply find more energy and vitality. The natural make-up of HGH enhancers and their benefits beyond just HGH production make them attractive to people looking to live a healthier lifestyle. The lack of side effects, low cost and ease of use make these products, the supplement of choice for many people seeking HGH therapy. HGH enhancers come in pill, oral spray, effervescent powder or tablets, or sublingual drops. Usually the L-series amino-acids are contained in the HGH enhancers. L-Glutamine, L-Arginine, L-Glycine, L-Lysine, L-Leucine, and L-Tyrosine are some of the more popular ones. A variety of vitamins and minerals to support, and enhance the function of, the pituitary glands are often included. Antioxidants are important to reverse any damaging effects from the ageing process as well. GABA and Broad bean may also be found in the cocktail mix of HGH enhancers.

The slow results and lack of the "Wow" effect turns some people away. Many people are just not patient enough to wait for an enhancing product to work. They want immediate results. The addition of essential vitamins, minerals and antioxidants in human growth hormone enhancers provide additional support for the proper function of not only the pituitary and hypothalamus, but also the other important organs of the body. HGH enhancers combined with a solid nutritional plan and exercise regimen may help you reach your goals. Make sure you speak to your doctor first.

The Signs of Ageing Linked to Declining HGH Levels

- Increased Body fat
- Decreased Lean Muscle Tissue
- Decreased Energy
- Diminished Immune System
- Decreased Sexual Performance
- Decreased Cardiac Output
- Decreased Libido
- Loss of Hair or Hair Colour
- Decreased Skin Elasticity
- Wrinkles and Cellulite
- Decline in Mental Function
- Decline in Memory
- Decline in Vision/Eyesight
- Decreased Bone Mass and Density
- Decreased Strength
- Decreased Exercise Performance
- High Blood Pressure
- Undesirable Cholesterol Profile
- Poor Sleep
- Slower Rate of Healing
- Joint Pain

Some other Hormones in Anti-ageing Medicine

Insulin-like growth factor 1 (IGF-1) is another hormone that may play a role in ageing and can be purchased as a dietary supplement. Other hormones whose production decreases with age are DHEA and melatonin. DHEA has been reported to improve the well being of the elderly by a variety of ways: improved memory, immune system, muscle mass, sexual appetite, and benefits to the skin. Pregnenolone is a mother hormone to DHEA and other hormones and is even safer. Melatonin is a hormone mostly involved in sleep and circadian rhythms. It appears to have antioxidant functions. Although it can be used for jet lag and some sleep disorders, it may also cause sleep disorders such as nightmares and vivid dreams. Recently, a study claimed that melatonin levels do not decrease with age, except maybe at night, although due to diseases or drugs elderly persons can have low levels of melatonin. Melatonin may also aggravate asthma. For women, estrogen is a popular anti-ageing therapy. This hormone is generally used in conjunction with others in hormone replacement therapy. It does reduce the effects of menopause, protecting against heart disease and osteoporosis. Weight gain and thrombosis are side effects and that it should not be taken for long periods.

DHEA

Imagine a natural substance that creates feelings of well-being and slows the ageing process. DHEA can prevent or reverse the diseases that anti-ageing experts have identified as the most prominent markers of accelerated ageing: atherosclerosis (hardening and clogging of the arteries), cancer, diabetes, and reduced immunity. But can the hormone actually extend human life span? While the literature strongly supports this claim, it remains unproven.

Adrenal glands are responsible for manufacturing DHEA. In fact, Pregnenolone is transformed into DHEA. And DHEA serves as the raw material from which all other important hormones—including the sex hormones estrogen, progesterone, and testosterone and the stress hormone cortisol—are synthesized. DHEA is the most abundant hormone in the body. Its production peaks at around age 20. By the time you reach 40, your body makes 50% of DHEA. By 65, output drops to 10 to 20 percent of optimum; by age 80, it plummets to less than 5 percent of optimum.

The immune system is especially sensitive to diminishing DHEA output, opening the door not just to viruses, bacteria, and other microbes but also to free radicals and the Pandora's box of degenerative diseases. If levels of DHEA decline with age, can replacing the hormone reverse ageing in humans? Nobody knows for sure. A host of studies suggest that the lower a person's level of DHEA, the greater his risk of death from age-related disease. The study found a close correlation between higher DHEA levels and reduced risk of death from all causes.

Living Better

Most people who take DHEA do so because the hormone helps them deal better with stress, gives them more well being, and makes them feel young again. In a study, researchers gave people 50 milligrams of DHEA every day for six months. Sixty-seven percent of the men and 84 percent of the women reported improvements in energy, sleep, mood, feelings of relaxation, and ability to handle stress—overall, a remarkable increase in subjective experience of physical and psychological well-being.

DHEA's power to invigorate the immune system is closely linked to its potential to fight ageing. Remember, heightened immunity translates directly into protection against oxidation, which in turn translates directly into protection against degenerative disease. So anything that strengthens your immune system also has the capacity to lengthen life. Immune deterioration with age is accompanied by increased incidence of atherosclerosis, autoimmune diseases, cancer, cataracts, and infections—all evidence of accelerated ageing.

DHEA protects your body from the hormone cortisol and the stress that triggers its production. Like DHEA, cortisol is secreted by the adrenal glands. If oversecreted, cortisol injures your body's tissues. When you're under stress, your adrenal glands release large amounts of cortisol. People under chronic stress have high cortisol levels. The presence of too much cortisol leads to age-accelerating damage. As stress accumulates over decades, cortisol levels tend to rise as well. Many people over age 40 have elevated cortisol. DHEA and cortisol have an inverse, or adversarial, relationship. When you're faced with prolonged stress, your cortisol/DHEA ratio—a measure of health status and ageing—can rise by a factor of 5. This means that the excess cortisol is battering DHEA's protective shield. DHEA supplementation increases your stress tolerance, lowers your cortisol/DHEA ratio, and protects you against cortisol-induced cellular damage.

Mending a Broken Heart

In healthy males given a clot-promoting substance (arachidonic acid, found in abundance in meat), DHEA blocked an increase in clotting. In men, DHEA lowered total cholesterol and "bad" low-density lipoprotein cholesterol better than and more safely than the "statin" drugs such as clofibrate and gemfibrozil. DHEA is also nontoxic.

Beating Cancer

Women with breast cancer consistently have lower-than-normal DHEA level. DHEA may help protect against breast cancer by inhibiting glucose-6-phosphate dehydrogenase, an enzyme required for cancer growth. Also, because DHEA has antioxidant properties, the hormone probably defends against free radical cancer initiators.

Good to Bones

Among the anti-ageing hormones, DHEA stands out as a multitalented star with amazing ways of outsmarting osteoporosis. DHEA is the only hormone that can both inhibit bone breakdown and stimulate bone formation. Plus, DHEA is a precursor to estrogen, progesterone, and testosterone, all of which prevent bone loss in their own rights. The higher the women's DHEA, the denser their bones. As DHEA levels decline with age, osteoporosis may appear. People with osteoporosis have significantly lower DHEA levels than people without the disease.

Protect the Mind

Don't be surprised if, in the next few years, you start seeing reports that DHEA is being used to treat Alzheimer's disease and other degenerative brain diseases. Strong evidence exists that the hormone is essential for maintaining healthy brain cells. Studies show that even very small doses of the hormone reduce amnesia while improving long-term memory.

The Lupus Link

Blood vessels, connective tissues, joints, kidneys, the nervous system, and skin may be affected in cases of Lupus. Lupus is commonly treated using immunosuppressive steroids and cancer chemotherapy agents. The treatment damages the immune system and thus undermines the healing process. But with DHEA's immune-enhancing effects, about two-thirds of the women reported some alleviation of their symptoms, including reduced frequency and severity of joint pain, headaches, rashes, and fatigue.

Dosage of DHEA

The recommended daily dose range is 10 to 50 milligrams for women, 25 to 100 milligrams for men. It may be prescribed for certain medical conditions, including Alzheimer's disease and other organic brain diseases, chronic fatigue syndrome, depression, diabetes, heart disease, immune deficiency syndromes, lupus and other autoimmune diseases, osteoporosis, and stress-related disorders. Men with prostate cancer and women with reproductive cancers should consult their doctors before taking DHEA, even though no adverse effects have been reported.

The Observations

Pregnenolone

Less is known about pregnenolone than DHEA because, until recently, research interest in it has not been as intense. In the meantime, pregnenolone has demonstrated its potent rejuvenative effects on the body and brain. It boosts energy, elevates mood, and improves memory and mental performance. It creates a sense of well-being while improving the ability to tolerate stress. Perched atop the adrenal family tree, it is the stuff from which all other steroid hormones are made. Your adrenal glands manufacture pregnenolone from cholesterol. Your body either uses pregnenolone as it is or converts it to one of its two "daughter hormones": DHEA and progesterone. These, in turn, spawn dozens of hormones, the most important and prevalent of which are the three estrogens (estriol, estrone, and estradiol), testosterone, and cortisol.

Thus, pregnenolone; the Feel-Good Hormone influences cerebral function, energy level, the female reproductive cycle, immune defenses, inflammation, mood, skin health, sleep patterns, stress tolerance, wound healing, and much, much more. Taking pregnenolone therefore normalizes and rejuvenates the entire adrenal cascade.

Your ability to tolerate stress is directly linked to your health and longevity. Responsibility for coping with all of this stress falls to your adrenal glands—or, more specifically, to the hormones they make. Pregnenolone is a powerful anti-stress hormone in its own right, and it provides the raw material for all of the other anti-stress hormones. Pregnenolone also protects you against chemical stress. Your liver contains enzyme systems that are responsible for removing toxins from your body. By protecting these enzymes from cortisol, which degrades them, pregnenolone reinforces your body's detox power.

Neuro-nutrient

Pregnenolone is a potent neuro-nutrient that improves memory, concentration, and mood. It supercharges your brain by facilitating the transmission of nerve impulses so that brain cells can communicate with each other more easily. Humans given pregnenolone became more productive on the job, felt better, and coped with stress better. Many neuroscientists now believe that pregnenolone is the most potent known memory-enhancer, perhaps many times more powerful than any other memory-enhancer. Pregnenolone fights depression, too.

Several studies described the hormone's effectiveness in reducing the swelling and pain of rheumatoid arthritis. The effective dose was fairly high by today's standards: 500 milligrams daily. Other reports told of pregnenolone's success as a therapy for lupus, psoriasis, and scleroderma. Now the hormone is making a comeback, as more and more people experience the adverse effects of anti-inflammatory steroids like prednisolone.

Pregnenolone is amazingly safe. You'll find pregnenolone in health food stores. Make certain that you are getting a pharmacologically pure product. A very safe dose is upto 100 milligrams per day.

Blood Tests are necessary before hormone administration

Since it is normal for an ageing person to have imbalances of hormones, it is recommended to assess the hormones. The recommended "Male Panel" consists of a complete blood count (CBC)/chemistry test, homocysteine, free testosterone, estradiol, prostate-specific antigen (PSA), and DHEA. The recommended "Female Panel" consists of the complete CBC/chemistry test, estradiol, progesterone, free testosterone, DHEA, and homocysteine. In addition to these special male and female panels, the following tests are especially important for men and women over 40: Fasting Insulin, Ferritin, Cortisol, Fibrinogen, Thyroid Stimulating Hormone (TSH), and Free triiodothyroxine (T3). If a serious abnormality is detected—such as elevated homocysteine, hormone imbalance, high PSA—testing should be repeated more often to determine the benefits of whatever therapy you are using to correct the potentially life-shortening abnormality.

7

Mid-Life Crisis: Men or Women

Good Understanding can Prevent Ill Health in Old Age

It is well recognized that men as well as women, both suffer from mid life crisis either due to decreased hormonal level or emotional deprivation, as they near the age of 40. Two events, i.e. menopause/andropause and mid life crisis are similar, but not the same. While the former is hormone based the latter is circumstantial. The menopause is a well-known event for women, though this has been late in coming to the understanding of men. What is much less known is that men have to endure a similar biological and emotional experience. However, it is perceived as less than masculine to admit to such feelings. It is vital that women appreciate what is happening to their loved husband and that doctor get to grips with this aspect of growing older. There is a male hormonal shut-down, akin to the menopause, which is therefore named the "andropause". Let us consider first the andropause.

The Andropause

It starts, usually, in the fifth decade. There are true biological changes, which can be measured in the laboratory. Testosterone levels fall. The resulting symptoms are like those experienced by a woman at the menopause:

- fatigue
- depression
- aches and pains
- sweating and flushes
- reduced libido
- loss of erectile function.

The latter is particularly disturbing to a man and difficulty in talking about this problem is one of the reasons why the andropause has been little heard.

Mid-life crisis

This often comes in the fourth decade. Typically, it occurs in response to some outside challenge in a man's life: a breakdown of the marriage, career failure, bankruptcy, death of a peer or loved parent, redundancy and so on. Essentially, it is an emotional crisis. It can be a time of great anguish, despair, inadequacy and feelings of guilt or futility. The man who suffers the mid-life crisis is typically one who has been challenged and cannot come to terms with his life. In trying to rationalize the unhappy feelings he may begin to see his life partner in negative terms or blame his boss and work dissatisfaction. He may contemplate change in one or more areas. Unfortunately, alcohol may often be seen as the answer. This may be the start of a slippery slope to abuse, addiction and early demise. Man in a mid-life crisis wants to boast of sexual prowess and seeks new thrills or has an affair with his secretary in her twenties. On the other hand the andropause man lacks energy or drive and cannot be bothered with sex, for want of testosterone. The mid-life crisis occurs to women as well. Almost all of what is said here applies equally. Even the search for new loves, thrills and adventure can lead to women too becoming unfaithful. Obviously it needs to be distinguished from the onset of the menopause.

A great deal depends on the response of the life partner at this time of upheaval and change in case of both genders. A man may be rehabilitated from the suffering, discover a vision for the future and come home once again to feelings of family. If the trigger was a financial collapse, he may recover the determination to work hard and rebuild his assets. Sadly, many do not do so but give in to what they see as an overwhelming tide of misfortune. Similarly the man has to give due care and support to the physical and emotional health of his wife to let her recover from the midlife crisis.

What the man can do?

The first step in case of andopause is to have blood tests to check up on the man's hormones. If this reveals there is a deficiency, testosterone supplements are needed and will work a satisfying change. The fatigue and depression will lift, life becomes worthwhile, energy levels and zest return to former levels, potency problems recede. What is more, testosterone improves circulation, protects against heart disease, aids weight loss, improves skin condition, increases muscle strength and works in a host of healthy ways to rejuvenate the man. Testosterone saves lives and saves hearts and minds.

The first sensible step towards dealing the mid-life crisis is having the problem identified and understood. Kindness, tact and sympathy are required, despite outrageous and often destructive behaviour by the affected individual. Any crisis is a time of great stress and stress shortens life. Bitter acrimony and rejection from relatives, even though badly affected in turn, are counter productive and simply make everyone suffer more. At all costs keep the communications flowing; it's the only hope for a sane future and rebuilding relationships. Kind of man likely to suffer a mid-life crisis is one with an unhappy childhood, maybe abusive or with cold and unloving parents. Such early formative experiences often bring a feeling of unworthiness which emerges later in life, at a time of crisis. Society at large and the media in particular, often impose ridiculous standards of standing/value in society. In the younger generation, there is a cult of greed, materialism and celebrity worship in vogue, which is very dangerous and tends to create envy, desire, inadequacy and misery in those parents who do not have all the trappings of a luxurious film-star lifestyle. The irony is that the people we are supposed to envy, have disastrous, miserable and often very sick lives.

The HGH deficiency

Medical scientists list the following symptoms of HGH deficiency: Decreased energy levels, Social isolation, Lack of positive well-being, Depressed mood, Increased anxiety, Increased body fat particularly at waistline, Decreased muscle mass, Decreased bone density, associated with an increased risk of fracture, Increased LDL cholesterol (bad cholesterol) and decreased HDL (good cholesterol), Decreased cardiac muscle mass, Impaired cardiac function, Decreased insulin sensitivity (disposition to diabetes), Accelerated atherogenesis (hardening of the arteries).

If you are deficient in growth hormone, you will benefit from supplementing it. The question is: are you deficient? Unfortunately, there are no easy tests to detect this. HGH appears in the blood at night and is present for a matter of minutes. A blood sample tested in such cases is a 'hit and miss'. A better test is to use the marker IGF-1 (insulin-like growth factor 1). No doubt that we lose production of HGH as the decades pass, therefore, one can safely assume that one is likely deficient. We would be far healthier with the HGH of a younger person than the one in decline. Supplements in later decades make sense. One should take HGH for no more than a year. The idea is to wind the clock back as far as you can while taking HGH and then let it roll forward, in the natural way. There are plenty of steps you can take to help release HGH naturally, including weight loss, exercise, plentiful sleep, diet changes and nutritional supplements. Start with a daily dose of HGH, starting at 0.8 unit/day. The main reported side effects are headache, visual disturbance, nausea/vomiting, carpal tunnel syndrome and mild hypertension. Such side effects would be exceptional in the low dose regime.

Natural hormone precursors; means of naturally stimulating HGH release are lysine, arginine, ornithine and glutamine. Arginine is an essential aminoacid, i.e. it is not manufactured in the body; it has to be supplied in the food. Claims for arginine therapy include an increase in fat burning and muscle building. Arginine strengthens the thymus gland, increasing its weight and activity, boosting immunity and fighting cancer, and it enhances male fertility.

Hormonal deficiency in women: menopause

In simple language menopause means age-related stoppage of monthly menstrual bleeding, permanently. The mean age has remained 48-50 years. Now the post-menopausal phase covers over one-third of a woman's life. In this region most of the women experience menopause around 45 years of age, and undernourishment may be a cause for the early development. Women who reach the menopause stage prematurely or suddenly due to the surgical removal of ovaries suffer more distressing symptoms. The cause of menopause and the associated symptoms is believed to be hormonal changes, having occurred at this age/stage. This stage requires care and attention by the husband and other family members of the woman, besides her gynecologists, to keep her in good mental and physical health. This will also give a peep into the health status of her husband, which may otherwise be neglected. Neglect can mean an unhappy and uncomfortable living, besides the risk of several serious ailments.

At this age most women start suffering from one or more unwelcome symptoms—hot flushes, mood swings, irritability, lack of concentration, lack of decision-making power, lack of sleep, night sweats, loss of sex desire, pains in bones and muscles, chest pain with or without breathlessness, lack of control on urination, headaches, distention of abdomen, putting on weight, protrusion of tummy and hips, etc. Also menstrual periods become irregular. Other symptoms may be bouts of rapid heart-beat or actual cardiovascular disease, sudden tears in the eyes, loss of libido, crashing fatigue, anxiety, feeling ill at ease, feeling of dread, apprehension, doom, disorientation, mental confusion, disturbing memory lapses, itchy-crawly skin, sore joints, muscles and tendons, increased tension in muscles, rough and inelastic skin, gastrointestinal distress, indigestion, flatulence, gas pain, nausea, depression, hair loss or thinning of hair on head, pubic, or whole body; increase in facial hair, dizziness, light-headedness, episodes of loss of balance, changes in body odor, electric shock sensation under the skin and in the head, increased bleeding in gums, burning tongue, burning roof of mouth, bad taste in mouth, change in breath odor, changes in fingernails; tinnitus; ringing bells in the ears, etc. More importantly, with the advent of the menopausal age, the incidence of actual heart disease and fractures due to bone weakening also rise manifold.

To prevent unwelcome symptoms and serious health hazards, the middle age women have to institute lifestyle and attitudinal changes, well in time. The best time to make first visit to your gynecologist is at the onset of peri-menopause—a few years before the menses stop, but with the onset of some symptoms like hot flushes or even if you have not suffered symptoms but crossed the age of 40. At this stage some investigations to rule out certain ailments like breast/genital cancers would be required. This would also be the best time to discover any ailment—diabetes, hypertension, obesity, bone weakness, heart changes, thyroid function tests, urinary changes, sex-related complaints, eye-related problems, early detection of genital and other concerns, etc.

What is menopausal Zone?

The phase of a woman's life that extends from 40 years of age to the last day of life has been called a menopausal zone by some experts. It includes peri-menopause, the event of menopause, the post-menopausal phase and the older age after that. Menopause (the cessation of menses or monthly ovulation), generally occurs between the ages of 45 and 55 though this can be earlier or later. The removal of the uterus and smoking can also cause an earlier menopause. It is less certain why some women have a very early menopause or cease ovulating after sudden shock but it is clear that the hypothalamus (at the base of the brain) is the controlling centre for menstruation The hypothalamus acts by releasing a hormone called GnRH (gonadotrophin releasing hormone) to the nearby pituitary gland. During the reproductive years the pituitary, triggered by GnRR, produces two hormones, follicle stimulating hormone (FSH) and luteinising hormone (LH) which determine the amount of oestrogen and progesterone hormones being prepared by the ovaries for reproduction Whatever the reasons for the menopausal state, high FSH and LH levels indicate that the ovaries are no longer producing eggs as the body continually increases these hormones to try to promote egg production

These high FSH and LH levels are signals to the adrenal glands near the kidneys to supplement the body's supply of estrogen and progesterone hormones. While the ovaries continue to produce some hormones after menopause, the body's fat cells can also be a source of estrogen.

HRT and the uterus

Estrogen has been found to be carcinogenic, so it is not given alone. It is given in combination with progesterone. First it started as a sequential therapy, i.e. estrogen in the first half of menstrual cycle and progesterone in the second half. Now one prefers continuous combined therapy, i.e. both the hormones for the entire cycle. Continuous progesterone is much safer and can be given for a long time, after one year of the onset of menopause. However, the hormones cannot be taken like vitamin pills or aspirin tablets. HRT can be taken under close supervision only. Agreement was reached on the following issues on the basis of several international studies:

- All women should receive a comprehensive assessment before HT, including mammography and bone densitometry.
- The primary indication remains the treatment of vasomotor symptoms.
- When estrogen therapy is considered solely for vaginal dryness, topical (not systemic) therapy should be considered first-line therapy.
- Women without a uterus should not be prescribed a progestogen with estrogen, and progestogen is not generally indicated for low-dose estrogen therapy administered locally for vaginal atrophy.
- There is insufficient evidence regarding the off-label use of long-cycle progestogen (eg. every 3-6 months for 12-14 days) and vaginal or intrauterine administration as an alternative to EPT.
- Estrogen/EPT use for primary prevention in relation to timing of menopause needs further evaluation, and disparities about CHD prevention exist in relation to the proximity of menopause.

- Data do not currently support EPT use for secondary CHD prevention.
- The data show a reduction in CHD in women 50 to 59 years old who initiate EPT within 10 years of menopause, and an increased risk in women who initiate after 10 years.
- The attributable risk for CHD remains very low in younger postmenopausal women.
- The risk for thrombo-embolism is highest within 1 to 2 years after initiation of systemic HT.
- Both estrogen and EPT increase stroke risk, with 8 additional strokes for EPT and 12 additional cases per 10,000 per year for estrogen therapy.
- Large randomized trials suggest a reduction of diabetes risk with HT, with a 21% to 35% relative risk reduction (RRR) for EPT (15 fewer cases per 10,000 per year) and a 12% RRR (14 fewer cases per 10,000 per year) for estrogen therapy.
- Breast cancer risk is slightly increased with EPT use beyond 5 years for 4 to 6 additional invasive cases per 10,000 per year.
- Estrogen and EPT reduce risk for osteoporotic fractures and should be considered an option for women at high risk for fractures within 5 to 10 years.
- Evidence is insufficient to support the use of estrogen/EPT for depression.
- Initiating EPT after age 65 years is not recommended for the primary prevention of dementia or cognitive decline because risk can be increased during the ensuing 5 years.
- Lower than standard doses of estrogen/EPT should be considered, such as 0.3 mg of oral conjugated estrogens or 0.25 to 0.5 μg of poral micronized β-estradiol, but these have not been tested in long-term trials.
- The long-term risk-benefit ratio for non-oral administration has not been tested.

- Extended use of the lowest effective dose is acceptable, provided the benefits of relief outweigh the risks in those at high risk for osteoporotic fractures and for further prevention of bone loss when alternative therapies are not available.
- "Bioidentical" hormones should be used with caution in absence of regulatory oversight and batch-to-batch variation in quality and purity.

The panel could not reach consensus on the following:

- Whether cessation of HT should be abrupt or tapered.
- Whether there is a difference in breast cancer risk for continuous *vs.* sequential progestogens.

Other diseases in this phase of life

During mid-life painful Menstruation can be a warning of Pelvic Inflammatory Disease (PID) or Endometriosis (excessive shedding of the cells lining the womb) when it needs medical treatment. These can also lead to pain during intercourse. Abdominal pain caused by Irritable Bowel Syndrome should not be confused with menstrual problem. If these attacks recur they may be identified with certain foods. Tiredness can also be caused by anemia due to bad nutrition, heavy bleeding or low thyroid function. Weight gain and dry skin can also be an indication of under active thyroid function particularly if accompanied by poor circulation and coldness and depression. When tiredness, on the contrary, is accompanied by anxiety and loss of weight in spite if a healthy appetite this can indicate an overactive thyroid. Fatigue and weight loss accompanied by high blood pressure may warn of diabetes. All these conditions should receive medical attention.

Peri-menopause

In the years preceding menopause many women suffer similar symptoms: water retention and breast swelling, irregular cycle and mood swings as well as heavy bleeding and hot flushes and sweats and sometimes cravings for sweet food. These can be signals of hormonal imbalance where estrogen levels are disproportionately high. HRT drugs containing even more estrogen will only worsen the problem. The symptoms can be alleviated by natural progesterone therapy. Nutritional supplements and a well balanced diet and exercise can also help rectify hormonal imbalance.

Thrombosis and heart disease

Although men have more heart disease than women, women suffer no less duiring menopausal zone. There is no substantial research that shows that HRT drugs protect the heart. On the contrary, excess estrogen can cause the accumulation of fibrin, an insoluble protein that promotes blood clotting As fibrin increases so does the risk of thrombus-embolism, a disease caused by clots forming in the blood vessels. Vitamin B can prevent clots from increasing as well as dissolve existing clots and research has shown that supplementation with this vitamin can reduce heart disease by 40 per cent. Magnesium has also been shown to be helpful in reducing high blood pressure and angina. Excessive weight caused by fluid retention can also put pressure on the heart and increase the risk of angina. A healthy balanced diet with plenty of fruit and vegetables is essential for a healthy heart with regular exercise.

Osteoporosis

Women start losing bone density well before menopause but do not generally suffer osteoporosis (or brittle bone disease) until they are in post-menopausal phase, unless they have undergone removal of the ovaries. Since there are no obvious symptoms for this disease, a woman can be diagnosed with osteoporosis but still appears to live healthy lives. It is only when the skeletal frame becomes so fragile that falls or even knocks lead to fractures.

While the hormone estrogen can prevent loss it does not build new bone and any beneficial effect gained from HRT drugs is lost as soon as these drugs are stopped. The other female sex hormone progesterone in its natural form can help build new bones. Minerals like calcium and magnesium are vital for healthy bones as is vitamin D, which is activated in the skin by sunshine and helps the kidneys to reabsorb calcium from the urine. Certain B vitamins are also believed to be important in maintaining bone structure. Red meat, soft drinks, caffeine, alcohol, sugar, fried foods as well as smoking can be detrimental for health of bones. Adequate weight bearing exercise also protects against this disease which has been shown to have a hereditary link. An overactive thyroid can increase bone loss by producing too much hormone as can thyroid medication. Steroid drugs also increase bone loss.

Research has also shown that women who have healthy diets and take plenty of exercise, do not suffer the menopausal symptoms, heart disease and osteoporosis. The importance of a healthy diet and proper exercise during this stage cannot be overstated and can eliminate many symptoms of hormonal imbalance as well as helping to protect the heart and the bones. Vitamin E has been shown to help relieve hot flushes and headaches, relieve itching and inflammation and normalize blood sugar levels, the Soya-based Lecithin can aid memory loss, relieve anxiety and depression as well as insomnia The B vitamins as well as vitamin C are also vital during this time to help the adrenal glands, which regulate stress. When women are stressed during the menopause they can produce more androgens or male hormones and this can lead to an increase in hair loss and the growth of facial hair.

What is PMS and how does it relate to peri-menopause?

Excess estrogen can lead to symptoms of pre-menstrual tension (PMS), when there is an imbalance of estrogen and progesterone hormones. PMS type symptoms can also be produced by HRT drugs. The most common symptoms include weight gain, bloatedness, breast tenderness, migraine, fatigue and mood swings as well as nausea and food cravings, which can be made worse by coffee, alcohol and stress. In the case of PMS such symptoms are not continuous but often worsen before menstruation and disappear after the monthly cycle. A drop in blood sugar levels can also block the transport of natural progesterone. It is essential to keep the two female sex hormones in balance.

Alarm signals that the body is suffering a chemical overdose of HRT, include chronic headaches, muscle pain, indigestion, depression, tingling in the hands and feet, skin problems and chronic fatigue. Toxins produced by bacterial and yeast in the gut can also build up toxicity. The liver eliminates toxins by neutralizing them or excreting them. Fasting is the best way to help the liver perform its function and eliminate toxic substances from the body. During fasting it is vital to drink much water. High potency multivitamin and mineral supplements help detoxification, particularly with 1000 mgs vitamin C taken 3 times a day.

Some frequently asked questions (FAQs) and their answers are given below.

1. What is menopause?

Menopause is the transition between a woman's childbearing years and her non-childbearing years. It is the last stage of a biological process during which the ovaries gradually produce lower levels of sex hormones—estrogen, progesterone, and testosterone. By the time natural menopause is complete, hormone output decreases significantly. In post-menopausal women, estrogen levels are about one-tenth the level in pre-menopausal women and progesterone is nearly absent.

2. What hormones may be used after menopause?

Post-menopausal hormone use usually involves treatment with either estrogen alone or in combination with progestin to compensate for the decrease in natural hormones that occurs at menopause. Among women who use hormones, women who have had their uterus removed use estrogen alone, whereas women with a uterus take a combination of estrogen plus progestin.

3. Why are hormones used after menopause?

Doctors may recommend using hormones to counter some of the possible effects of menopause on a woman's health and quality of life. Symptoms of menopause may include hot flashes, night sweats, sleeplessness, and vaginal dryness. Women should discuss risks and benefits of combined hormone use with their doctor before selecting hormones for use in preventing osteoporosis.

4. What are the effects of post-menopausal hormone use on the uterus?

Some studies have shown increase in endometrial cancer risk with the combined regimens if progestin is used for less than ten days per month.

5. What is known about the effects of hormones on heart disease?

A study concluded that estrogen in combination with progestin has no beneficial effects on the heart. Although earlier results from this study had suggested such benefits might exist, longer follow-up (6.8 years) found no overall reduction in the risk of heart attacks and coronary deaths with use of estrogen and progestin.

6. What is known about the effects of hormones on bone health?

Post-menopausal osteoporosis is characterized by decreased bone mass, deterioration of bone tissue, and increased bone fragility, making bone fractures of great concern. Low levels of estrogen are a risk factor for osteoporosis in women. Estrogen alone and estrogen combined with progestin have been shown to protect against osteoporosis. However, some studies have shown that the beneficial effects of short-term therapy are not permanent; short-term use (three to five years) of estrogen to relieve symptoms of menopause did very little to prevent fractures from osteoporosis in women when they reached ages 75 to 80 years old. Women who take estrogen to maintain bone density must continue taking estrogen because its beneficial effects on bone health disappear after hormone use is discontinued.

7. How does hormone use affect breast cancer risk?

While studies indicate that both groups of hormone users have a higher risk of breast cancer than non-users, the risk appears to be greater among women using combined therapy than in women using estrogen alone. One recent observational study found that risk increased with longer duration of hormone use. A recent re-analysis of over 90 percent of breast cancer studies throughout the world showed an increased risk in breast cancer for women who used postmenopausal hormones for five years or longer.

8. Is there a risk of ovarian cancer with hormone use?

A study that women who used estrogen alone for 10-19 years were twice as likely to develop ovarian cancer than women who did not use hormones. For women who used estrogen for 20 or more years, the risk of ovarian cancer increased to three times that of women who did not use post-menopausal hormones. In this study, the increased risk appeared to be limited to women who used estrogens for 10 or more years.

9. Are there other reported benefits or risks associated with hormone use?

Estrogen is very effective for treating menopausal symptoms such as hot flashes, sleeplessness, and vaginal dryness. Post-menopausal hormones may improve mood and psychological well-being in women who have hot flashes and sleeplessness during menopause, but should not be used to treat the symptoms of major depression. There are reports that estrogen prevents memory loss, delays the onset of Alzheimer's disease, and improves urinary incontinence. Women who use estrogen plus progestin are at increased risk for blood clots, gallbladder disease, and stroke. Increased cases of blood clots in the lung (pulmonary embolisms) and inflammation of veins have also been reported with hormone use.

11. What are the risks of hormones for women who have a previous cancer history?

One of estrogen's primary roles is to promote the growth of cells in the breast and uterus. For this reason, there is concern that use of estrogen after cancer may promote further tumor growth. Only a small amount of research has been done to look at the risks associated with post-menopausal hormones for women who have a history of endometrial cancer.

12. Does the route of administration of hormones make a difference?

Several routes of administration of hormones are available, such as oral, transdermal patches, estrogen gels, and vaginal creams and rings. There is evidence to suggest that transdermal estrogen patches have beneficial effects on blood lipids, cholesterol, and bone, although many of these benefits are less as compared to hormones administered orally. Several studies have found the benefit of transdermal products on bone density and bone metabolism to be comparable to that of oral therapy.

Generally, vaginal administration of hormones will result in lower levels of circulating hormones compared to an equivalent oral dose. Because the vaginal epithelium will respond to very small doses of estrogen, low-dose estrogen-containing creams can be used to correct vaginal atrophy. Vaginal estrogen therapy does not appear to protect against bone loss or cardiovascular disease.

13. Are there any alternatives for women who choose not to take hormones?

Such women can adopt a healthy lifestyle, such as not smoking, regular exercise, and good nutrition. In addition, other prescription drugs, such as statins or beta-blockers, are available to lower blood lipid levels or blood pressure levels. A healthy lifestyle can also help decrease a woman's risk of bone loss. In addition, doctors also recommend calcium and vitamin D supplements as a means of preventing osteoporosis. Other drugs, such as raloxifene, tibolone, alendronate, and risedronate have been shown to prevent bone loss. Many women find relief from short-term menopause-related changes with non-prescription remedies, such as estrogen-containing foods (soy products, whole-grain cereal, seeds, certain fruits and vegetables) and creams, certain herbs such as black cohosh, and vitamin E and vitamin B complexes. Short-term menopause-related changes may resolve on their own and frequently require no therapy at all.

14. What is elder abuse and how to check it?

Elder abuse occurs when someone knowingly or unknowingly causes harm or a risk of harm to an older adult. Elder abuse can take several forms, including:

Physical abuse

Physical abuse is the use of physical force, such as hitting, pushing, shaking or burning, with the intention of causing pain or injury.

Sexual abuse

Sexual abuse involves any non-consensual sexual contact, such as inappropriate touching, rape or pornographic photography.

Emotional abuse

Psychological or emotional abuse is the use of tactics, such as harassment, insults, intimidation or threats, that cause mental or emotional anguish or isolation.

Financial abuse

Financial or material exploitation involves improperly using an older person's resources for the benefit of another person, for example, by stealing, trickery or inappropriate use of government checks. Inappropriate use of financial power of attorney is another common example.

Neglect

Neglect occurs when a caregiver refuses or fails to provide the level of care necessary to avoid physical or mental harm. Examples include inadequate attention to food, water, shelter and personal hygiene.

The abuser is typically a family member—an adult child or a spouse. In institutions, such as nursing homes or group homes, professional caregivers may be abusers.

Signs that an older adult is neglecting himself or herself include:

- Neglecting personal hygiene
- Wearing soiled or ragged clothes

- Lacking food or basic utilities
- Refusing to take medications

Contact resources in your area if you know older adults who may be neglecting their own needs and putting themselves in danger.

8

Anti-Ageing in Women

Can Gender make a Difference?

As you look in the mirror you find a few more wrinkles and gray hairs, than you saw last time. As you age, your metabolism generally slows, meaning that your body burns fewer calories. Calories that were once used to meet your daily energy needs instead are stored as fat, resulting in unwanted weight gain. This can herald several ailments. Many consider ageing as a deficiency disease that is characterized by a gradual enfeeblement of mind and body. While women are biologically superior gender and on the average women live longer than men, women get poor nutrition and less care in the old age. Slogans such as "Age Adds Value," "Growing Older Getting Better", "Positive Ageing", "It Gets Better", and "Older and Bolder" are meant to project age as a time of fulfilment. The older woman may get confused. We are aged in a society where the norm is considered to be young; retired in a society where identity is invested in occupation; where quality of lifestyle is equated with the ability to consume; and where negative terms like "has been," "over the hill," "past it", "down hill", are commonly used when referring to older people. Probably the youth is gone for ever; grow old gracefully!

What world health organization (WHO) says on women ageing and health?

Most ageing women are living in the developing countries. Currently, more than half of the world's women aged 60 years and over are living in developing regions, 198 million compared with 135 million in the developed regions. And the percentage of older women living in developing regions will grow dramatically in the future, since two-thirds of the women in the age group 45-59 currently live in developing countries as compared with only one-third in the developed countries.

In the developed nations of the world, women live on average six to eight years longer than men. Life expectancy for women now exceeds 80 years in at least 35 countries and is approaching this threshold in several other countries.

Longer lives are not necessarily healthier lives

Since the likelihood of disability increases with age, it is hardly surprising that national surveys reveal increasing numbers of disabled women among the older populations. In a few developed countries, however, recent data reveals that the rates of disability among the older population are steadily declining. The available data, on the other hand, is still insufficient to assess the real extent of disability among the world's older women.

Among the types of disabilities, walking disability is currently acknowledged as one of the most important quality of life and public health concerns of older women. Slow walking speed is a risk factor for falls and other accidents, resulting in fractures, further disability and loss of independence. In developing countries, loosing the ability to walk may be associated with even greater risks of adverse outcomes as walking is often the most common means of transportation.

It is inaccurate to say that older women are generally frail

Recent studies in developed countries have shown that the prevalence of disability for both women and men to be less than 5 per cent for persons aged 60 to 64, less than 10 per cent for persons aged 70 to 74, and then rising to slightly more than 20 per cent among those aged 85 and over. There are powerful economic, social, political and cultural determinants, which influence how women age, with far-reaching consequences for health and quality of life, as well as costs to the health care systems. For example, poverty at older ages often reflects poor economic status earlier in life and is a determinant of health at all stages of life. Poverty is also linked to inadequate access to food and nutrition and the health of older women often reflects the cumulative impact of poor diets. For example, years of child bearing and sacrificing her own nutrition to that of the family can leave the older woman with chronic anemia.

In many countries, access to health care is tied to coverage by national social security and health insurance systems which in turn is linked to employment in the formal sector of the economy. As many older women in developing countries have worked all of their lives in the informal sector or in unpaid activities, access to health care often remains unaffordable and difficult at best.

Cessation of smoking, promotion of exercise and improved diet are in fact primary prevention strategies for many causes of death and disability. In addition, it is of paramount importance that younger women have the opportunity to build and maintain strong bones in order to maintain bone density and prevent osteoporosis at later ages.

Another example of preventable diseases is heart disease and stroke which are the major causes of death and disability in ageing women, accounting for close to 60% of all adult female deaths. For many types of cancer, particularly breast cancer and cervical cancer, early detection is the main strategy for prevention. For breast cancer early detection include physical examination of the breasts by trained health workers, breast self-examination and mammography. As general screening programmes by mammography are still far beyond the resources of developing countries, there is an urgent need to improve the effectiveness of breast self-examinations strategies.

WHO's response to maintain the health of older women

WHO's Ageing and Health Programme (AHE)

recognises that gender is one of the major determinants of health. In addition to biological differences, a gender approach to health includes an analysis of how different social and economic roles, decision-making power and access to resources affect the health status of men and women at older ages. Ageing which stresses that older people are a resource for their families and communities and that policies should be developed which enable older people to remain active for as long as possible in their later years. To facilitate the implementation of Active Ageing policies and strategies at all levels—national and community—gender sensitive guidelines and strategies are being developed.

Heart muscle becomes a less efficient pump

Over time, heart muscle becomes a less efficient pump, working harder to pump the same amount of blood through your body. The natural loss of elasticity, in combination with atherosclerosis, makes your arteries stiffer; causing your heart to work even harder. This can even lead to high blood pressure. As you age, your bones shrink in size and density. Gradual loss of density weakens your bones and makes them more susceptible to fracture. Muscles, tendons and joints generally lose some strength and flexibility as you age. There is a general slow down in the digestive organs as well. You might notice more constipation. With age, your kidneys become less efficient in removing waste from your bloodstream. About 30 percent of people aged 65 and older experience a loss of bladder control (incontinence). Incontinence can be caused by a number of health problems, such as obesity, frequent constipation and chronic cough. Women are more likely than men to have incontinence. Women who've been through menopause might experience stress incontinence as the muscles around the opening of the bladder lose strength and bladder reflexes change. As estrogen levels decline, the tissue lining the tube through which urine passes becomes thinner. Pelvic muscles become weaker, reducing bladder support. In older men, incontinence is sometimes caused by an enlarged prostate, which can block the urethra. This makes it difficult to empty your bladder and can cause small amounts of urine to leak. With age Women's vaginas tend to shrink and narrow, and the walls become less elastic. Vaginal dryness is a problem. All of this can make sex painful.

As you age your memory becomes less efficient. Your reflexes tend to become slower. You also tend to become less coordinated. With age, your eyes are less able to produce tears, your retinas thin, and your lenses gradually turn yellow and become less clear. In your 40s, focusing on objects that are close up may become more difficult. Cataracts, glaucoma and macular degeneration are the most common problems of ageing eyes. Hearing loss is one of the most common conditions affecting adults who are middle-aged and older. Also, the walls of your auditory canals thin, and your eardrums thicken. You may have difficulty hearing high frequencies. As you age, you'll likely find that you sleep less soundly, meaning you'll need to spend more time in bed to get the same amount of sleep. By age 75, some people find that they're waking up several times each night. Most adults can keep their natural teeth all of their lives. But with less saliva to wash away bacteria, your teeth and gums become slightly more vulnerable to decay and infection even if you're meticulous about brushing and flossing. If you've lost most or all of your natural teeth, you might use dentures or dental implants as a replacement. Dry mouth can also make speaking, swallowing and tasting difficult. Decreased production of natural oils may make your skin drier and more wrinkled. Age spots can occur, and skin tags are more common. Your hair may gray and thin. You are at increased risk of heat exhaustion and heat stroke. The most significant factor is sun exposure over the years. The more sun your skin has been exposed to, the more damage you may attain. Smoking adds to skin damage, such as wrinkles.

Certain modes of anti-ageing therapies are given below:

1. Botox

A botox injection can effectively reduce wrinkles and greatly improve your physical appearance.

2. Body Makeover

A body makeover consists of multiple cosmetic surgeries performed by a plastic surgeon to improve your appearance and make you look younger.

3. Early Menopause

Early menopause can occur in some women and the symptoms may be severe. Menopause symptoms can be treated with hormonal replacement therapy (HRT), herbal preparations or dietary estrogens (soy products).

4. Exfoliating Cleanser

An exfoliating cleanser is effective in removing the build up of dead skin cells thus preventing acne and hyper pigmentation.

5. Eye Makeup

Eye makeup can greatly improve your facial appearance, enhance your own natural beauty, and help to conceal the signs of facial ageing.

6. Facial Care

A good facial skin care regimen requires daily moisturizing, weekly exfoliation and a skin lightener to unify skin tone. Facial exercises can help to reduce facial wrinkling, especially when combined with an effective anti-ageing skin care treatment. Damage from free radicals can cause the skin to loose its natural elasticity, resulting in fine lines and wrinkles. A facial mask can improve the appearance and health of your skin by making it more vibrant and radiant. The daily use of a facial moisturizer can significantly reduce the loss of moisture from the skin, thus preventing dryness and wrinkling of the skin. Restylane is a hyaluronic acid-based filler that is effective in erasing wrinkles and giving the face a youthful contour. A face lift can make you look younger, but it cannot restore your face to its original youthful state. Microdermabrasion is a non-invasive cosmetic procedure used to improve the quality and texture of the skin by promoting renewal of the skin's surface cells. DDF wrinkle relax helps to prevent fine lines, reduce the appearance of wrinkles, and increase the production of collagen and elastin. Face Creams containing copper peptides utilize the collagen, elastin, glycoaminoglycan promoting capabilities of copper to revitalize dull, lifeless skin, reduce fine lines and wrinkles.

7. Hair Restoration/Removal

Hair loss can have a devastating affect on one's self-esteem and confidence. The earlier you start treatment the better. Hair restoration can be achieved successfully in men and women through the use of medications and hair replacement surgery. Hair transplant surgery is a safe and effective means of permanently restoring hair loss. Hair removal lasers work by selectively targeting the melanin pigment in the hair follicles to prevent future regrowth of hair. Laser hair removal works by selectively targeting the melanin pigment, which destroys the hair follicle and prevents future regrowth.

8. Skin Lighteners

Natural skin lighteners are very effective in reversing the excessive skin pigmentation that is associated with ageing. Increased skin pigmentation is the result of the build up of dead skin cells and the overactive production of melanin.

9. Teeth Bleaching

Teeth bleaching can significantly improve the appearance of discoloured teeth resulting from external stains. Teeth whitening performed under the supervision of a cosmetic dentist can greatly improve the appearance of teeth that are discoloured by external stains and yellowing caused by plaque. Vitamin C Cream acts as an antioxidant to combat the harmful effects of free radicals, revitalizing your skin.

10. Anti-Ageing Diet

The best anti-ageing diet is one that is low in carbohydrates, low in fats, high in proteins and rich in vitamins, antioxidants and phytochemicals.

11. Breast Lift

A breast lift is an aesthetic surgical procedure aimed at

reshaping and lifting sagging breasts. Breast augmentation is a surgical procedure to enlarge breasts by inserting a fluid or gel-filled implant between the breast tissue and the chest wall.

12. Dry Skin Care

Dry skin care involves gentle cleansing, moisturizing, protection from the sun, selecting the right make up, eating a healthy-balanced diet and hydrating the body. A chemical peel is a type of cosmetic skin treatment that uses various chemical solutions of varying concentrations to remove the top layer of the skin to improve its radiance and remove wrinkles

13. Human Growth Hormone

In adults, the effects of human growth hormone are to maintain and repair the body's muscle mass, decrease body fat and it has been proven to have anti-ageing benefits.

14. Eating Healthy

Eating healthy means eating a diet that is low in carbohydrates, low in total fat, high in proteins, and foods that are rich in vitamins, antioxidants, fiber and phytochemicals.

Why Women live longer?

Some thinkers blame the ageing on the body iron. They say the cause of early ageing and several ailments is excess iron in the body of males since they cannot get rid of it every month like a woman. Women live longer because they are better designed to withstand the rigors of life. Women, being the baby carriers of the species, must be protected from disease for human life to skirt extinction. Women better control iron in their bodies and thus outlast men. But once full growth has been achieved, around age 18, the demand for iron is relaxed and about one excess milligram of iron per day of life accumulates thereafter in the body. But at this point females avoid iron overload by virtue of their monthly menstrual cycle. About 80 percent of the iron stores in the body are in the red blood cells and females will lose about

30-60 milligrams of iron with the monthly cycle. On the other hand, males have no direct route for the disposal of excess iron. A 40-year old male will have twice the iron load as a female and will experience twice the rate of diabetes, cancer, heart disease and infections. Bacteria, viruses and fungi all utilize iron as a primary growth factor, so lower iron levels in females protect them from infection.

Females who have undergone early hysterectomy or who have entered early menopause lose their control of iron and begin to experience the same rate of disease as males. Females at age 45 have an advantage of about 5-8 more remaining years of life than males. But at age 80 this advantage shrinks to just two years. This is because now both sexes have lost any direct outlet for iron. Those who regularly donate blood are healthier. Even blood letting, practiced long ago, and is returning to conventional medicine to treat Alzheimer's disease, Parkinson's disease, cancer and diabetes. Blood-sucking leaches could theoretically protect against age-related iron overload and thus promote longevity.

Is it Calorie or iron restriction?

Anti-ageing researchers recognize calorie restriction as the only proven method of slowing down the ageing process. it would take a 30% reduction in calories over a human lifespan to significantly slow ageing in humans. Calorie restriction lowers body temperature, reduces cholesterol, triglycerides and blood pressure, elevates HDL cholesterol and reduces artery stiffness. Studies of fruit flies may help to understand the supremacy of iron control in the ageing process. Fruit flies are often used in ageing studies because of their short life span, may be 50-70 days. Insects have inborn mechanisms to control iron similar to humans. Excessive iron has been found to be the initiator of ageing in fruit flies. The lifespan of the fruit fly has been found to be proportional to the iron content in the diet. So calorie restriction may not be the only way to prolong human life. Supplemental iron should be avoided for full-grown males and post-menopausal females. Taking an aspirin a day to prevent heart attacks and strokes causes blood loss via the digestive tract of the order of about a tablespoon per day. This results in iron loss. By exercising, a person loses about 1 milligram of iron through sweat. Fasting and vegetarian diets, both of which promote longevity in animals and humans, limit iron consumption because plant foods provide non-hem iron which is poorly absorbed. Green tea will reduce iron absorption even further, by 62 percent. The diet also provides some potent iron binders. Iron-binding pigments found in berries, coffee, green tea, pine bark, onions and the rind of citrus fruits, and phytic acid (a component of whole grains and seeds such as sesame and rice bran) bind to iron and other minerals in the gastric tract and help to limit iron availability. They advocate that Chelation therapy is needed, for the removal of the excess iron.

Take care of your face

No lady wants to see an 'old woman' in the mirror or her husband likes her wrinkles and gray hair. You'll see plenty of compelling ads for plastic surgery, injections and treatments aimed at helping look younger. A good anti-ageing treatment regimen can make a huge difference in the appearance of ageing facial skin. Your appearance and your sense of well-being are linked. Every woman wants to look great and feel good about her. This desire can be fulfilled through an effective anti-ageing treatment regimen, one that will leave you with a clear, radiant, vibrant, and healthy skin. Look at the mirror again. Be alone. How do you appear? Facial exercise is one of the easiest ways to incorporate into a daily routine. Yes, the magic of facial exercise works from the inside out, first making an important shift in the shape and contour of the muscles supporting your skin, but most importantly, there is magic when you shift your thinking to acceptance, love and peace of mind.

The softness and flexibility of the skin is dependent on its moisture and oil content. As the skin ages, there is a decreased production of oil and perspiration by the sebaceous and sweat glands, respectively. Thus, the skin becomes drier. Because dry skin is more prone to wrinkling than oily skin, ageing skin requires daily moisturizing. A moisturizing cream is essential to any anti-ageing treatment plan. Daily moisturizing of the skin will make it softer, vibrant, and healthier. As a woman ages, there is an overall slowdown in the skin renewal process. Ageing skin loses the ability to regenerate new youthful skin cells and to shed dead ones. A build-up of dead cells on the surface of the skin can give it a dull and lifeless appearance.

An exfoliating cleanser is essential to an anti-ageing treatment regimen. An exfoliating cleanser can effectively remove the build-up of dead cells from ageing skin. After the dead cells are scrubbed from the skin's surface, immediately left under it is a revitalized, radiant, healthier, and a more youtful appearing skin. In addition, exfoliation is good skin hygiene. An exfoliating cleanser removes impurities and dead cells from the surface of the skin. Periodic exfoliation can greatly improve the appearance of ageing skin. Increased skin pigmentation is also associated with ageing. Melanocytes are specialized skin cells that produce a pigment called melanin. As the skin ages, splotching occurs. Splotching is due to an uneven deposition of pigment in the outer skin. The skin is no longer a uniform colour when compared to the skin of a young healthy adult. A skin lightener is essential to an anti-ageing treatment regimen. A skin lightener smoothes out skin tones and splotches. They also improve the clarity and radiance of ageing skin. A skin cream containing vitamin C can effectively reduce the hyperpigmentation associated with ageing skin and unify skin colour. Vitamin C reduces hyperpigmentation of the skin by decreasing the production of melanin by the melanocytes.

Menopausal weight gain

Obesity during menopause increases the risk of diabetes, heart disease, and has been strongly linked to increased incidence of breast and other hormone-related cancers, post-menopause. These healthcare concerns have led to the conception of specific products that target menopausal weight gain.

Estrothin is one of the newer weight-loss products on the market, it consists of a heavy mix of xanthine (caffeine) based stimulants such as yerba matte and green tea. It also consists of a compilation of herbal ingredients such as damiana, guarana, eleuthero root, rhodiola, stevia and ginseng. All of these ingredients are intended to help curb appetite, provide a sense of fullness, contain hormonal swings, and increase resting metabolic rate. There is little doubt as to the quality of the product's ingredients. However, one must be cautious, as there is a substantial amount of caffeine-based stimulants (yerba matte and green tea) in the product. For many people, consuming high amounts of caffeine can lead to elevated heart rate, increased blood pressure, nervousness, sweating among other symptoms. This is an obvious drawback with caffeine-based products. According to many physicians specializing in the treatment of menopause, increased levels of caffeine intake can exaserbate symptoms such as hot flashes, night sweats, and insomnia precipitously worse. Caffeine can also increase the risk of osteoporosis that affects many menopausal women. Given that fact, Estrothin may not be the right product for someone experiencing menopausal weight gain. Zalestra is another commercially popular menopausal weight-loss product. Estrolean was one of the first menopausal weight loss products on the market. Its formula is somewhat dated but it does contain some ingredients that have shown to be beneficial in alleviating menopausal symptoms. Estrolean also contains naturally occurring estrogen which addresses the hormonal imbalance responsible for symptoms associated with menopause and weight gain.

Overall, many of the ingredients contained in these formulas can be beneficial in minimizing uncomfortable symptoms, such as weight gain, hot flashes, night sweats, and mood swings that are associated with menopause. Menopause easing ingredients, as well as, hormonal supporting nutrients can be coupled with standard weight loss components producing beneficial effects of both weight loss and symptom relief. Estrothin targets primarily the symptom of menopausal weight gain. EstroLean targets primarily symptoms related to hormonal imbalances such as hot flashes and night sweats, while being a relatively mild weight loss product. Zalestra is a more comprehensive formulation because it addresses not only the weight gain but the symptoms associated with hormonal imbalances, such as hot flashes, night sweats, and mood swings, seen in the menopausal woman. These products may be worth a try for women who are experiencing weight gain or other negative symptoms associated with menopause.

DHEA

DHEA has long been touted as an anti-ageing therapy, used to ward-off chronic illness and maintain energy and vigor. However, an October 2006 study by K. Sreekumaran Nair, published in the New England Journal of Medicine has found no evidence that taking DHEA reverses the effects of ageing in rats. Similarly, they gave to the study participants DHEA for two years, it showed no physiologically significant beneficial effects in men and women in their 60s and 70s. The adverse effect of its long-term use in the general population is uncertain.

Peak blood levels of DHEA occur at approximately age 25, decreasing progressively thereafter. Thus, scientists have been looking at ways of restoring DHEA to youthful levels, and are now discovering mechanisms by which this hormone protects against age-related decline. In 1981, the Life Extension Foundation introduced DHEA (dehydro-epi-androsterone) and described the multiple benefits that this hormone might produce. DHEA became credible to the medical establishment when the New York Academy of Sciences published a book entitled DHEA and Ageing.

A study focused on the various benefits of DHEA, noted that its protective effect could be of benefit to the normal ageing brain. Some studies have reported DHEA may improve mood and alleviate melancholy. In still another investigative study doctors noted that DHEA is one factor that determines lumbar spine density. In women, it has been shown that DHEA helps to protect bone mineral density.

A DHEA-S (dehydroepiandrosterone sulfate) blood test may be taken three to six weeks after initiating DHEA supplementation regimen to help determine optimal dosing. When having your blood tested for DHEA, blood should be drawn three to four hours after the last dose. DHEA testing may save you money if it shows that you can take less DHEA to maintain youthful DHEA serum levels. The DHEA is calculated in micrograms per deciliter (mcg/dL) of blood.

The youthful ranges of DHEA are as follows (mcg/dL):

Men	400-560
Women	350-430

Men

Before attempting to restore DHEA to youthful levels, men should know their serum PSA (prostate specific antigen) level and have passed a digital rectal exam. Men with prostate cancer or severe benign prostate disease are advised to avoid DHEA since it can be converted into testosterone. Therefore, men are advised to have a PSA and digital rectal exam before initiating DHEA to rule out existing prostate disease. When taking DHEA we also recommend taking the following other nutrients:

Vitamin E	400-800 IU daily
Selenium	200 mcg daily
Mega Soy Extract (40% isoflavone extract)	135 mcg twice daily
Lycopene Extract	20-30 mg daily
Saw Palmetto Extract	160 mg twice daily
Pygeum Extract	50 mg twice daily
Nettle Extract	120 mg twice daily
Gamma tocopherol	200 mg daily
Boron	3-10 mg daily

Men should also periodically check their blood levels for free testosterone and estrogen to make sure that DHEA is following a youthful metabolic pathway:

Women

When taking DHEA it is also recommended take the following other nutrients to maintain a healthy balance.

Melatonin	300 mcg to 3 mg nightly
Vitamin E Succinate	400-800 IU daily
Mega Soy Extract (40% isoflavone extract)	135 mg twice daily
Indole-3-carbinol	200 mg two to four times daily

Vitamin D3	1000-1400 IU daily
Gamma tocopherol	200 mg daily

Women should consider estrogen and testosterone testing when they take their DHEA blood test in order to evaluate DHEA's effect on their blood levels of these hormones. Women who have been diagnosed with an estrogen-dependent cancer should consult their physicians before beginning the DHEA restoration process. Generally, take one to four capsules in the morning and/or afternoon. Taking DHEA with fat or an oil capsule enhances absorption. DHEA serum blood tests are suggested 3 to 6 weeks after initiating DHEA replacement therapy to optimize individual dosing. Do not take in the evening as it could interfere with sleep.

Stem cells taken from the umbilical cord tissue is not ethically wrong in any way. In the US, you are asked if you would like to donate the tissue for medical use when giving birth. Some clinics, who are using harvested embryos are not exactly ethical, but it is going on, has been going on, and will continue to happen. Deal with it.

9

Ageing and Skin Care

Is it Just Skin Deep Approach?

People spend billions of dollars on skin care products that promise to erase ageing marks like wrinkles, dryness, lighten age spots, and eliminate nuisance like itching, flaking, redness or just to give more youthful look to the face. Age is the enemy of elastic, healthy, young-looking skin. As we age, our skin stops producing collagen, which in turn leads to wrinkles. The factors that lead to wrinkles include—prolonged unprotected sun exposure, unhealthy lifestyle habits like smoking and overindulging, and the simple passage of time. Although many skin creams claim that they contain collagen, the fact is that collagen is too large to be absorbed directly through the skin. But collagen production can be stimulated by peptides; the chains of amino acids that are found naturally in the body. This stimulation makes it possible to slow down the effects of ageing and diminish facial wrinkles.

The skin; gatekeeper to health

An adult's skin comprises between 15 and 20 percent of the total body weight. Each square centimeter has 6 million cells, 5,000 sensory points, 100 sweat glands and 15 sebaceous glands. Skin is constantly being regenerated. The skin constitutes first line of defense against dehydration, infection, injuries and temperature extremes. As gatekeeper, the skin absorbs and uses nutrients applied topically. The skin may absorb the chemicals often present in soaps and lotions, which at best it has no use for and at worst can be toxic or irritating. It makes sense to choose nourishing natural skin care products. The epidermis consists of many layers: The stratum corneum, or outer layer, the translucent or transitional layer, the supra-basal layers, the basal or cell-division layer. Since the human epidermis is renewed every 15-60 days, proper surface nutrition feeds the cells of the basal layer. The dermis is the middle layer of the skin located between the epidermis and subcutaneous tissue. It is the thickest of the skin layers and comprises a tight, sturdy mesh of collagen and elastin fibers. The dermis also contains capillaries and lymph nodes. The former are important for oxygenating and nourishing the skin, and the latter—for protecting it from invading microorganisms. The dermis also contains sebaceous glands, sweat glands, hair follicles as well as a relatively small number of nerve and muscle cells. Sebaceous glands, located around hair follicles, are of particular importance for skin health as they produce sebum, an oily protective substance that lubricates and waterproofs the skin and hair. When sebaceous gland produce too little sebum, as is common in older people, the skin becomes excessively dry and more prone to wrinkling. Overproduction of sebum, often leads to acne. Wrinkles arise and develop in the dermis. Subcutaneous tissue is the innermost layer of the skin located under the dermis and consisting mainly of fat. Subcutaneous fat acts as a shock absorber and heat insulator, protecting underlying tissues from cold and mechanical trauma. The loss of subcutaneous tissue, often occurs with age, leads to facial sag and accentuates wrinkles. You sweat less, leading to increased dryness. As your skin ages, it becomes thinner and loses fat, so it looks less plump and smooth. Underlying structures—veins and bones in particular—become more prominent. Your skin can take longer to heal when injured. You can delay these changes by staying out of the sun. Common Skin Diseases are: Acne,

Baldness, Contact dermatitis, Eczema, Impetigo, Lichen planus, Lichen simplex chronicus, Psoriasis, Ring worm, Seborrhoeic dermatitis, Seborrheic keratosis, Shingles, Skin cancer, Tinea, Viral warts, Vitiligo.

Some common conditions consequent to ageing are as follows.

- Wrinkles
- Textural Changes
- Brown Spots
- Loss of Elasticity
- Coarse Texture
- Dryness
- Blood Vessel Damage—Broken Thread Veins
- Skin Growths
- Breakdown of Collagen—Sagging Skin

Wrinkles

The breakdown of elastin fibers due to ageing causes the skin to lose its ability to snap back, as a result, wrinkles form. Gravity also is at work, pulling at the skin and causing it to sag, most noticeably on the face, neck, and upper arms. People who smoke tend to have more wrinkles than non-smokers. Smoking also plays a role in damaging elastin. Tretinoin cream (Renova), a vitamin A derivative, is approved for reducing the appearance of fine wrinkles, mottled darkened spots, and roughness. However, it doesn't eliminate wrinkles, repair sun-damaged skin, or restore skin to its healthier, younger structure. The CO_2 and Er: YAG lasers are approved to treat wrinkles. The doctors use the laser to remove one layer of skin at a time.

Dry Skin and Itching

Many older people suffer from dry skin, particularly on their lower legs, elbows, and forearms. The skin feels rough and scaly and often is accompanied by intense itchiness. Low humidity—caused by overheating during the winter and air conditioning during the summer—contributes to dryness and itching. The loss of sweat and oil glands as you age also may worsen dry skin. Anything that further dries your skin—such as overuse of soaps, antiperspirants, perfumes, or hot baths will make the problem worse. Dehydration, sun exposure, smoking, and stress also may cause dry skin. Dry skin itches because it is irritated easily. Dry skin and itching can affect your sleep, cause irritability, or be a symptom of a disease; diabetes and kidney disease. Some medicines make the itchiness worse.

The most common treatment for dry skin is the use of moisturizers to reduce water loss and soothe the skin. Moisturizers come in several forms—ointments, creams, and lotions. Ointments are mixtures of water in oil, usually either lanolin orpetrolatum. Creams are preparations of oil in water, which is the main ingredient. Creams must be applied more often than ointments to be most effective. Lotions contain powder crystals dissolved in water, again the main ingredient. Because of their high water content, they feel cool on the skin and don't leave the skin feeling greasy. Although they are easy to apply and is more pleasing than ointments and creams, lotions don't have the same protective qualities. You may need to apply them frequently to relieve the signs and symptoms of dryness. Moisturizers should be used indefinitely to prevent recurrence of dry skin. A humidifier can add moisture to the air. Bathing less often and using milder soaps also can help relieve dry skin. Warm water is less irritating to dry skin than hot water.

Age Spots

These flat, brown spots are caused by years of sun exposure. They are bigger than freckles and appear in fair-skinned people on sun-exposed areas such as the face, hands, arms, back, and feet. They may be accompanied by wrinkling, dryness, thinning of the skin, and rough spots. A number of treatments are available, including skin-lightening, or "fade" creams; cryotherapy (freezing); and laser therapy. Tretinoin cream is approved for reducing the appearance of darkened spots.

Shingles

Shingles is an outbreak of a rash or blisters on the skin that may cause severe pain. Shingles is caused by the varicella-zoster virus, the same virus that causes chickenpox. After an attack of chickenpox, the virus lies silent in the nerve tissue. Years later, the virus can reappear in the form of shingles. Although it is most common in people over age 50, anyone who has had chickenpox can develop shingles. It also is common in people with weakened immune systems due to HIV infection, chemotherapy or radiation treatment, transplant operations, and stress. Early signs of shingles include burning or shooting pain and tingling or itching, generally on one side of the body or face. A rash appears as a band or patch of raised dots on the side of the trunk or face. The rash develops into small, fluid-filled blisters, which begin to dry out and crust over within several days. When the rash is at its peak, symptoms can range from mild itching to intense pain. Most people with shingles have only one bout with the disease in their lifetime.

Bruising

Many older people notice an increased number of bruises, especially on their arms and legs. The skin becomes thinner with age and sun damage. Loss of fat and connective tissue weakens the support around blood vessels, making them more susceptible to injury. The skin bruises and tears more easily and takes longer to heal. Sometimes bruising is caused by medications or illness. If bruising occurs in areas always covered by clothing, see a doctor.

Skin Cancer

Skin cancer is a common type of cancer. The risk is greater for people who have fair skin that freckles easily. UV radiation from the sun is the main cause of skin cancer. In addition, artificial sources of UV radiation—such as sunlamps and tanning booths—can cause skin cancer. Basal cell carcinomas are the more common, accounting for more than 90 percent of all skin cancers. They are slow-growing cancers that seldom spread to other parts of the body. Melanoma can spread to other organs, and when it does, it often is fatal. Both basal and squamous cell cancers are found mainly on areas of the skin exposed to the sun; the head, face, neck, hands, and arms. All skin cancers could be cured if they were discovered and brought to a doctor's attention before they had a chance to spread. The most common warning sign of skin cancer is a change on the skin, especially a new growth or a sore that doesn't heal. Skin cancer can start as a small, smooth, shiny, pale, or waxy lump. Or it can appear as a firm red lump. Sometimes, the lump bleeds or develops a crust. Skin cancer also can start as a flat, red spot that is rough, dry, or scaly. In treating skin cancer, the doctor's main goal is to remove or destroy cancer completely, leaving as small scar as possible. Treatment for skin cancer usually involves some type of surgery. In some cases, radiation therapy or chemotherapy (anticancer drugs) or a combination of these treatments may be necessary.

How to protect against harmful ultraviolet (UV) rays of the sun?

Sunscreens are rated in strength according to a sun protection factor (SPF), which ranges from 2 to 30 or higher. A higher number means longer protection. Buy products with an SPF number of 15 or higher. A hat with a wide brim shades your neck, ears, eyes, and head. Look for sunglasses with a label saying the glasses block 99 to 100 percent of the sun's rays. Wear loose, lightweight, long-sleeved shirts and long pants or long skirts; when in the sun. Don't use sunlamps and tanning beds, as well as tanning pills and tanning makeup. The large amount of colour additive in tanning pills may be harmful.

If you find any changes that worry you, see a doctor.

Plastic Surgery

The principal areas of plastic surgery include two broad fields.

Reconstructive Surgery

Focuses on undoing or masking the destructive effects of trauma, surgery or disease. Such surgery may include closing defects by transplantation of tissue from other parts of the body. Common cases of reconstructive surgery are breast reconstruction for women who have had a mastectomy, facial and contracture surgery for burn victims, closing skin or mucosa defects after removal of tumors in the head and neck region.

Cosmetic Surgery

Despite criticism, cosmetic surgery is becoming popular as less expensive and better techniques are being developed. The most prevalent are listed below:

- Facelift, brow lift, neck lift
- Augmentation Mammoplasty (or "breast enlargement")
- Chemical Peel: Removal of acne scars and sagging skin—not technically surgery and can be performed by a cosmetologist
- Mastopexy (or "breast lift"): Raising of sagging breasts
- Rhinoplasty: Reshaping of the nose
- Rhytidectomy (or "face lift"): Removal of wrinkles from the face
- Suction-Assisted Lipectomy (or liposuction): Removal of fat from the body
- Abdominoplasty (or "tummy tuck"): reshaping and firming of the abdomen
- Otoplasty (ear surgery)
- Fat injections
- Blepharoplasty (or "eyelid surgery")

Botox can produce dramatic anti-ageing results, similar to surgery, without the devastating side effects. Botox is a neurotoxin produced by the bacterium Clostridium botulinum. It causes a slight paralysis of the muscles around the wrinkles. This can diminish the appearance of "wrinkles," such as laugh lines and crow's feet. The procedure to have Botox injected under the skin can be quite costly and its effects are temporary, so it must be repeated several times a year. Botox; depending on the area can cost $ 250 to $ 600 per treatment. Also available are collagen injections, Restylane injections, Perlane Injections, and Sclerotherapy.

Dermabrasion utilizes micro-crystals or other sanding equipment to scrape away facial skin around the affected area. It is a costly procedure that my actually require a recovery of several weeks.

Laser surgery is a technique that uses a controlled laser beam to remove the upper layer of damaged skin. It can visibly reduce the appearance of fine line and in come cases, deeper wrinkles. It is one of the most popular procedures in cosmetic surgery today. However, it is an invasive surgical procedure that also has risks such as excessive scarring, infection, loss of normal skin pigmentation, skin redness and dryness.

Chemical Peels involve applying a chemical substance to your skin that "burns" off the damaged layers. The gentlest type of chemical peel available is the glycolic acid that removes dead skin cells from the upper layer of skin only. These treatments are quick and are often referred to as "lunch time peels," as they may only require ten to fifteen minutes in the doctor's office. However, the results of chemical peels are only temporary and the procedure must be repeated frequently.

Facial Skin

The skin on your face is exposed to a barrage of toxins and environmental damage on a daily basis. It must withstand pollution, ultraviolet rays, wind, and debris, as well as the harmful chemicals in skin cosmetics. Basically, facial skin is categorized as either normal, oily, dry, sensitive, or combination. The pores of normal skin are small and the overall skin tone is even. Oily skin, on the other hand results in medium to large pores that are prone to blockage and breakouts. Oily skin is moderately greasy and is thicker and firmer than normal skin. Dry skin feels tight and itchy, especially in the winter. Sensitive skin is prone to rashes and breakouts from any kind of irritants such as sun, perfumes, shaving cream, temperature extremes, and even soap. Avoid products with dyes, perfumes, or unnecessary chemical ingredients in all skin conditions.

Cosmetics

The role of modern cosmetics is to simulate youthfulness, health and, to an extent, arousal. The various forms of cosmetics include lipstick and lip gloss (used to colour the lips); foundation, powder, and rouge (used to colour the face); mascara (used to enhance the eyelashes) and eyeliner (used to colour the eyelids); and nail polish (used to colour the fingernails and toenails). If the market is extended to include cosmetic surgery, health and fitness and dieting it is worth $ 160 billion every year, specifically cosmetics—perfume is $ 15 billion, make-up is $ 18 billion, skin care is $ 24 billion and hair-care is $ 38 billion.

Skin toners offer extra cleaning and help to restore the pH balance of facial skin; but can be quite drying. Facial creams made of antioxidants (particularly vitamins C and E), vitamin A or alpha-hydroxy acids (AHAs), that are commonly used to help reduce the wrinkles and restore luster to the skin. Eye creams are specifically made to pamper the delicate skin around the eyes. They help to tighten under eye skin and they can reduce fine lines and wrinkles. Moisturizers help to hydrate skin and reduce the effects of ageing over time. Sunscreen is the most important facial skin care product for the health and protection of skin. The fragile skin on face needs a gentle cleanser that is designed for facial skin. Facial cleansers may come in liquid, foam, gel, towelette, or bar form. Alpha Hydroxy Acids (AHAs) work wonders at smoothing out the texture of skin and reducing the visibility of fine lines. These products work by sloughing-off dead skin cells to unblock and cleanse pores, to improve oily skin or acne, and to improve skin condition in general. Exfoliators utilize a variety of ingredients such as nuts, alpha hydroxy acids, and microcrystals to gently remove dead skin cells and reveal the healthy, radiant skin underneath. They are best used occasionally to restore luster to dull or dry skin.

Anti-Ageing and Beauty

Commercialism and media has placed high emphasis on beauty, thus nowadays everyone is trying to look like Ashwariya. Argireline is sold on the market, and the product supposedly produces powerful actions, while producing youthful skin in about one month. The product claims to diminish wrinkles greatly, while hydrating the skin in minutes. The first step requires that you cleanse the face, and apply the solution. It is recommended that the solution is massaged into the skin. The aroma is of melon and after washing the skin, the skin supposedly feels completely renewed and downy soft.

For around $ 90, you could purchase a 2-ounce pump bottle of Vitamin C Ester. The product is known as Amine Complex Face Lift. The product includes resourceful hydrator, which assists in balancing the skin to its natural moisturizing level. The product claims provide radiance to the face. PROPYLENE GLYCOL is specifically employed in antifreeze and brake fluids, which are very harmful chemicals.

Skin Care Treatments

The following active ingredients found in topical cosmetics are useful in prevention and treatment of premature ageing:

1. Vitamin A (retinol)

One of the few anti-ageing-pharmaceuticals with a scientifically proven efficacy. When applied topically, it is transformed to retinoic acid by human keratinocytes. Retinol stimulates collagen production in the skin, and its application can result in a reduction of wrinkles and skin pigmentation.

2. Vitamin C

It stimulates collagen production and has a photo protective effect. Its wrinkle-improving effect has been proven in clinical studies. One problem is its instability in various topical products, as vitamin C is prone to oxidation, and may lose its efficacy this way. Furthermore, some topical products do not penetrate through the stratum corneum, and thus are not able to render the desired effects.

3. Alpha-lipoic acid

It has antioxidative effects and has been shown to significantly reduce symptoms of skin ageing and skin roughness in a clinical study.

4. Flavonoids

Group of substances found in many foods, e.g. green-tea phenols. They have a photoprotective effect.

5. Copper

Copper peptides seem to have effects on skin ageing. Clinical studies showed wrinkle reduction and improvement of elasticity.

6. Vitamin E

There are almost no data on the antioxidant effects of Vitamin E from clinical studies, although some studies indicate a reduced wrinkle depth and a decrease in skin roughness. Confirmation of this data is still lacking. Vitamin E is found in various cosmetic products, however, in some of these its concentration is so low that no effects on the skin can be expected.

7. Coenzyme Q10

A lipophilic antioxidant which is reduced in ageing humans. Only few scientific data is found regarding its clinical anti-ageing effect. Further double-blind placebo-controlled studies are necessary to establish its efficacy.

8. Growth Factors

A relatively new concept is the topical application of growth factos such as EGF (Epidermal Growth Factor) and TGF-beta (Transforming Growth Factor beta). EGF is supposed to accelerate the cell turn-over rate and thus increase the speed of skin regeneration. TGF-beta seems to be effective in reducing wrinkles due to photoageing. Further controlled studies are needed to establish their effects in the long run.

9. Phyto-oestrogens

These are plant-derived substances with a hormone-like effect on the skin, such as isoflavones. They are found in soy products, grapes, and tropical fruits. A controlled study showed positive effects on skin tightness and wrinkle reduction after topical application of isoflavones in post-menopausal women.

10. DMAE

Dimethyl aminoethanol has supposedly a positive effect on periorbital oedema (swelling of the eyelids) and on skin tightness. Some studies show an anti-ageing effect on the skin.

11. Emblica

This antioxidant is extracted from the plant Phyllantus emblica and is said to reduce free radicals.

12. Polypeptides

Studies have shown that topically applied polypeptides may induce an acceleration of collagen synthesis. A clinical study demonstrated a positive effect on skin thickness and skin density after the application of a product containing palmitoyl pentapeptide for three months.

Home remedies for skin care

1. Zap blemishes

Tea's tannic acid absorbs oils that lead to blemishes. Saturate a tea bag in warm water and press on the affected area for about 5 minutes. Rinse.

2. Facial steam

Combine 1 cup fresh rose petals with 2 cups boiling water. Tent a towel over your head and let steam penetrate face for 10 minutes. Stay several inches away from the bowl.

3. Home-made exfoliator

Mix 1/8 cup of olive oil and 1 heaping tablespoon of sea salt. Use on knees and elbows in the shower and rinse off. Pat dry with a soft towel.

4. Home-made clay mask

Use 100% clay kitty litter (ground to a powder), mix with water, apply to face, let dry, then rinse. Eye mask—Grate 1/4 of an apple and a small raw potato and combine. Apply mixture to eyes for 15 minutes, cover your eyes with a warm washcloth and relax with some soothing music.

5. Home-made toner

In a blender, blend 1 peeled kiwi and 1 and 1/2 teaspoons lime juice. Add an equal amount of water and blend until smooth. Use a cotton ball to apply to face. Refrigerate any leftover toner in an airtight container.

6. Seal your pores

Close your pores with a skin tightening all natural clay or mud mask, or try this recipe: Mix 1 egg white with a few drops of lemon juice. Using a brush, massage onto clean skin. Leave on for 5 minutes then rinse with warm water.

7. Chapped lips

Exfoliate your lips by using an old toothbrush and a menthol-based lip balm. Apply lip balm first, and then brush gently with the toothbrush.

8. Moisturize your room

To keep skin from drying use humidifiers and keep the room temperature moderate. Also, get some green plants; they add moisture to your room!

9. Protect your skin

Photo-ageing is responsible for as much as 80% of skin damage—wrinkling, sagging, and discolouration or age spots. Use a safe sunscreen and apply it before exposing your skin to the elements.

10. Skin cream

Applying a skin cream 2-3 times per day helps to protect clean skin from daily assault. The most beneficial skin cream contains such anti-ageing ingredients as DMAE, Ascorbyl-Palmitate, ALA, Green Tea Extract and Vitamin E. Amway has started marketing a skin cream to prevent ageing of skin by blocking uv rays and free radicals. It will act as a barrier to prevent moisture loss and assault by the environmental factors. It contains time defiance intensive serum, rosemary extract, hexose and hydrolysed oats, sunflower extract, deep night action complex, etc. It repairs and revitalizes the skin from premature ageing by preserving collagen endonuclease for DNA repair.

Skin Care or Toxic Chemicals?

What may be palmed off as a skin care product may in fact be a toxic chemical.

Here are a few in particular to avoid:

Methyl Sulfonyl Methane (MSM)

Methyl Sulfonyl Methane (MSM) is one of the many products used to deal with wrinkles. Nevertheless, studies reveal it is leading to harm. Calcium Magnesium and Zinc, conversely work to reduce wrinkles. Collagen is one more of the anti-ageing products accessible, which comes in supplement form, creams, gels, foams, and so on; but can callagan penetrate the skin?

Products that use Ethoxylated surfactants as foaming agents or emulsifiers often produce 1, 4-doixane in the manufacturing process. This chemical is considered toxic if it is inhaled, absorbed through the skin or ingested. Alcohol, Isopropyl (SD-40); drying agent strips-off the outer most protective layer, exposing the body to bacteria, fungus, molds, and other toxins. It is derived from petroleum and may promote brown spots or premature ageing.

Surfactants are used in about 90% of foaming personal care products. They are also used in car washes, garage floor cleaners, and as engine degreasers. Common anionic surfactants include: Sodium Lauryl Sulfate (SLS), Sodium Laureth Sulfate (SLES), Ammonium Lauryl Sulfate (ALS), Ammonium Laureth Sulfate (ALES), Sodium Methyl Cocoyl Taurate, Sodium Lauroyl Sarcosinate, Sodium Cocoyl Sarcosinate, Potassium Coco Hydrolysed Collagen, TEA (Triethanolamine) Lauryl Sulfate, TEA (Triethanolamine) Laureth Sulfate, Lauryl or Cocoyl Sarcosine, Disodium Oleamide Sulfosuccinate, Disodium Laureth Sulfosuccinate, and Disodium Dioctyl Sulfosuccinate. Avoid all of these ingredients. Other surfactants commonly used in hair conditioning products are synthetic, irritating to hair follicles, and toxic and cause hair to become dry and brittle. Common cationic surfactants include Stearalkonium chloride, Benzalkonium chloride, Cetrimonium chloride, Cetalkonium chloride, and Lauryl dimonium hydrolysed collagen.

Chloromethylisothiazolinone and Isothiazolinone

These two harmful chemicals can be corrosive to the eyes and skin. Long-term exposure can cause permanent eye damage and third degree burns to skin. They can be fatal if ingested and they can cause damage to the mucous membranes of the lungs if inhaled.

DEA (diethanolamine), MEA (Monoethanolamine), and TEA (triethanolamine)

These chemicals are often used in personal care cleansers to adjust the pH of the formula. They can cause allergic reactions, eye irritation, dryness, and toxicity if used over long periods. Diazolidinyl urea and DMDM Hydantoin: These chemicals contain formaldehyde, a toxic carcinogen, and it can cause dermatitis, burning, irritation of the mucous membranes, inflammation, and watering of the eyes.

Ethoxylated surfactants

These surfactants are commonly used in cosmetic formulas as foaming agents, emulsifiers, and humectants. They may be listed on the ingredient label as "PEG", "polyethylene", "polyethylene glycol", "polyoxyethylene", "-eth-", or "-oxynol." These chemicals form 1,4-dioxane (a known carcinogen) as a byproduct in the manufacturing process.

The synthetic colour pigments are made from coal tar. They contain heavy metal salts that leave toxic byproducts on the skin. These chemicals have been tested on animals and found to cause cancer. Formaldehyde is another cancer causing agent that is commonly found in commercial make-up products. It can cause allergic reactions, headaches, and chronic fatigue.

Lanolin is used in many commercial cosmetic formulas, and it is often considered harmless. Since it is obtained from the wool of sheep and is therefore contaminated with the pesticide DDT. Liquid paraffin, is a byproduct of petroleum that coats the skin like plastic. It disrupts the skin's natural ability to purge itself of toxins, slows down cell function and can cause premature ageing. It can also be found in paraffin wax, paraffin oil and petrolatum.

Chemicals that cause nitrosamine contamination have been found in laboratory tests to cause cancer. Nitrosamines can be found in the following chemical ingredients: 2-bromo-2-nitropropane-1, 3-diol, Cocoyl Sarcosine, DEA compounds, Imidazolidinyl Urea, Formaldehyde, Hydrolysed Animal Protein, Lauryl Sarcosine, MEA compounds, Quaternium-7, 15, 31, 60, etc. Sodium Lauryl Sulfate, Ammonium Lauryl Sulfate, Sodium Laureth Sulfate, Ammonium Laureth Sulfate, Sodium Methyl Cocoyl Taurate, and TEA compounds.

Paraben preservatives (methyl, propyl, butyl, and ethyl)

These chemicals are often used in cosmetic formulas to inhibit microbial formation and extend the shelf life of the make-up products. They are commonly used in commercial applications even though they are known to be highly toxic and to cause allergic reactions and skin rashes.

Propylene/Butylene Glycol

This chemical compound is considered so toxic by the EPA that it mandates that its workers wear protective equipment when handling it. It is a petroleum product that penetrates the skin easily and can cause brain, liver, and kidney malfunctions. This ingredient is often found in stick deodorants where it can cause acute and chronic health hazards.

Rancid Natural Emollients

Creams and other commercial cosmetics made from refined vegetable oils contain harmful transfatty acids. Polyunsaturated oils can also oxidize quickly, causing free-radical damage to the skin and premature ageing. They are also missing the essential nutrients, fatty acids, and vitamins that help protect and moisturize the skin.

Silicone derived emollients

Like other emollients, these products coat the skin like plastic wrap, and disrupt the skin's ability to breathe and release toxins. They can accumulate in the liver and lymph nodes and promote the development of tumors. Common silicone derived emollients include Dimethicone, Dimethicone Copolyol, and Cyclomethicone.

Sodium Laureth Sulfate (SLES) Ammonium Laureth Sulfate (ALES)

When combined with other ingredients, these chemicals form nitrosating agents and have a carcinogenic effect on the body. Be especially wary of semi-natural products that claim to be derived from coconut oil. These chemicals can alter the immune system and cause damage to the eyes, digestive system, nervous system, lungs, and skin. They are commonly found in foaming personal care products. Stearalkonium Chloride: Originally developed as a fabric softener, this chemical is often found in hair conditioners and creams. They are toxic chemicals that can cause allergic reactions on contact.

Toluene

This chemical can be particularly dangerous if inhaled or absorbed through the skin. Aspiration can cause chemical pneumonitis, a fatal disorder. It is highly flammable in both liquid and vapor form and it may affect the liver, kidneys, nervous system, and blood. Overexposure can cause fatigue, confusion, headache, dizziness, or numbness. Severe overexposure can cause coma and death. Exposure to toluene can also affect the proper development of a growing fetus.

10

Scourge of Obesity

The Fat Looks Older and Ugly

It is estimated that 30% population in the developed nations is suffering from this syndrome and now the developing countries are following suit. This is caused by excessive intake of food and less of exercise. Metabolic syndrome is a cluster of conditions that occur together, increasing your risk for heart disease, stroke and diabetes. A WHO criterion entails evidence of insulin resistance. Having just one of these conditions—increased blood pressure, elevated insulin levels, excess body fat around the waist or abnormal cholesterol levels—contributes to your risk of serious disease. In combination, your risk is even greater. An overweight person gives an older look than his/her actual age. This is one of the most common diseases found all over the world. A billion people (world's population is six billion) are presently considered overweight. The World Health Organization has reported that for every four adults in the world who are malnourished five more are overweight. Body-mass index (BMI) is the international standard for determining obesity, which is

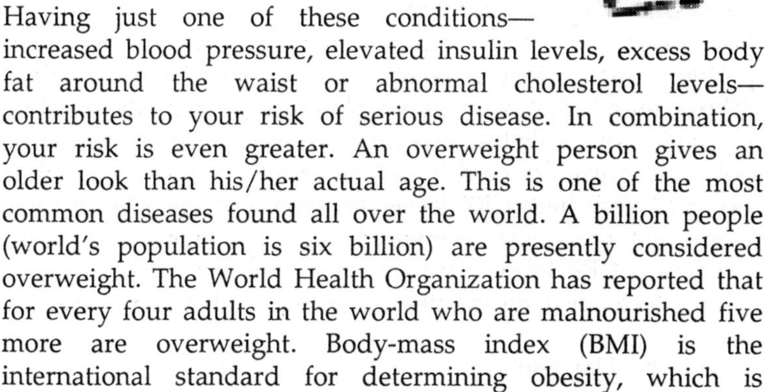

defined as one's weight in kilograms divided by the square of one's height in meters. 30% of adults in the United States are said to be clinically obese while in Europe Britain has 23% of its adults as obese, which is nearly twice the rate in Germany (12%). Italy counts only 8% of its population as severely overweight. Less than five percent of the population in China, Japan and some African nations is obese. India is also falling prey to increasing obesity in a big way. Obesity rates have started to climb towards epidemic levels as the sedentary lifestyles and rich diets—laden with sugar, fats and salt—common in many Western countries, take hold in all age groups in India. In developing countries it is more prevalent in the wealthy society, whereas in developed countries it is more common in lower-socio-economic groups. Obesity tends to run in families. Eighty percent of the offsprings of two obese parents become obese. What ever the cause you must avoid becoming fat and in case you are overweight, shed the extra kilos.

Indian women/men are falling prey to obesity

As per latest study sponsored by ICMR and conducted by AIIMS, shows that 48.7% women have apple shaped obesity and the general figure is more than 50%. A waist to hip ratio of 0.6 or more is indicative of obesity in women (men the limit is 0.8 to 1). Obesity decreases life expectancy 12 fold.

Sedentary life style, coupled with rich food and lack of exercise is slowing down metabolism and is exposing to depression, hypertension and a host of other chronic diseases. You suffer from heart attacks, diabetes, cancers and other problems more often. A recent study by the Harvard Medical School found that women who ate large amounts of high-glycemic (or diabetes promoting) carbohydrates, including potatoes, breakfast cereals, white bread, muffins, and white rice, had very high CRP levels. Women who ate a lot of these foods and were also overweight had the highest and most dangerous CRP levels. Obesity brings economic problems too.

Mechanical disabilities associated with obesity are:

- Flat feet

- Osteoarthritis of knees, hips
- Lumbar spine
- Abdominal hernia
- Varicose veins
- Exertional healthlessness
- Respiratory infection
- Accidents

Metabolic syndrome X

As the name suggests, metabolic syndrome is tied to the body's metabolism, possibly to a condition called insulin resistance. Besides abdominal obesity, raised cholesterol level, raised blood pressure, other components of this syndrome include: raised CRP and cytokine levels, prothrombotic state with raised levels of PAI 1 and fibrinogen. Doctors have talked about this constellation of risk factors for years and have called it many names, including syndrome X and insulin resistance syndrome. Whatever it's called, and however it's precisely defined, this collection of risk factors is apparently becoming more prevalent. If you have metabolic syndrome or any of its components, you have the opportunity to make aggressive lifestyle changes that can delay or derail the development of serious diseases. In addition to the lifestyle modifications some patients may require one of the two drugs to reduce weight. Orlistat works by reducing fat absorption by the intestine. Sibutramine is another; which is an appetite suppressant.

Neurological diseases such as multiple sclerosis (MS) and Parkinson's disease may be far more common than had previously been thought. A recent survey has found that one out of every 100 elderly Americans has Parkinson's, and nearly one out of every 1,000 Americans has MS. Just as the obesity epidemic continues to grow, so are the incidents of these serious neurological diseases. Do you think there is any connection? Fortunately, eating the right foods based on your body's unique metabolic type in tandem with a regular exercise program will do wonders to protect you from the underlying factors that precipitate chronic degenerative diseases like Parkinson's and Alzheimer's.

- Follow the nutrition plan paying special attention to avoiding sugar
- Eat plenty of high-quality omega-3 fish oil
- Avoid most fish and remove mercury
- Eat plenty of vegetables
- Avoid flu vaccinations
- Keep your mind active
- Since worry accelerates your risk of Alzheimer's, learn an effective energy psychology tool like the Emotional Freedom Technique

Be prepared to lose weight first of all. You're ready to lose weight, if you say yes to the following questions?

- Are you motivated to make long-term lifestyle changes that require eating healthy foods and exercising more?
- Do you currently have distractions in your life that may prevent you from committing to your weight-loss program?
- Do you truly believe that slower is better? Losing weight at a relatively slow pace has proved safe, healthy and effective over the long-term.
- Are you realistic about your weight-loss goal? Remember, losing 5% to 10% of your body weight can reap health rewards.
- Do you have family and friends to support your weight-loss efforts?
- Do you believe that you can change your eating habits? It can be difficult.
- Are you willing to become more physically active?
- Do you have time to keep records of your food intake and physical activity?
- Are you willing to look at past successes and failures in weight loss?
- Do you view a healthy-weight program as a positive experience?
- Have you resolved any eating disorders that make it difficult for you to achieve a healthy weight?
- Do you believe that a healthy weight is a lifelong commitment?

The two most important strategies to control weight are increased physical activity and balanced food.

Make whole grains foods a habit

Whole grains are a great source of important nutrients, including protein, fiber, vitamins, minerals, and, especially, carbohydrates that are low on the glycemic index (GI), a ranking of carbohydrate foods on the basis of how they affect blood sugar (glucose). This is important for many people because eating a lot of foods that are high on the glycemic index will produce spikes in blood sugar that can lead to insulin resistance over time. Insulin resistance is associated with obesity, high blood pressure, elevated blood fats, and an increased risk of type 2 diabetes, and other chronic diseases.

Grains in their natural form have a low glycemic index, while processed carbohydrates, including those made with flour or puffed grains, have a high GI. The reason is that it takes longer for digestive enzymes to reach the starch inside whole grains or grains cracked into large pieces, slowing down the conversion of starch to sugar. True whole grains include wild rice, barley, quinoa, millet and wheat berries. You can be pretty sure you're eating a natural grain with a low GI ranking if you have to chew it or can see grains or pieces of grains in food products. The more your jaw has to work, the better. But when grains are pulverized into flour, whether whole or not, their surface area expands dramatically, providing a huge, starchy surface area on which the enzymes can work. Consequently, the conversion to sugar happens very quickly. Whole wheat bread and products labeled "whole grain" are usually made with flour. If you check a list of the glycemic index of various foods you'll see that finely textured whole wheat bread has the same GI as white bread—about 70, making both high GI foods. It is recommended to cut down on all products made with flour and increasing consumptions of grains in their more natural state.

Health Benefits of Physical Activity/Exercise

Biological process called AMP-activated protein kinase (AMPK), which boosts muscles, begins to fail with advancing age. This leads to a need for increased effort to achieve the same effects from exercise, and could help explain the link between ageing and type 2 diabetes. AMPK stimulates the body to burn off fat by producing mitochondria, the power sources of cells. The skeletal muscles of athletes have been found to contain a much higher number of mitochondria, which is likely linked to AMPK activity. Older people have more fat in their muscles and livers than younger people do. These fat cells have been linked to insulin resistance and type 2 diabetes.

Major benefits from regular exercise include the following:

- favourable effects on fats in the blood
- better handling of blood sugar
- improved breathing
- better endurance
- improved balance
- greater strength
- stronger bones
- improved sense of well-being
- clearer thinking
- better sleep

Physical activity reduces the risks of heart disease, high blood pressure, diabetes, obesity, osteoporosis, and colon cancer. There is also much evidence that physical activity can reduce loss of muscle related to age, depression, injuries related to falls, and stroke. In addition, physical activity has been linked to a decreased risk of gall stones, sleep problems, and ability to fight-off infections. Remember—even if a person has some health problems, exercise is still beneficial.

Physical activity can improve symptoms of depression, with one study suggesting that strength training can improve symptoms of depression as much as medication. Regular physical activity can also improve sleep. Exercise is a vital part of the treatment of arthritis, and studies have found that exercise reduces pain without causing damage in people who have arthritis of the knee. Exercise is also useful to lower blood pressure in people with high blood pressure, to reduce falls, and to improve bone strength in people with osteoporosis. Regular physical activity delays the loss of function and can keep you living independently longer. Higher levels of physical activity are also associated with fewer years of disability before death. Exercise in older adults decreases functional limitations and increases quality of life. Inactive older adults who have lost some function probably benefit the most from increasing their level of exercise.

Different Types of Exercises

Walking and aerobic activities

Walking is the core activity in most exercise plans for older adults. It is, by far, the most common and popular form of physical activity for older adults. Walking reduces the risks of death and heart disease, as well as the risk of falling. Of course, some older adults prefer other forms of aerobic activity, such as swimming, biking, dancing, and racket sports.

Stretching exercises

Stretching exercises and other activities that improve flexibility are recommended for older adults. Flexibility can be increased by specific stretching exercises, by exercise programs that include stretching exercises, or by some daily activities such as walking. Current recommendations encourage stretching at the end of a bout of activity, or after gentle warm-up activities.

Reducing muscle loss

Muscle loss contributes to functional limitations and dependence in older adults. We don't completely understand why the loss develops, but nerve damage, decreased blood supply, and injury to cells may be involved. Several studies suggest that regular physical activity among older adults can prevent much loss of muscle mass. In a study, everyday physical activities, such as household work, walking, and gardening, maintained skeletal muscle strength well enough for independent living.

Resistance training

Strength training has become a standard part of many exercise programs, including programs for heart and lung rehabilitation. It also improves function and joint symptoms of older people with arthritis. In addition, strength training can improve control of blood sugar in older adults with diabetes. These programs typically use free weights, such as weight cuffs or dumbbells. Typically, regular training for 3-6 months can increase strength by 10-30%. In general, 2 days per week of resistance training is enough, doing, for example, 8-10 exercises 10-15 times each. Strength training also improve overall physical function, including improved balance and gait and less risk of falling. Some older adults may want to go a step further and explore more strenuous or high-intensity resistance training. Older adults involved in these programs can gain strength steadily for many months. It can cause low levels of muscle inflammation and, if improperly done, cause injury.

Reducing osteoporosis, falls, and fractures

Resistance and high-impact exercises are probably the most beneficial for slowing bone loss but they may be associated with injury. Weight-bearing aerobic activities can also help maintain bone mass. Increasing physical activity is regarded as an effective part of programs to prevent falls. Overall, exercise improves balance and reduces the risk of falls and hip fracture. Studies also suggest that even daily activities, such as walking and climbing stairs, can reduce the risk of hip fracture.

Consult your doctor

Your doctor can help you establish an activity program that is right for you. Key things for you to work on together include:

- Evaluating your current level of physical activity.
- Setting goals that consider your health status, preferences, and life style.
- Identifying and overcoming barriers to activity. Common barriers for older adults include symptoms of disease, concern about neighborhood crime, being too busy for a variety of reasons, and the weather.

- Identifying sources of support. These include social support, telephone follow-up, community programs that provide encouragement. Your doctor may also help you identify resources, such as information sheets, senior's activity programs, shopping malls that open early for "mall walkers," etc. that could be useful to you.

Take care to promote all aspects of your fitness

1. Aerobic fitness

Any activity you do—from taking a walk to washing the dishes—requires oxygen. Regular aerobic fitness exercise increases your body's ability to use oxygen. How well you use oxygen is termed your "aerobic capacity." When your aerobic capacity is high, your heart, lungs and blood vessels efficiently transport and deliver large amounts of oxygen throughout your body.

Aerobic exercise helps you in your daily activities. It helps your heart, blood vessels, lungs and muscles complete routine tasks and rise to unexpected challenges, such as running to your car in pouring rain.

The key to achieving aerobic capacity is to find fitness training activities that you enjoy and can do regularly. You needn't limit yourself to a single activity, such as running. Add variety and increase your motivation by trying different types of aerobic activity, such as dancing, bicycling or water aerobics. Aerobic exercise at least 10 minutes in length is required to obtain health benefits.

2. Muscular fitness

Muscular fitness refers to the strength and endurance of your muscles. The more fit your muscles are, the easier your daily tasks become, whether they include lifting groceries, raking the yard or pushing a vacuum cleaner.

Strength training can help you improve your muscular fitness. It also enables you to increase your body's lean muscle mass, which helps with weight loss.

Training options include using free weights, resistance bands, weight machines or your own body weight to increase muscular strength and endurance. Fitness training that includes more than one option will help ensure greater overall muscular fitness.

3. Flexibility

Flexibility is the ability to move your joints through their full range of motion. You maintain your body's flexibility through stretching. When you're flexible, routine tasks, such as lifting packages, bending to tie your shoe and hurrying to catch a bus, are easier and less tiring.

Fitness training activities that lengthen your muscles increase your flexibility. One way to become more flexible is to include stretching exercises in your fitness routine. Yoga and tai chi, if performed correctly, can be effective for improving flexibility. No matter what type of stretching exercises you choose, make flexibility training an integral part of your fitness plan.

4. Stability and balance

Stability and balance are associated with your body's core muscle strength—the muscles in your lower back, pelvis, hips and abdomen. These core muscles provide the support system for almost any activity or motion your body makes. They help you maintain stability and balance during your daily activities.

You can improve your stability and balance through core exercises that strengthen the muscles at the center of your body—the area around your trunk—where your center of gravity is located. A strong mid-section helps combat poor posture and low back pain. It also helps prevent falls, especially in older adults.

Whether you create your own fitness training plan or work with a personal trainer, make aerobic fitness, muscular fitness, flexibility, and core strengthening for stability and balance a part of your overall exercise plan. Factoring in these four fitness elements can help you live a longer, healthier life.

Healthy Diet for Everyone

The traditional Japanese diet is very low in cholesterol,

fat, and calories and high in fiber and proteins. Emulate it for better health. Here are the eight secrets of success of Japanese diet:

1. Eat brown Rice

How many times in a week do you eat rice? For the Japanese it is normally daily. Rice is rich in carbohydrates and proteins it is the basis of the Japanese diet.

2. Eat More Fish

The Japanese eat about 70 kg of fish per person per year, that's four times as much as the average for the rest of the world. Eating fish lowers the risk of disease and increases vitality.

3. Eat Soya

The Japanese eat 10 times more Soya produce than any other nation. Low in calories and fat and high in protein Soya is also packed with plant estrogen.

4. Variety

A recent study showed that Japanese people eat an average of 100 different foods a week, compared to just 30 in other western countries. This well balanced diet provides all the nutrients the body needs. A premium is also placed upon freshness and natural flavor; people like to eat ingredients at their "shun" or "now-in-season" in Japanese.

5. Portion Control

Portions tend to be smaller and are savored, and it is this portion control that stops binging and over eating. Each portion is eaten slowly, so the stomach has more time to register when it is full. Eating slowly also aids digestion and absorption of the nutrients in the food.

6. Breakfast

Breakfast is the most important meal of the day, giving a boost of energy and preventing hunger pangs later. A typical breakfast might include green tea, steamed rice, soup with tofu, spring onions and may be omelette and grilled salmon.

7. Cook Light

In the Japanese diet, food is usually steamed, pan-fried, simmered or stir fried over intense heat. This method of cooking helps the food retain more of the nutrients and particularly anti-ageing antioxidants.

8. Eat Sweets with restraint

The Japanese diet has room for these treats. They love chocolate, pastries, ice cream and cookies. The difference is they view them as a regular treat and do not overdo the portions.

Cutting calories

If you eat more calories than you burn, you gain weight. Because 3,500 calories equals about 1 pound of fat, you need to burn 3,500 calories more than you take in to lose 1 pound. Carbohydrates, fats and proteins are the types of nutrients that contain calories and thus are the main energy sources for your body. The amount of energy in each varies: Proteins and carbohydrates have about 4 calories per gram and fats have about 9 calories per gram. Alcohol is also a source of calories, providing about 7 calories per gram. Regardless of where they come from, calories you eat are either converted to physical energy or stored within your body as fat. Unless you use these stored calories—either by reducing calorie intake so that your body must draw on reserves for energy, or by increasing physical activity so that you burn more calories—this fat remains stored within your body. Skipping one or two high-calorie items that you might have otherwise eaten is a good place to start when cutting calories.

Here are 20 ideas to reinforce your healthy lifestyle and to keep you committed to permanent weight loss.

1. Exercise 30 to 60 minutes each day. If time is limited, exercise for several brief periods throughout the day—for example, three 10-minute sessions rather than one 30-minute session.
2. Eat three healthy meals during the day, including a good breakfast. Skipping meals causes increased hunger and may lead to excessive snacking.

3. Focus on fruits and vegetables. Top off your morning cereal with sliced strawberries or bananas. Stir berries or peaches in yogurt or cottage cheese. Liven up your sandwiches with vegetables, such as tomato, lettuce, onion, peppers and cucumber.
4. Weigh yourself regularly. Monitoring your weight can tell you whether your efforts are working and can help you detect small weight gains before they become even larger.
5. Don't keep comfort foods in the house. If you tend to eat high-fat, high-calorie foods when you're upset or depressed or bored, don't keep them around. Availability of food is one of the strongest factors in determining how much a person eats.
6. Plan a family activity. Get the family together to go for a bike ride, play disc golf or kick the ball around in the yard.
7. Eat healthy foods first. Eat foods that are healthy and low in calories first so that when it comes time to enjoy your favorites—sweets or junk food, for example—you won't be so hungry.
8. Pay attention to portions. Serve meals already dished onto plates instead of placing serving bowls on the table. Take slightly less than what you think you'll eat. You can always have seconds, if really necessary.
9. Create opportunities to be active. Wash your car at home instead of going to the car wash. Bike or walk to the store. Participate in your kid's activities at the playground or park.
10. Sit down together for family meals. Avoid eating in front of the television. TV viewing strongly affects how much and what people eat.
11. See what you eat. Eating directly from a container gives you no sense of how much you're eating. Seeing food on a plate or in a bowl keeps you aware of how much you're eating.
12. Vary your activities. Regularly change your activity routine to avoid exercise burnout. Walk a

couple of days, swim another and go for a bike ride on the weekend. Seek out new activities—karate, ballroom dancing, cross-country skiing, tennis or Pilates.

13. De-stress your day. Stress can cause you to eat more. Develop strategies that can help you relax when you find yourself becoming stressed. Exercise, deep breathing, muscle relaxation techniques and even a good laugh can ease stress.
14. Eat at home. People eat more food in restaurants than at home. Limit how often you eat at restaurants. If you do eat out, decide what and how much you're going to eat before you start and have the rest boxed to go.
15. Plan healthy snacks. The best snacks include fruits, vegetables, whole grains and low-fat dairy products. Fruit smoothies, sliced fresh fruit and yogurt, whole-grain crackers, and carrot and celery sticks with peanut butter are all good choices.
16. Start your day with a high-fiber breakfast cereal, such as bran flakes, shredded wheat or oatmeal. Opt for cereals with "bran" or "fiber" in the name. Or add a few tablespoons of unprocessed wheat bran to your favorite cereal.
17. Walk for 10 minutes over your lunch hour or get up a few minutes earlier in the morning and go for a short walk.
18. Plan a week's worth of meals at a time. Make a detailed grocery list to eliminate last-minute trips to the grocery store and impulse buys.
19. Look for a distraction when you're fighting a craving. Call a friend, put on music and dance or exercise, clean the house, pull weeds in your garden, or run an errand. When your mind is occupied with something else, the cravings quickly go away.
20. Reward yourself. Losing weight and keeping the pounds off is a major accomplishment. Celebrate your success with non-food rewards, such as new clothes or an outing with friends.

FAQ about obesity

Q. Does obesity causes complications?

Yes. Obese patients are at a risk of developing Diabetes mellitus, cardiovascular diseases and Hypertension in the long-term.

Q. What is the relation between obesity and heart attack/high blood pressure?

The adverse effects of obesity are more pronounced when the fat is concentrated in the abdomen. A study in Europe found that 63% cases of heart attack had abdominal obesity. South Asian men have 41% of central obesity; though they are 3 times suffer less from general obesity. Women are more often obese. Diabetes is a serious risk factor.

Q. Does low calorie diets help in losing weight?

Yes. Weight reduction can be achieved by reducing food intake and by regular exercise. A low calorie diet should constitute a low carbohydrate, high fiber, moderate protein and a low fat diet.

Q. Does exercise help in losing weight?

Yes, there are several advantages of exercise: 1. Most obese people are capable of moderate aerobic exercise such as walking, swimming, gardening, dancing, provided it does not exceed their cardiovascular capacity. 2. Because of their heavy weight obese people expand more food energy than lean people doing exercise of this type. 3. Regular daily exercise will help in reducing than exercising once in a while.

There are various appetite suppressing drugs but should be taken only on recommendation by the doctor. Surgery also may be an option but usually as a last resort, only recommended in case of gross obesity.

Q. What are the methods in surgical treatment?

1. Wiring the jaws together to prevent eating has been used to treat those who have found it impossible to adhere to a low calorie diet.

2. Although this usually results in marked loss of weight, many patients regain weight when the procedure is reversed.
3. An alternative and fairly safe operation (major) is to reduce the size of the stomach, by stapling, which can be undone.
4. Small intestine bypass, aimed at inducing mal-absorption, has been undertaken in some centers for the treatment of severe obesity, but complications can be severe and sometimes fatal.
5. It should be emphasized that surgery should be considered only for those with gross, intractable obesity.

Q. Is Your Food Ageing You?

Over-indulgence in certain types of food causes the body to prematurely age. We are advised by nutritional experts to eat plenty of fruit and vegetables. This is because they are rich in antioxidant phytonutrient substances that neutralize free radicals and so help protect the body. One of the essential tasks of free radicals is in producing energy from the food you eat. Every time you eat, free radical activity is intense. The more food you eat, the more free radicals are formed, and the more antioxidants your body needs to neutralize them. Big meals are big trouble! Carbohydrates are root vegetables, pasta, rice, bread, grains, fruit, pastries, cakes, biscuits, crisps, sweets, etc. They are easy to prepare, filling, tasty and cheap. When you eat carbohydrates you're eating a form of sugar. Carbohydrates make up an excessive proportion of the diet, add together a lack of exercise and excess sugar and the inevitable result is excess weight. Reduce intake of carbs. You could choose to eat less.

Q. How much should I exercise?

A moderate amount of physical activity has major health benefits and is recommended for all adults, regardless of age. Regular day-to-day activities may provide enough activity for older adults. For example, these activities might include walking, gardening, or performing household chores.

Indeed, surveys show that older adults do not prefer this option. However, for people who are trying to increase their level of activity, exercise classes can be useful because they provide supervision, instruction, and motivation. Nearly all agree that adults should include a total of 30 minutes of moderate physical activity in their daily routine.

Q. What is meant by "moderate" activity?

Definitions of a "moderate" amount of activity differ, even among experts. A moderate amount of activity expends about 150-200 kcal (i.e., calories) per day, over 30-45 minutes, on at least 5 days per week. In less technical terms, a common example of a moderate amount of activity is a brisk 30-45 minute walk, 5 days a week. Moderate activity has also been defined based on maximal heart rate. Several equations have been developed to predict maximal heart rate:

- Max heart rate = 220 minus your age
- Max heart rate = 208 minus (0.7–your age)

Using these definitions, moderate activity for most adults (all ages) would increase heart rate to 70% of maximal. However, a realistic, practical goal for currently inactive older adults is 30-45 minutes of activity at 55% to 69% of maximal heart rate. Increasing activity level by running is not generally recommended for older adults. Running and other high-intensity activities carry a greater risk of both sudden cardiovascular problems and injury to bones and muscles. People are also less likely to continue this type of exercise program.

Q. What if I can't exercise a lot?

Although bouts of activity 30-45 minutes long, are recommended, several bouts as short as 10 minutes each may substitute for one 30 to 45 minute bout. Short bouts fit into daily schedules more easily. They are also often preferred by older adults who may have symptoms of conditions that limit exercise, such as arthritis pain. Even low amounts of activity have important health benefits and are better than an inactive life style. The generally recommended activity level of about 30-45 minutes a day reduces the risk by more than 50%.

Q. Do I need to work up a sweat?

Yes. Whether activity causes perspiration depends on several factors, including the following:

- the duration of activity
- the temperature in the environment
- the person's clothing
- the person's sex

Monitoring either heart rate or symptoms with exercise is probably a better way to guide level of exercise than working up a sweat. In group programs, an exercise leader can help older adults monitor themselves to maintain moderate levels of exercise intensity.

Q. What if I want to do more?

Older adults who already are active may want to increase their level of exercise to maximize health benefits and improve all aspects of fitness, including endurance, strength, balance, and flexibility. So long as the number of calories used up is about the same for less strenuous bouts of exercise that are done for a longer time as for more strenuous bouts that are done for a shorter time, the health benefits are similar.

11

Memory Loss and Ageing

Use it or Lose it!

Failing memory is a common problem with ageing. The ability to encode new memories of events or facts and working memory shows decline as you age. These deficits may be related to impairments seen in the ability to refresh recently processed information. In addition, even when equated in memory for a particular item or fact, older adults tend to be worse at remembering the source of their information, a deficit that may be related to declines in the ability to bind information together in memory. In contrast, implicit or procedural memory typically shows no decline with age and semantic knowledge, such as vocabulary, actually improves somewhat with age. In addition, the enhancement seen in memory for emotional events is also maintained with age. The key to keep a healthy memory quotient is exercise of the body and mind 'use it or lose it'.

Most research on memory and ageing has focused on how older adults perform less well at a particular memory task. However, recently researchers discovered that simply saying that older adults are doing the same thing, only less of it, is not always accurate. Brain imaging studies have revealed that older adults are more likely to use both hemispheres when completing memory tasks than younger adults. In addition, older adults sometimes show a positivity effect when remembering information, which seems to be a result of the increased focus on regulating emotion.

CARE your mind and body; both

Your quality of life will improve if you take steps to age gracefully and take care of your mind and body. Determine to do your best at slowing the ageing process and you will feel better and continue to be able to do more activities for a longer period of time. Deep breathe and meditate to counteract ageing. Deep breathing and meditation slows your thinking and makes your body calm. If you suspend time, you will counteract the effects of ageing. Exercise regularly to slow ageing. Do the types of exercise that you enjoy. Do them regularly. Do not strain or injure yourself while doing them. Choose activities that are fun and safe. Even walking is excellent for your health. Do whatever is possible. Perhaps speak with a physician on the type of exercise program that you can engage in without overstraining yourself. Deep breathing, meditating, and exercise, will aid in your state of relaxation. Sleep also helps. Relaxing all parts of your body all the time will definitely slow the ageing process, and give you fewer diseases and illnesses. Listen to soothing music, watch soothing scenery, do whatever it takes to relax you.

Do some relaxation exercises before going to bed. Also, when going to bed, just sleep. Forget about everything else. People who have difficulties sleeping often think about certain things when going to bed. Just stop thinking, and you will fall asleep. There is probably no need for sleeping pills. Certain foods also help people sleep, drinking some milk before going to bed may help. Lotus beans also have a sedative effect. Conversely, do not drink tea, coffee, or other types of stimulants four to five hours or more before going to bed. Those stimulate the body and reduce the sedative state of your body. It is also helpful to take an afternoon nap, as it is quite relaxing and is good for the body.

Applying lotion after washing, such as Vaseline, is a good way to reduce your wrinkles. If you stop worrying, or frowning, that will most likely reduce wrinkles on your face too. Be a kind person, forgive don't forget, and you will be happier, and have fewer wrinkles.

If you stop worrying, you will also reduce how much you get ill and how much you age. Just calm down. Most things will work out if you just leave them the way they are without doing anything.

Try to maintain the rhythm of your body by maintaining schedules when you do certain activities. For example, try to eat and sleep and approximately the same time each day. Of course, you can deviate from it mildly once in a while, but it would be good to generally follow the routine. The body enjoys a regular rhythm. Look at your heart, for instance—it beats at a regular rhythm. Eat nutritious foods such as vegetables and fruits. Regularly see your physician and dentist. Make sure you monitor your health regularly and follow their advice. If you wish, you may also consider getting a second opinion from other doctors.

As you age, you may not be able to do or not as efficient do, some of the things that you once did. Remember to slow down. Your body sometimes gives signs, but that may be too late. Try not to carry those heavy things, don't hurt yourself, don't strain. Relax, calm down, and slow down.

You may require vitamin pills, or calcium tablets. However, in general, anti-ageing medicine does not exist. If it did, people would not need to die. Just use your common sense when you hear about miracle anti-ageing pills. For smokers, quitting is the single best thing they can do for their health at any age. Doing all these things will definitely help. It'll also allow you to enjoy life more. It will also not affect your memory.

Want to keep your memory intact?

Exercise is Your Right. If you're fit, you're less likely to be chronically ill, disabled or dependent on others. Being inactive approximately doubles your risk for coronary artery disease. In addition, people who exercise reduce or even eliminate blood pressure medications. Exercise also reduces LDL (bad) cholesterol and triglycerides (fat), while increasing

HDL (good) cholesterol. People who exercise are less likely to develop Type II diabetes, also known as non insulin-dependent diabetes mellitus, or adult-onset diabetes. A long-term conditioning program may also significantly decrease your insulin dose. You can lose about five to 10 pounds a year merely by adding a one-mile daily walk to your routine. Researchers divided 235 sedentary men and women into two groups. One group did traditional structured exercise 20-60 minutes continuously. The other group incorporated into their day brisk walks, stair climbing and other moderate-intensity lifestyle activities. After 6 months, both groups had similar improvements in blood cholesterol, blood pressure and percentage of body fat. The structured exercisers gained more cardiovascular fitness. But the point is that the moderate-intensity-folks also did benefit. Structured exercise in longer sessions is better for you. But something is better than nothing. Try doing four 10-minute increases at least five days a week. The idea is to just do more of what you are already doing.

Here are some great ideas on getting motivated:

- Walk, don't drive.
- Take the stairs at the office—not the elevator.
- Play with your kids instead of watching them play.
- Bike to the store.
- Stretch while you watch TV.
- Get up from the sofa to change the channel. Channel surfers get quite a workout.
- Park at the opposite end of the mall from where you're headed.
- If you've got an exercise bike at home, peddle away for 5 minutes while you're talking on the phone or waiting for the washing machine to finish.
- Walk the treadmill while watching a favourite TV program.
- Listen to music and dance your way through housecleaning.

- Start slow—a few minutes at first. Then, pick up the pace and go longer.
- Workout clothes are not necessary, but wear good walking shoes.
- Don't let missing a few days become your excuse to quit.
- Even if you miss a few days, you won't lose all the benefits you've gained.
- Be flexible. Do what you can when you can.
- Take advantage of opportunities. If you're watching your child's soccer game, walk around the field.
- Playing golf? Skip the cart.
- Find a partner. Climbing stairs at the office will be far more interesting if you chat away the minutes with a co-worker.

Instead of building your life around exercise, build exercise around your life.

Aerobics

The word aerobic literally means "with oxygen" or "in the presence of oxygen." Aerobic exercise is any activity that uses large muscle groups, can be maintained continuously for a long period of time and is rhythmic in nature. Aerobic activity trains the heart, lungs and cardiovascular system to process and deliver oxygen more quickly and efficiently to every part of the body. As the heart muscle becomes stronger and more efficient, a larger amount of blood can be pumped with each stroke. Fewer strokes are then required to rapidly transport oxygen to all parts of the body. An aerobically fit individual can work longer, more vigorously and achieve a quicker recovery at the end of the aerobic session.

2. Mind Quietening

A disciplined mind is a free mind. Gain control over your thoughts and you maintain control over your life. Retrain your mind and you regain your freedom. Calming the mind is a behavioural technique used to interrupt, minimize and eliminate "psychological noise". Obsessive, repetitive thoughts, anxiety and fears are all apart of negative, self-destructive patterns that can benefit from the power of music and mind quietening.

3. Breathing

Breath is life! Air is the primary nutrient. Survival without it is measured in minutes. It is so important that you do it without thinking. Your breathing is the voice of your spirit. Its depth, smoothness, sound, and rate reflect your mood. If you become aware of your breath and breathe the way you do when you are calm you will become calm. Practicing regular, mindful breathing can be calming and energizing. With the addition of music and it's rhythm, the "musical breath" can even help stress-related health problems ranging from panic attacks to digestive disorders. Fall into the rhythm of the music and breathe. Focus on your breathing and the music.

4. Weight Bearing

Exercise stimulates tissue growth in bone and muscles, strengthening the body's structure. A stronger skeleton reduces the risk of osteoporosis, arthritic joint pain and other bone conditions. Also known as resistance training, weight-bearing exercise can be any activity that involves carrying, lifting or pushing a heavy object. Walking is considered to be weight bearing, as muscles and the skeleton support body weight. You do not need to 'pump iron' to benefit from this form of exercise.

5. Yoga

Many different types of yoga workouts exist. But many times in our quest for fitness and a hard body, at some point it becomes just a workout and not yoga. If you come to this path with fitness in mind that is important, but Yoga is extremely powerful. If you try to rush it, you will only slow yourself down. Yoga is not mind over body. It is harmony between them. In yoga, the mind is used to perceive (diagnose) and guide (heal) the body. Not to "control" it and never to force it. Wearing clothes like a 'saint or guru' has no co-relation to the degree of efficacy in yogic exercises.

6. Stretching

Just as there are different types of flexibility exercises, there are also different types of stretching exercises. Stretches are either dynamic (meaning they involve motion) or static (meaning they involve no motion). Dynamic stretches affect dynamic flexibility and static stretches affect static flexibility (and dynamic flexibility to some degree).

7. Power Walking

Studies have suggested a link between increased physical activity and a decreased chance for developing disease in general. Exercise of any kind trims your odds by improving the body's sensitivity to insulin—a hormone, helps control cholesterol, weight, and blood pressure, which further guards you from adult-onset of disease.

8. Swimming

It's hard to beat swimming when it comes to a sport that builds the body, soothes the mind, regulates breathing, stimulates circulation, and puts no stress on the joints. That's why it's an ideal exercise for just about everyone—old people, overweight people, young people, people with hip, knee and ankle problems, and active people with no health problems at all. Plus, swimming has a calorie-burning potential of 350-420 calories per hour. No wonder it's one of the most popular fitness sports around.

9. Tai Chi, Qi Gong, Aikido

These Asian martial art forms have been practiced for centuries. QiQong is one of the four pillars of traditional Chinese medicine: Acupuncture, Massage, Herbal Medicines and Qi gong. Of these, Qi gong is the one that can be most easily self initiated. Both massage and herbal remedies can also be done as self care, however, Qi gong is the mother of Chinese self healing. Patients who use Qi gong faithfully need less medication, less acupuncture and heal faster. Tai Chi is a martial arts form that enhances balance and body awareness through slow, graceful, and precise body movements, can significantly cut the risk of falls among older people and may be beneficial in maintaining gains made by people age 70 and older who undergo other types of balance and strength training. Aikido is a Japanese martial art developed by Morihei Ueshiba (often referred to by his title 'O Sensei' or 'Great Teacher'). On a purely physical level it is an art involving some throws and joint locks that are derived from Jujitsu and some throws and other techniques derived from Kenjutsu. Aikido focuses not on punching or kicking opponents, but rather on using their own energy to gain control of them or to throw them away from you.

10. Elastic Bands

Resistance training is the benefit of elastic bands or tubing. As long as we have gravity, we can challenge our muscles effectively. Doing a push-up is one example of a resistance exercise. Instead of using weight from another source, you're using your body weight to challenge your chest and arm muscles, and you will get toned up. Elastic tubing and bands are great for those who want to get the benefits of weight training without using traditional weights.

12

Futuristic Technologies

Years into the Life or Life into the Years?

In the past it was thought that physical ageing is inevitable. New scientific discoveries have shown that we can live longer, healthier and more enjoyable lives. Our longevity is not purely genetic—inherited factors account for only 30% of longevity. It is our health behavior—that is, the choice of food, environment and physical activity that accounts for 70 percent of living longer. Improved healthcare and standards of living also mean we are seeing the growth of an active elderly population over the age of 65, and a new group of 85 years and older. Twenty percent of the world's elderly population or 61 million people are 85+. By 2020, this group will double to 146 million. So we should all take preventative measures with out diet and exercise to ensure we not only live longer but also we are as happy and healthy as we can be.

Doctors are learning more about how to extend human life through new discoveries such as stem cells and cloning. Scientists support both embryonic and adult stem cell research. Adult stem cell research is further along in human trials, because it has been far easier to get these trials organized. When you look at animal studies, it is quite clear that both embryonic and adult stem cell-based research have potential. Embryonic stem cell-based therapies have been used to treat the mouse versions of Parkinson's, nerve damage and diabetes. Adult therapies have been used to treat heart disease, nerve damage and forms of blindness.

What is cloning?

Cloning is a science for many species, and it could hold the answer for the majority of problems of ageing humans. In a major new paper published in the April 28, 2000 issue of the journal '**Science**', a group led by Dr. Michael West has reported, what may be the most revolutionary advance in cloning research so far. They have found that cloning can totally reverse cellular ageing. This could give us the solution to several ailments that remain unaddressed as of now viz. Alzheimer's, Angina, Arthritis, Cancer, Diabetes, Heart Disease, High blood pressure, Obesity, Osteoporosis, Stress, Stroke.

Healthy young calves at five months of age, with telomeres longer than normal, all produced by cloning from highly senescent skin cells. Their nicknames are Lily, Daffodil, Crocus, Forsythia and Rose

Gregory Fahy, Ph.D. and Saul Kent, President and founder of the Life Extension Foundation (LEF), interviewed Dr. West on March 18th, 2000. Dr. West is the founder of Geron. He is currently President and CEO of Advanced Cell

Technology in Worcester, Massachusetts, where the research reported in **'Science'** was conducted.

Life Extension Foundation (LEF)

Q. What is cloning?

Mike West: Cloning, as it is used in popular language, means the process we call nuclear transfer, which is an asexual way of reproducing an animal. Rather than using a sperm and an egg cell and getting a genetic mix between two animals, making a unique offspring, cloning uses an egg cell which is stripped of its DNA and a cell from the body of an existing animal. That body (somatic) cell is then placed into the egg cell.

What we typically do is take the whole somatic cell and transfer it into an egg cell whose DNA has been removed. The result is a cell that has the entire DNA from an existing animal, so the resulting embryo and then, eventually, the animal is genetically identical to the original animal from which the cell was taken, unlike normal sexual reproduction, which leads to a unique new animal. In a sense it is being born again. It's a rebirth of a genetically identical copy of the original animal.

Q.. LEF: Are there different ways of doing cloning?

West: It is possible to clone an animal from cells that are usually easily accessible, such as skin cells or mucosal epithelial cells from the inside of the cheek.

Q. LEF: How could cloning impact the field of anti-ageing medicine?

West: Over the course of ageing, we may need to have cells and/or tissues and organs replaced

Q. LEF: What is therapeutic human cloning?

West: It is for recreating young cells and tissues genetically identical to the person, who needs them in order to replace worn out cells and tissues. What we are proposing as an ethical and moral use of cloning technology in the arena of human medicine is the creation of microscopic balls of cells, called blastocysts. These are aggregates of about 100 cells that exist up to about 14 days of development. At 14 days, small aggregations of cells begin to individualize. By that, we mean the cells begin to become the various cells and tissues of the body, or that they've committed themselves to become. The blastocyst is often called a pre-embryo to distinguish it from an embryo which is committed to becoming a given individual. And because of that primitive state of the cells, the majority of ethicists have agreed that the creation of such an aggregate of cells to benefit people who are sick and in need of therapy, would be a good and moral use of technology.

We believe we can even take a cell from a patient, and put it back into an egg cell, and that egg cell would be like a time machine, taking what was once a skin cell back in time, making it young again and erasing its memory of what it was, taking it back to the state of complete power, or as we say, "totipotency," such that the cell can then become any cell in the body. Now we can go in two directions. First, we could implant this small ball of cells into a uterus, and it could become a human being, or two human beings, forming identical twins. That would be reproductive cloning of a human being. The second path, which is the path that we are advocating, would be to use the cells to create specific cell types that a particular patient needs. So if the patient has Parkinson's Disease, we would create just the dopaminergic neurons that they have lost, the loss of which is causing their Parkinsonian symptoms or islets of langerham cells in the pancreas to treat diabetes. This could be done in tissue culture, growing individual cells, without creating a cloned human being.

Q. LEF: What are embryonic stem cells?

West: Technically, an embryonic stem cell is a cultured

inner cell mass. So the blastocyst is a little ball of cells, and inside it is a cluster of cells called the inner cell mass, and surrounding them is a shell of cells called the trophectoderm. The trophectoderm will become the placenta, and the inner cell mass will become the entire animal. The inner cell mass cells are totipotent. They have complete power. And because they have not yet committed to either becoming the germ line or the body (soma), they have not yet committed to the mortality of the soma, so they still have the immortality of the germ line. As you know, germ line cells have the ability of proliferating indefinitely, and that is why the species is immortal. We keep making babies generation after generation, so these cells are in this immortal germ line. in a state of total power. When they are grown in the dish, they are called embryonic stem cells.

Q. LEF: Has anyone taken these embryonic stem cells and turned them into specialized cells in tissue culture? And what was done in this study?

West: Yes. It was the first time human embryonic stem cells were ever grown in the dish. Also in this publication was evidence that they could be shown to differentiate into skin, neurons, heart muscle cells, blood cells, and all of the many different kinds of cells in the body.

Q. LEF: So to summarize what you've said, basically you can take a totipotent cell and instead of letting it commit itself to form of an individual, you can take that cell and, direct it to become any type of cell. As you said, you can make brain cells to treat Parkinson's disease or perhaps skin cells to treat facial ageing or isolate the beta cells in relatively pure form, and put them into a mouse and cure diabetes.

West: I think that is an accurate statement. Second level of amazement is the fact that not only does the development go in reverse, but the animal is actually made young again in the process, for example, a patient who has lost heart tissue because of a heart attack and needs new heart tissue could receive tissue to restore normal heart function.

One could imagine creating in a laboratory, virtually all of the components of the human body by cloning, making you a new heart, a new kidney, new lungs, new skin and replacing virtually your entire body in parts or in conglomerate. Cloned animals, even when they are made from very old animals, appear to be young and are able to reproduce. There is no evidence of premature ageing. There is no reason we couldn't find ways of applying this technology to transplant cloned young cells and tissues into an aged person.

New stem cell technologies actually offer the promise of distributing new young cells throughout the body. One could imagine, for instance, the transplantation of mesenchymal stem cells into the bone marrow. Those cells have been shown to travel throughout the body to seed muscle tissues with new muscle cells, bone with new bone cells and so on.

Q. LEF: So in other words, you would inject a particular kind of cell that is not muscle and not bone, and it would then find places where there is a deficiency in muscle cells and bone cells, somehow sensing this deficiency, then turning into muscle or bone cells to overcome the deficiency?

West: Correct. That is all published data (16,17). These technologies could potentially allow you to restore back into ageing patients stem cells that are the patients' own cells and would not be rejected, which have their whole life span ahead of them, and have the potential of distributing themselves throughout the body, seeding cells and tissues with new, young cells to replace those that are worn out. There are potentially many applications for diseases that are not normally thought of as a part of ageing. One could think of muscular dystrophy as an example, or even diseases such as AIDS. We think both are examples of cells reaching the end of their life span in a premature manner because of an accelerated turnover of cells.

Q. LEF: What would be the full impact of this sort of technology if it could be brought into full use?

West: Well about half of all health care expenditures in the United States, now upwards of 500 billion dollars a year, can be attributed to transplantation-related costs. And given an ageing population, the numbers are expected to increase. It is important, of course, to point out that a lot of current health care expenditures are for conditions not treated by transplantation. A salient example would be diabetes. We don't have the ability to cure diabetes by replacing the beta cells that are lost (and cause type 1 juvenile onset diabetes), so we give insulin instead, which is not a cure for the disease. As another example, Parkinson's disease is typically not treated by replacing the neurons that are lost and whose loss causes the disease, it is treated instead with L-DOPA. So what would be potentially useful would be to find a way of meeting this already significantly large need, representing upwards of half of all health care expenditures, with transplantable cells and tissues that are identical to the patient, and would not require immunosuppressive therapy. Therapeutic human cloning could enable us to meet this need.

Q. LEF: Would replacement cells have to be human cells, or could they be cells from other species?

West: The whole field of xeno-transplantation, obtaining tissue from other species, is increasingly promising with the recent cloning of the pig for instance. Cloning allows us to create sophisticated genetic modifications in animals, making those tissues potentially acceptable into patients. What therapeutic cloning, making tissues and organs directly from the patient's own cells, offers is perhaps the ultimate solution to the problem of transplant rejection.

Q. LEF: One of the things that happens with ageing is not just a wearing out of cells and tissues, but a change in the hormonal environment that affects tissue and cell function. One often-cited example is the diminution of the secretion of growth hormone with ageing. This may be due to damaged cells in the base of the brain which could be replaced, but it may be due to some sort of ageing clock. If it is the latter, do you see the possibility of cloning your own body cells with genetic modifications that could then be transplanted into the body to change that type of ageing program?

West: Well, there certainly are such possibilities. The beauty of cloning technologies is that everything starts with a single cell. Whether it be a skin cell or a blood cell from the patient, from that single cell, stem cells would be created that would then be turned into whatever cell or even complex tissue the patient needed.

Q. LEF: What about the cells that comprise our identity and our memories? Most cells are interchangeable, but in this case, a brand new cell or a group of cells would not contain the information originally there. How do you deal with that?

West: I think one of the strongest arguments for cloning, beyond the obvious issue of preventing tissue rejection, is the issue of identity. One can imagine in a world without human therapeutic cloning, engineering cow heart valves, pig kidneys and pig hearts. As you know, there are people walking around today with pig neurons in their brains for Parkinson's Disease. One can imagine ones' self as a patchwork of tissues from animals and nieces and nephews, and one wonders at some point, are we in a sense becoming someone else? I think therapeutic cloning offers the best approach to maintaining ones' identity in the face of a very clear need for cell and tissue transplantation. Stem cells planted in the brain can also distribute themselves throughout the brain. It is possible to imagine technologies that would seed new embryonic stem cells into the brain that would graft into existing tissue. What this would mean in terms of memory and the preservation of psychic identity remains to be determined. It might lead to the infusion of rejuvenate cells that are ageing. There is a recent paper in the Proceedings of the National Academy of Sciences showing reversal of age-associated neuronal atrophy by growth factor, and gene therapy in aged monkeys.

Q. LEF: Are you contemplating using bovine egg cells for therapeutic human cloning and, if so, are there mitochondrial or other problems that you would be concerned about?

West: We share, I think, the present concern about mixing DNA across species. There have been reports over the last few years of the transfer of whole human chromosomes into animals such as mice, and there are, I think, ethical concerns about what kind of life forms we might create. Rather than getting human egg cells, we propose using cow egg cells, which are widely available from slaughter houses at a dollar or two per egg, and removing the genetic information from the cow's egg cell, so that we put a human cell into it, we would provide the genetic information from the human nuclear DNA and mitochondrial DNA, which would then completely transform the resulting cells into human cells. We do not believe that any animal DNA would remain, either mitochondrial or nuclear. As far as the cow egg cell proteins are concerned. As you know, protein does not make one a cow. Drinking cow's milk does not make you a cow. DNA, the blueprint of life, confers those characteristics, and we're not talking about mixing DNA across species.

Q. LEF: What about human therapeutic cloning?

West: On the human therapeutic front, it is likely that the early products are going again to be human therapeutic protein drugs made in cloned transgenic animals. We are now making human medicines in the milk of cloned and genetically

engineered cows for instance, such as human serum albumin. Human therapeutic cloning is a long-term project.

Persephone, an older clone made from a senescent cell, still going strong at the age of 10 months.

Q. LEF: What about acute conditions?

West: when it comes to acute conditions, it's a different story. For example, with skin burns the patients need immediate treatment. In the future we will likely have cells taken from people and reprogrammed, back to a toti-potent state as well as young differentiated cells and tissues kept frozen in waiting for sudden trauma needs.

This procedure requires time. The nuclear transfer to create the stem cells will take a couple of weeks. The creation of specialized cells and tissues will take about seven additional weeks. So what we envision for chronic long-term disease, such as Parkinson's disease, heart failure, kidney failure, and so on, is plenty of time to create cells and tissues to help the patient.

Telomerase; the wonder enzyme

Telomerase is an enzyme that appears to overcome cellular senescence. Some have reasoned that if telomerase can avoid ageing in cells, may be it can avoid human ageing too. Though products are yet to reach the public, there are serious efforts to develop telomerase-based therapies to fight ageing. Our knowledge of telomerase is in its infancy. Moreover, telomerase is important in cellular proliferation but many of our organs, such as the brain, are mostly composed of cells that do not proliferate. Scientists doubt about the efficiency and safety of telomerase-based anti-ageing therapies.

Where are the ethical issues?

She has been given the final go-ahead to travel abroad for a cutting edge non-surgical treatment that promises to make her look ten years younger. She doesn't care if the treatment is expensive, involves babies and is controversial, it is not allowed to be performed in her country. The attractive brunette has opted for a controversial stem-cell therapy where umbilical cord tissue from new-born babies will be injected into her body

It may seem distasteful, but thousands of women have already done it and it is organized by a seemingly respectable British clinic then carried out in Rotterdam, Holland, where rules regarding stem cell therapies are not so strict. Stem-cell therapy has been big business for beauty doctors since scientists discovered the strong healing and rejuvenating potential of stem cells for medical conditions such as Alzheimer's and Parkinson's. But there has also been a furious ethical debate. In America, President Bush has denounced stem-cell therapy. So what is it about stem cells that have set tongues wagging? They are the building blocks of every human body but are far more plentiful in embryos, which are still growing, human fetuses, or newborn babies, than in adults. They are immature but powerful cells that, once extracted, can be stimulated in a laboratory to develop into any type of body cell or organ, including bone, muscle and nerve tissue. When injected, these powerful cells target the organs that are not functioning at their optimum and encourage them to produce new tissue. But scientists agree that further research is required to substantiate the claim that injecting stem cells can diminish wrinkles or reverse the signs of ageing.

Many unregulated companies have mushroomed across the globe offering 'aesthetic stem-cell therapies' at exorbitant prices to anyone willing to pay. They claim that stem cells have the ability to rejuvenate the body and renew the cells. There is much room for unethical and morally dubious treatment by unqualified doctors. And if anything goes wrong afterwards, it is hushed up to prevent damage to the business. Yet hundreds of women are visiting such clinics, desperate for the new elixirs of youth. Medical tourism on account of stem cell therapy is in the upswing. The aim is to attract wealthy British and American stem-cell tourists for treatment, avoiding the strict ethical barriers to such treatment enforced in Europe and America. Such clinics have a waiting list of more than 1,000 patients for cosmetic treatments. They claims that the fetal tissue derived from elective abortions at six to 12 weeks is rich in regenerative stem cells. they inject the cells taken from the liver tissue of human fetuses directly into the vein in the back of hand. 'The results are incredible. You'll feel and look different after a month because these cells help the body to regenerate it. The effects last for a year before it needs to be "topped up"'. Ukrainian stem-cell researchers have secretly pioneered stem-cell studies at Barbados Institute for Regenerative Medicine. The past 12 months have seen this popular holiday resort become the stem-cell capital of the developed world, treating hundreds of patients in a year. 'You think better, sleep better, and look better. Your quality of life improves and your libido improves.' But what such clinics are doing raises serious issues. For a start, it is not regulated by any medical board and there is no documented evidence or controlled clinical trials to back up their claims.

Another destination is The Cellulite Clinic at Moscow. It offers anti-ageing injections of stem cells from aborted fetuses into thighs, buttocks and stomach at a cost of £10,000 to £15,000 for a course of six. More than 50 clinics have sprung up in Russia's capital over the past three years to meet the demand from wealthy Westerners who flock to the global capital of cosmetic stem-cell therapy. RUSSIA and the Ukraine currently top the world abortion league, with more of the operations carried out here than anywhere else on earth. Medical risks from complications can include infection, tumors and rejection of tissue.

A similar destination is Medra Clinic in Dominican Republic. They have arranged for hundreds of patients to be injected with cells taken from six to 12-week-old aborted fetuses, since the clinic opened its doors. 'Stem-cell therapy is the future. It's just unfortunate that there is so much opposition to it in the West,' they say. Patients risk at best wasting a lot of money on a treatment that is not proven in clinical trials and at worst one that is putting their health at serious risk.

Another destination is Rotterdam Holland, where Anti-ageing treatment is carried out. Treatment involves being injected with stem cells extracted from the umbilical cords of babies who have had a natural birth to full term. "To inject cells from one human being into another, a range of checks must be made to make sure they genetically match each other."

A clinic at New York offers Frozen in time Stem-Cell for Facial beauty treatment. The facial involves an exfoliation and steam. The face is then covered in a moisturizer composed of cells harvested from the embryonic fluid of pregnant cows. The spa claims that introducing live stem cells from cows helps your skin cells—which may be damaged by 'environmental factors'—restore and replicate themselves, creating healthier, stronger, and more youthful-looking skin. After six days your skin becomes radiant. Skeptics argue that the treatment is useless. If people can be fatally allergic to the latex in food packaging, imagine the potential for allergic or other immune reactions to the proteins of stem cells from cows.

Turning Back the Clock?

Real anti-ageing medicine does not yet exist. Efforts should be made for human benefit, to develop biomedical interventions that can delay ageing in people and improve their health. So what scientific approaches are more suited to cure ageing?

One crucial aspect of research on ageing, which is sometimes overlooked by researchers, is that our work should deal with human ageing. Once we know more about which mechanisms to target, we can consider the development of therapies (Fig.). It is somewhat speculative to consider anti-ageing therapies at present, since we know little about what interventions will be necessary, but a few ideas are given bellow.

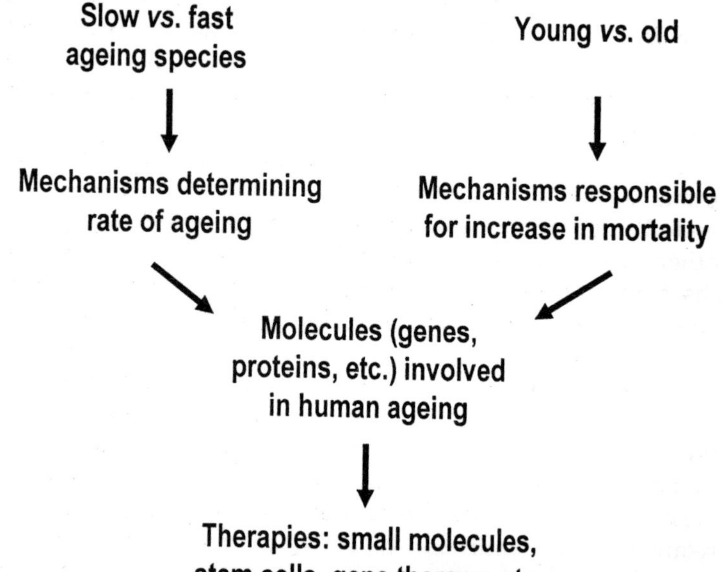

Identify therapeutic targets by studying why we become frailer with age and/or why we age slower than most other mammals; develop technologies capable of targeting the molecules, cells, or tissues necessary to revert ageing.

Even if we do not know the underlying mechanisms of ageing, if we can engineer the reversal of all the major molecular and cellular changes that occur with age, we will be able to achieve rejuvenation. These include stem cells to replace old cells, the application of enzymes—including bacterial enzymes—to degrade certain forms of "cellular junk," gene expression technologies that allow the incorporation of transgenes with a high efficiency and viability, and the ablation of old cells. SENS, however, promises radical results: a cure for ageing. The idea that we can cure a complex process like ageing without knowing its underlying mechanisms is, of course, debatable, even though it is plausible that if the technologies in which SENS is based on—e.g., stem cells, tissue engineering, and gene therapy—reach a high level of efficiency then anti-ageing research will greatly benefit.

The Brain in Anti-Ageing

Perhaps our brain just ages because the other organs in the body can no longer support it. If we could change the body at regular intervals to keep it always young, it might happen that our brain would never age. It is also possible, though speculative, that future developments in cybernetics and therapeutic cloning will make it possible to replace all other organs as well. For now, we must focus on trying to discover a way to stop ageing in all the body, having, of course, the brain as top priority. Short-term memory loss, personality and cognitive changes with age, dementia, general decline of the nervous system and senses, and many other changes are likely to occur with ageing. Until recently, it was thought that neuronal loss, due to the accumulation damage—such as oxidative damage—was the main cause of brain ageing. Nowadays, it appears that neurons can remain relatively healthy through life. Instead of seeing brain ageing as a mere consequence of the death of neurons, it appears that, even without neuronal death, biochemical and structural changes compromise neuron function.

The Road Ahead

"By the year 2030, we will have (1) developed a complete model of all human cells types, obviating the need for many laboratory experiments; (2) lowered the cost of doing a complete genomic sequence for an human individual to less then $ 1,000 each; and (3) catalogued all the genes involved in ageing. Therefore, human clinical trials to extend life would be a reality.

If we can understand the genetic factors that determine the rate of ageing among similar species, like primates and rodents, then it may be possible to develop interventions that extend the human lifespan even further. Eventually, however, the genome holds all answers; all we need to do is ask the right questions. Overall, determining the genetic basis of ageing will be a monumental task. Still, I feel confident that scientists will be able to identify all the genetic mechanisms that cause ageing within next 1-2 decades by the combination of approaches mentioned earlier.

Lifespan

13

Critiques of Anti-Ageing Medicine?

Is it a Myth or Fact?

Many critics are crying to crack down on the anti-ageing industry, especially on the cheats who are taking the middle aged and elderly men and women for a ride. "False to illegal," says Dr. Thomas Perls, associate professor of medicine and geriatrics at Boston University, who has been an outspoken opponent of the anti-ageing industry.

HGH is by far the most controversial weapon in the anti-ageing arsenal. The first products were approved by the FDA in 1985 to help short children grow taller. Lately the anti-ageing industry has latched on to HGH as a tool for boosting immunity, memory, heart function, muscle mass, and more. Critics believe that many players in the anti-ageing industry who prescribe it are violating laws and endangering patients. The drug industry formally opposes the efforts to link HGH with anti-ageing, but behind the scenes, companies promote it. There are concerns that anti-ageing promotions may be more like scams. Because ageing is not actually a disease. That leaves patients paying often substantial fees out of pocket. In U.S complete health assessment—a two-day process that includes meetings with a nutritionist and an exercise physiologist—costs $ 2,500 or more. The patient often walks away with a long shopping list of diet supplements and natural hormones that can run $ 250 a month. And HGH can suck as much as $ 2,000 a month. Many warn, "people are spending a lot of money to get treatments that is not a medically necessity." Rothenberg, who earlier practiced medicine in the Amazon, returned to U.S. at the University of California at San Diego, where he is still on the faculty. He first started injecting himself with HGH about a decade ago. "I was losing my memory. Libido-wise, it was take it or leave it." He says, "Ageing is a disease that can be prevented or reversed". Federal laws, bar doctors from prescribing HGH for uses not approved by the FDA. One disease in adults that does qualify is adults growth hormone deficiency. The disease carries symptoms such as depression and increased body fat. Blood tests can confirm the deficiency.

Cancer Risk

In response to concerns that too much HGH can cause cancer, Rothenberg flashes a reference to a study carried out by endocrinologist Dr. Mary Lee Vance and others that shows there's no cancer risk. However, other research has shown that HGH can promote tumor growth. What's more, the hormone can spark high blood pressure, blood clots, and structural changes in the hands and feet. Any one illegally selling HGH could face up to five years in prison, and $ 1 million in fines.

Anti-ageing doctors also prescribe testosterone, often in skin gels, and they recommend the hormone DHEA, which can convert itself to estrogen and testosterone in the body. They say the treatments enhance heart health, sexual performance, and memory in men, and fight menopause symptoms in women. Anti-ageing doctors run a battery of blood and saliva tests prior to prescribing testosterone, and say they're simply replacing what's missing. Too much testosterone can cause mood disorders and hair loss. In women, it can bring on acne, deepening voices, and unwanted hair growth. The hormones estrogen and progesterone have also given rise to controversy. FDA-sanctioned synthetic versions, such as Wyeth's Prempro and Premarin, got a bad rap in 2002, when a giant study by the

Women's Health Initiative (WHI) suggested the hormones might increase the risk of breast cancer and heart disease. Since then many traditional gynecologists have shied away from prescribing hormones.

The hormones prescribed by anti-ageing doctors are generally derived from plants such as soybeans and sweet potatoes, which may never be tested in human trials. Anti-ageing proponents say the substances are natural, safe alternatives to hormones. What's missing amid all this excitement, though, is any firm scientific proof that these regimens actually slow down or reverse the ageing process. A paper published in the Oct. 26, 2005, issue of The Journal of the American Medical Association describes the distribution of human growth hormone for anti-ageing as both rampant and illegal. The anti-ageing industry is fighting back. The public has little inkling about the expert bickering. Anti-ageing centers are popping up all over the country. Some patients are aware that anti-ageing is controversial, but they say they must answer to how they feel.

A handful of anti-ageing doctors now offer a treatment called chelation therapy, which was once commonly used to treat lead poisoning. Chelation involves infusing a patient with chemicals that are believed to bind to metals and clear them out of the body. The process may reverse heart disease, proponents say. But it can cost as much as $ 2,400 and take up to three months. And its heart benefits have never been proven. Critics say:

"Anyone purporting to offer an anti-ageing product today is either mistaken or lying". Aside from the fact that supplements have not been shown to have any influence on ageing, these products have no warnings about side effects that may result when taken either with or without approved medications. The experts warn that hormone supplements being sold at anti-ageing clinics are potentially dangerous and should not be used except with the advice of their physicians. There are several of Anti-ageing therapies that are currently being explored:

I. Caloric Restriction (CR)

This intervention proposes lessening caloric intake

while maintaining a normal diet regarding other nutrients such as vitamins and minerals. Studies have shown that CR increased their lifespan by 40 percent. These experiments have also shown that CR can reduce the frequency of age-related diseases and decelerate the appearance of ageing.

2. *Antioxidants*

When oxygen is used to make energy in human cells, compounds called free radicals are released. Human cells defend themselves from being invaded by these free radicals through antioxidants. Many of these antioxidants are synthesized or extracted and then sold in tablets as anti-ageing drugs. Common antioxidants include vitamins A, C, and E and co-enzyme Q10. However, the evidence is inconclusive as to whether or not they stop the ageing process.

3. *Hormonal Therapies*

Some of the most popular anti-ageing treatments are based on the assumption that hormonal levels fall in ageing. The most famous of these involves human growth hormone (HGH). Side effects of this therapy include weight gain, high blood pressure, and diabetes. The most commonly used bioidentical hormones include estradiol, progesterone, and testosterone. Other lesser-used ones are estrone and estriol, hydroepiandrosterone (DHEA) and melatonin.

Increase vitamins intake as you age

As we age; our bodies' process nutrients less efficiently, resulting in the need for us to increase our nutrient intake. You should gradually increase your intake of vitamin D, so that by age 60 or so you are up to around 600 IU. The need for B vitamins increases with age. Three B vitamins—folic acid, vitamin B6 and vitamin B12—are essential for keeping levels of a compound called homocysteine low in the blood; if allowed to rise, homocysteine contributes to heart-disease risk and possibly memory loss. As you age, increase your B6 dose from 2 mg to 5 mg; increase B12 over time from 2 mcg to 10 mcg. Women should take 400 mcg of folic acid daily. Women, in particular, should be aware that their calcium intake should increase as they age to prevent osteoporosis: according to the National Institutes of Health, during the middle years, 1,000 mg each day is adequate; 1,200 mg after menopause if you're on hormone replacement therapy; 1,500 mg if you are not on HRT.

Consume fruits and vegetables

People who consume diets loaded with fresh fruits and vegetables have lower disease rates, more energy and less risk for weight gain than those who skip these foods, according to numerous studies published over the years. With the exception of avocados, olives and coconuts, fresh fruits and vegetables have no fat, cholesterol or sodium. They are also fiber-rich: Eight servings of fruits and vegetables daily supplies approximately 27 grams of fiber, well within the daily target goal of 25 grams to 35 grams. Fiber-rich foods lower a person's risk for developing age-related diseases such as heart disease, cancer, diabetes and hypertension. Fiber-rich foods also are low in calories, yet satiating, so they help fill you up without filling you out: Fresh fruits and vegetables are nutrient-packed, providing ample amounts of calcium, iron, magnesium, vitamin C, beta carotene and folic acid, and they are low in calories.

The age-defying antioxidants

Fruits and vegetables also are gold mines of longevity-enhancing compounds called antioxidants; these include vitamins C and E and beta carotene. Antioxidants combat free radicals, oxygen fragments that attack and damage cell membranes, life-sustaining proteins and even our cells' genetic code, and in so doing bring about ageing and disease. Diets rich in antioxidants prevent disease and premature ageing. Antioxidants also stimulate the immune system and protect the nervous system and brain from the oxidative damage associated with age-related memory loss. Practice portion control and make every bite count Cut back on unnecessary calories, and you stack the deck in favor of living longer. Studies of small mammals have shown that in every case these animals have increased their lifespan from two- to four-fold by cutting back on food intake. Such animals have lower rates of all age-related diseases, including heart disease, diabetes, cancer, memory loss and dwindling immunity.

Get your fat from fish

Get your fat from fish, not from red meat. Omega-3 fatty acids, lower heart-disease risk, stimulate the immune system and might even reduce the incidence of depression. Even small amounts of fish were found to lower risk for cancers of the digestive tract.

Exercise, a Natural Medicine

A study reports that blood levels of estrogen, testosterone and growth hormone were significantly higher in women aged 19-69 years after 40 minutes of (either endurance or resistance exercise) versus a control group, who performed no exercise! What does this mean?

As populations are growing older, the pressure to develop treatments to allow people to live healthier lives is also rising. HRT trials have shown, such treatments harbor substantive risks. Two major trends are discernible: understanding the biological mechanisms of ageing to find potentially life-extending treatments, and improving the quality of life in old age. There's an economic aspect as well as a humanitarian one, for trying to break the link between old age and ill health. Healthier people could work longer and thus generate the money needed to pay for their own care.

What is worrying health institutions and experts, however, is the increasing use of testosterone as an 'anti-ageing tonic' among middle-aged and older men, particularly in the USA, for which the results have not been adequately assessed. In addition, many fear that the treatment could result in a higher risk of prostate cancer, benign prostatic hyperplasia and cardiovascular disease.

The efforts are on to evaluate the efficacy and safety of alternative approaches using phyto-oestrogens to treat hot flashes and night sweats in peri- and post-menopausal women. In the meantime, a growing number of women are turning to isoflavones and lignans-oestrogen-like compounds, which are naturally occurring in plants or available as dietary supplements—believing that they might mitigate menopause symptoms with fewer adverse effects. But both efficacy and safety data for these products, for which no licence is required, are virtually absent. Some claim that soy isoflavones attenuate cognitive decline in healthy post-menopausal women and improve memory and higher order cognitive functions in young adults. But others found no evidence that soy supplements containing isoflavones improve cognitive function, bone mineral density or plasma lipids in healthy post-menopausal women. On the basis of an article in the New England Journal of Medicine by Rudman, Chein developed and patented a therapy combining HGH with other hormonal injections, which he claims has remarkable rebuilding effects on muscle, skin and bone mass. Chein has stated that buying these hormone supplements at local health-food stores could be dangerous. There may be an irony in the fact that the most well-off in society are going to act as guinea-pigs. Whether hormone therapies will eventually become a part of the anti-ageing medical arsenal is not possible to say at this stage.

FAQs on hormones

Q. What are Hormones and how do they work?

Hormones are potent chemicals produced from cholesterol, amino acids and proteins in your endocrine glands. These glands include the hypothalamus, pituitary, pineal, thymus, thyroid, adrenals, pancreas, testes and ovaries. The endocrine glands secrete hormones into your bloodstream, from where they are carried to specific receptor sites in other parts of your body. The hormones serve as messengers from your brain, telling your internal organs how to function.

The hypothalamus, a walnut-sized gland, is considered the master hormone gland because it is the central link between your brain and your endocrine system. It controls many of your basic instincts, such as, thirst, hunger and sex. The pituitary, a pea sized gland at the base of your brain, acts as a liaison between the hypothalamus and other endocrine glands throughout your body.

Q. What are the advantages of natural hormone replacement therapy (NHRT)?

NHRT may be helpful in:

- Adjusting to natural changes that come with ageing
- Alleviating menopause and prostate symptoms
- Alleviating some of the bodily trauma resulting from these biological changes (e.g. osteoporosis, atherosclerosis, etc.)
- Rejuvenating mental speed and clarity
- Improving skin tightness and moisture
- Enhancing libido and sexual function
- Reducing unwanted side effects inherent in traditional HRT with synthetic hormone.

Q. How are the hormone levels monitored?

Saliva testing is utilized to monitor the hormones and has the following advantages:

- Saliva reflects the biologically active/free fractions of steroids in the blood, unlike the blood or urine, which measures total levels. It's the free form of the hormone that is physiologically active
- Collection time is more controlled which is crucial for baseline testing of hormones with diurnal variation and assessment of HRT dosing
- It is non-invasive, safe, stress free, and painless
- It is private and convenient for patient
- It allows for multiple collections
- Hormones are stable in the saliva at room temperature for weeks
- Transport of saliva to the lab is easy
- It is less expensive than blood testing

Q. When should HRT be started?

HRT should be started as soon as the levels decline. This can occur as early as at 40. Hormones should be replaced as they decline with age in order to prevent diseases of ageing. Symptoms such as anxiety, depression, memory deficit, chronic fatigue, sleep problems, hot flashes, decrease in libido, difficulty-loosing weight, all may be due to hormone imbalance. There are many forms of natural hormones available such as: oral capsules, creams, ointments, gels, suppositories and trans-dermal patches. The most preferred route is trans-dermal creams or ointments. These are rubbed in highly vascular areas, such as the forearms and are easy to titrate.

Q. Will I need to supplement the hormones for the rest of my life?

Your body can no longer produce adequate amounts of these hormones. If you want to prevent age related diseases and live a more youthful life, then you will have to continue with HRT.

Q. Can the cream hurt a child?

All medications should be kept out of the reach of children. However, single exposure to the cream is not harmful.

Q. Can one get pregnant on HRT?

HRT can increase fertility. However, if a woman is not ovulating, she cannot get pregnant.

Q. What if I'm already on synthetic hormones?

After testing the levels on the present hormones, it can be determined what dosages of natural hormones are needed to replace the synthetic ones. There are fewer side effects and more benefits with the NHRT.

Q. What side effects are there from NHRT?

There are no side effects from the hormones when given to achieve a normal physiological range. Most symptoms occur from increased or decreased levels of hormones. Hence the importance of monitoring.

Q. Should progesterone be cycled?

Cycling is preferred as it is more physiologic and may reduce the risk of endometrial cancer. Menses will occur with cycling. Cycling is advised if the woman is still having menses.

Q. What about breast cancer?

NHRT can prevent breast cancer as well as colon cancer. In NHRT, the 3 estrogens are given at a physiologic level; estriol is given at a ratio of 80% compared to the other estrogens. Progesterone and DHEA also balance the risk of cancer. If a woman has had cancer, estrogens should be avoided. However, if therapy is clearly indicated because of risk factors such as heart disease or osteoporosis, some physicians prefer to recommend progesterone, DHEA or estriol alone as therapy or combination therapy.

Q. Will testosterone increase the risk of prostate cancer?

Dhydro-testosterone (a break down hormone of testosterone that increases with age) is probably related to BPH. An individual with history of prostate cancer should not be taking testosterone. Prescreening (blood test—PSA) is required before therapy is initiated.

Q. Will testosterone increase the risk of testicular cancer?

Testosterone replacement does increase the risk for testicular cancer. Fortunately, the risk is low with the use of natural hormone in physiologic doses.

Q. Can Phytoestrogen replace natural hormones?

Phytoestrogens are plant varieties of estrogens, which are not bio-identical to the human hormone. Even the strongest phytoestrogen has at most 1-2% the potency of human estrogens. They do help relieve some of the menopausal symptoms, but do not have a greater beneficial effect on bone, heart and blood vessels and brain.

Q. What is anti-ageing medicine, and how did it come about?

Anti-ageing is a new subspecialty in which the ageing process can be slowed, suspended and in some cases reversed.

Q. How does anti-ageing medicine differ from wellness and holistic medicine?

It incorporates components of holistic and wellness medicine but goes beyond them.

Is this a "fountain of youth?"

Q. How do you measure ageing?

Medical tests called Biomarkers actually indicate signs of ageing at different levels down to DNA. At the functional level, we test such things as visual accommodation, auditory response, and memory succession. We do a skin biopsy at the cellular level. We test biochemicals such as hormones and cholesterol, and DNA is checked for damage to hereditary matter.

Q. What kind of anti-ageing supplements doctors prescribe?

As you age, you develop deficiencies in vitamins and minerals. A complete, balanced nutritional multi-vitamin, mineral and anti-oxidant complex is a major part of the treatment regime.

Q. What are cognitive enhancers?

Techniques to improve your mental acumen may involve natural herbs like ginko. Meditation is also an effective enhancer.

Q. How quickly will a patient see results?

Improvement in energy is almost immediate. Significant differences usually take four to six months for DNA to regenerate in the body.

Q. Does a patient have to adopt a vegetarian diet to be successful?

Yes, it is high in vegetable protein, fish and white-meat chicken. We tend to stay away from red meat.

Q. Can you get the vitamins and supplements you prescribe at a health food store?

You probably can if you know what you need, but even then some of them are not available through health food stores.

14

American Academy of Anti-Ageing Medicine (AAAAM)

Umbrella to Many Organizations in USA

American Academy of Anti-Ageing Medicine ('A4M') was established in Chicago in 1993. It is registered as a charitable organization and is dedicated to the promotion of research aimed at slowing and reversing the human ageing process. A4M has a current membership of over 11,500 physicians and scientists from over 65 countries and is recognized as a leading body in the science of anti-ageing medicine. On the other hand, World Anti-Ageing Academy of Anti-Ageing Medicine (WAAAM) was incorporated on 15 August 2001 in England/Wales. It is also not a commercial profit-making organization and is registered with the UK Charity Commission. This Academy has been established with the support and active involvement of the board of the American Academy of Anti-Ageing Medicine. A4M's large membership of physicians and scientists from 65 countries has no more disciplinary actions against them than does the membership, who are of the American Heart Association or American Medical Association. The overwhelming majority of A4M members who are practicing the clinical science of anti-ageing medicine are already board certified by a traditional medical board such as internal medicine, endocrinology, family practice, emergency medicine, OB-GYN, and is members in good standing of their boards, the AMA, and their state licensing boards. A4M in its short tenure of but 7 years has done more to advance the cause of advanced diagnosis and prevention of disease as well as the important new concept that ageing is a treatable condition, than have all other associations combined over the past 30 years. Far from being a questionable science, anti-ageing medicine is rooted in the best-published works from mainstream medical science.

Dr. Klatz and other founders of AAAAM hold that: "The A4M has, over the past fourteen years, established a worldwide leadership role in educating clinicians in life enhancing, life extending medical technologies. The A4M is a leading provider of post-graduate medical education, training more than 100,000 physicians and scientists. We are proud to announce that the A4M is expanding its mission to embrace regenerative medicine, a medical specialty that applies advanced biomedical technologies for the purposes of renewing body tissues with the goal of maintaining the human body in normal-to-peak function for a prolonged period of time. With futuristic technologies like stem cell therapeutics, scientists aim to beneficially alter the very basic cellular sources of dysfunctions, disorders, disabilities, and diseases. Via therapeutic cloning, scientists will develop ample sources of human cells, tissues, and organs for use in acute emergency care as well as the treatment of chronic, debilitating diseases. Genetic engineering and genomics are important advancements that permit the identification and alteration of genetics to ameliorate dysfunctions, disorders, disabilities, and diseases. And, with nanotechnology, we can deploy micro- and molecular-sized tools to manipulate human tissue biology for micro-surgical repair on a gross level, as well as microscopic nano-biology for repair at the most basic cellular level. Indeed, when taken collectively, the advancements offered by anti-ageing and regenerative medicine to improve the quality of, and/or extend the length of, the human lifespan, are the single most potent emerging biomedical technologies today." The founders of A4M claim that the efforts to deface and defame a young specialty that is offering new hope to overcome mankind's oldest and most debilitating disease—old age—is morally contemptuous, brutish and not in the service of humanity

Today it is big business: according to the American Academy of Anti-Ageing Medicine (A4M); the US anti-ageing industry alone rakes in $ 56 billion annually. Elderly consumers need some form of protection against this racket. For starters, the anti-ageing scam may be harmful in a number of respects. First of all, some treatments may be detrimental to health: for example, growth hormone 'supplements' can cause high blood pressure and tumor growth. Secondly, consumers may misguidedly use ineffective treatments in place of validated therapies that could really help them. Thirdly, people may hurt themselves financially by frittering away their limited resources on futile therapies.

The opponents of anti-ageing medicine have their own story to tell. "There is no evidence to show there is anything that will slow, modify, reverse or stop the ageing process. Anyone who says otherwise doesn't have the evidence to support it." Said Olshansky, a scientist who doesn't agree with the views of founders of A4M. Olshansky views A4M as doing great damage to the cause of legitimate science. A4M runs anti-ageing conferences that are widely criticized in the scientific community due to the presence of vendors from the fraudulent and adventurous marketing school of "anti-ageing" pills, potions and crystals. They have expressed the desire to see the "marketeers" vanish from the industry, and recognize the great harm they are doing to scientific progress. The founders of A4M view Olshansky as a member of an establishment unwilling to grant legitimacy to any of the "anti-ageing" industry, no matter what evidence is offered. The American Academy of Anti-Ageing Medicine and its Chicago founders, Drs. Robert Goldman and Ronald Klatz, have sued professors from the University of Illinois-Chicago and Harvard University, alleging they have trashed their reputations in an effort to discredit their anti-ageing works. S. Jay Olshansky and Thomas Perls are the targets of the $ 150 million lawsuit filed in Cook County Circuit Court.

Both sides are damaging the potential for progress.

While the founders of A4M are far more invested in seeing working become a reality than most conservative gerontologists, their credibility is being questioned. The reason being that fraudulent and frivolous business men view "anti-ageing" as a lucrative way to increase sales. In the medical and more reputable business community, anti-ageing medicine means early detection, prevention, and reversal of age-related diseases. This is quite different from tackling the ageing process itself and a wide array of strategies and therapies are currently available. Calorie restriction, for example, is a demonstrated way to lower risk for a wide range of age-related degenerative conditions. The war over the meaning of "anti-ageing" is being fought over money and the perception of legitimacy. It is this perception of legitimacy that determines funding for scientific research and revenues for businesses. Scientists feel that the noise and non-sense coming from the anti-ageing marketplace is damaging the prospects for serious, scientific research. If everyone knows that anti-ageing means high-priced cream from Revlon marketed to the gullible and brand-aware, no scientist is going to get funding for a serious proposal in ageing research that uses the word "anti-ageing."

The proponents' claim that this medicine is not a fraud, it is working. There are several therapies that can help you temporarily to lose weight, gain muscles, regain strength, increase energy, strengthen the immune system, stop or decrease loss of hair, decrease or vanish skin wrinkles, tighten skin, increase oxygenation, increase circulation, etc. it improves the quality of life. There are several therapies that . . . Among them one can mention plastic surgery, (makes wrinkles disappear), hyperbaric oxygen (repairs the nervous system, improves the circulatory system), injectable human growth hormone (increases energy, decreases fat, increases muscle mass, etc.), EPO (increases red blood cells and consequent oxygenition), insulin (improves blood glucose response), testosterone (increases sexual abilities, increases muscle mass). Add to the above a healthy life style viz. Correct Diet (to control blood glucose), Exercise, Vitamins, Skin care, Get rid of parasites, Get rid of toxic metals,

Hormone replacement therapy, care of the Brain and Nervous System.

What effects of anti-ageing medicine have been reported?

- Restoring lost hair
- Restoring hair colour
- Increasing energy
- Increasing sexual function
- Improving cholesterol profile
- Restoring size of liver, pancreas, heart and other organs that shrink with age
- Improving vision
- Improving memory
- Elevating mood and improving sleep
- Normalizing blood pressure
- Increasing cardiac output and stamina
- Improving immune function
- Restoring muscle mass
- Decreasing body fat
- Thickening the skin, reducing wrinkles

Conference Lectures

Several conferences of the academy have been organized. An illustrative programme is given below:

- Anti-Ageing Endocrinology and Metabolic Cardiology
- Lab Diagnostic and Evaluation of Hormonal Balance in The Ageing Body
- Functional and Biological Markers of Ageing
- Advanced Facial Sculpting with Botox® and Newer Filling Agents
- Allergy, Silent Inflammation and Immune Augmentation
- Antioxidants in Prevention of Brain Ageing
- Reproductive Endocrinology in The Ageing Body
- Nutritional Approach in Managing Degenerative Diseases

- Male and Female Sexual Enhancement
- Herbs, Nitrogen, Medicine and ED-Erectile Dysfunction: 1-2 Hr Erections
- The Relationship Between Serum IgF-1 with Several Ageing Parameters
- Treatment of Senile Dementia with Traditional Chinese Medicine (TCM)
- Spa Medic: Drugless Prevention of Ageing
- Ageing Vision Repair and Regeneration
- Alternative Interventions for Cardiovascular Disease
- Embryonic Cell Therapy
- Enhancing Metabolism and Handling Obesity in the Clinic
- Adipose Modulation with Mesotherapy
- Hyperbaric Oxygen Therapy
- Sleep Disorder and How it Impacts Ageing Process
- More . . .

Post-Conference Hands-on Workshops

- Advanced Hormone Optimization; Testosterone
- Melatonin Replacement Therapy
- Growth Hormone Replacement Therapy for Normal Ageing
- DHEA and Pregnenolone Replacement Therapy
- Bio-Identical Hydrocortisone Replacement in Cortisol Deficient Patients
- Estrogen and Progesterone Replacement Therapy
- Case Presentations; Questions and Answers
- Aesthetic Medicine-Lasers and Procedures
- The Cosmetic Use of Lasers: Hair, Veins, Wrinkles, Dyschromias
- Aesthetic Skin Care-Enhance Your Patients Cosmetic Results as well as Your Bottom Line
- Cosmeceutical Choices and Ingredients: Learn how to Incorporate Skincare into Your Practice

Other Academic Activities

- Poster and Oral Presentations
- CME Accreditations: Category 1 AMA/PRA 62 Credit Hours
- ABAAM Written Board Exams for Physicians
- ABAAHP Written Board Exams for Health Practitioners
- Sports Medicine and Fitness Professionals Certification
- Post-Conference International Hormone Society Hands-on Workshops

Post-Conference Cosmetic/Aesthetic Medicine Hands-on Workshops

Pre-Conference Workshops

- Integrating Bio-Identical Hormone Therapy in Clinical Practice
- Hormonal/Nutritional Laboratory Testing, Diagnostics and Monitoring
- Cosmeceuticals and Aesthetic Medicine

Polymorphism Diagnostics in HRT and HT

Handling Testosterone and Estradiol Risks—The Newest Approach to Anti-Ageing.

Conference Workshops

- Metabolic Syndrome and Obesity Management
- Sexual Health and Healing
- Musculoskeletal Muscle Sports Medicine
- Weight Training that Improves Quality of Life and Slows Ageing Process
- Mesotherapy: The Treatment of Cellulite and Fat

Setting-up Medical Spa and Anti-Ageing Clinic Operation

The Academies Collaborate to Advance Anti-Ageing Medicine World-Wide

Dr. Robert Goldman, WAAAM Director, and Heather Bird, WAAAM Board Member, attended meetings and award ceremonies, as A4M and WAAAM collaborated with the newly established Mediterranean Academy of Anti-Ageing Medicine to promote Anti-Ageing Medicine world-wide and plan for a conference in Catania, Italy. The goal is to unify global medical data and patient treatment information, sharing these developments in anti-ageing medical therapeutics in a centralized manner. Broadly speaking, the approach is to treat ageing as a disease in itself. Anti-Ageing research, while embracing sophisticated high-tech innovations, aligns itself mostly with low-cost preventative medicine. Practitioners believe that Biologically Identical Hormone Replacement, correct use of nutritional supplements and lifestyle changes, including stress management and exercise, can slow the ageing process. Anti-Ageing therapies have the potential to reinforce bodily self-maintenance and thus reduce the impact of the degenerative disease. Older individuals can therefore remain healthy and unencumbered by debility for a considerably longer period of time. Indeed, some studies suggest that if Anti-Ageing therapies are successfully employed, the average productive life of humans could be extended.

Bibliography

A. Zempleni J., Trusty T.A., Mock D.M., Lipoic acid reduces the activities carboxylases in rat liver. *J Nutr* 1997; 127: 1776-81.

Abbott A. (2004), Growing old gracefully. *Nature* 428: 116-118

Achenbaum WA. Crossing frontiers: Gerontology emerges as a science. New York: Cambridge University Press, 1995.

Aecherio A., Rimm E.B., Hernan M.A., *et al.*, Intake of potassium, magnesium, calcium and fiber and risk of stroke among U.S. men. Circulation, 1998; Vol. 98, pp. 1198-1204.

A.G.S., Panel on Chronic Pain in Older Persons. The management of chronic pain in older persons. *Journal of American Geriatric Society*, 1998; Vol. 46, pp. 635-51

Albanes D., Heinonen OP, Taylor P.R., Virtamo J., Edwards BK, Rautalahti M., Hartman A.M., Palmgren J., Freedman L.S., Haapakoski J., Barrett M.J., Pietinen P., Malila N., Tala E., Liippo K., Salomaa E.R., Tangrea J.A., Teppo L., Askin F.B., Taskinen E., Erozan Y., Greenwald P., Huttunen J.K. Beta Carotene and Lung Cancer, *J Natl Cancer Inst.*, 1996, Nov. 6; 88(21): 1560-70.

American Academy of Anti-Ageing Medicine (2002). About A4Mandendash; History and Overview. Retrieved June 13, 2002 from http://www.worldhelath.net/html/about_a4m-history_and-over.htm

Ammendolia C., Rehabilitation of the older patient: A Case Report. *Journal of the Canadian Chiropractic Association*, 1998; Vol. 42, No. 1, pp. 42-5.

Ansbacher R., The pharmokinetics and efficacy of different estrogens are not equivalent. *Am J Obstet Gynecol* 2001; 184:255-263.

Antioxidants and age-related macular degeneration. Age-Related Macular Degeneration Study Group. Journal of the American Optometric Association. January 1996—Vol 67, No. 1.

Argao E.A., Heubi J.E., Hollis B.W., Tsang R.C.. "d-Alpha-tocopherylpolyethylene glycol-1000 succinate enhances the absorption of vitamin D in chronic cholestatic liver disease of infancy and childhood." *Pediatr Res.* 1992 Feb. 31(2): 146-50.

Arlt W., Justl H.G., Callies F., *et al.*, Oral dehydroepiandrosterone for adrenal androgen replacement: pharmacokinetics and peripheral conversion to androgens and estrogens in healthy young females after dexamethasone suppression. *J Clin Endocrinol Metab*, 1998; 83: 1928-34.

Arthur C.K., Isbister J.P., Iron deficiency. Drugs 33:171-82, 1987.

Baker V.L., Alternatives to oral estrogen replacement. *Obstet Gynecol Clin North Am* 1994; 21(2): 271-97.

Beck J., *et al.*, Periodontal disease and cardiovascular disease. J Periodontal 67 (suppl): 1123-1137, 1996.

Beresford S., Weiss N., Voigt L., *et al.* Risk of endometrial cancer in relation to use of oestrogen combined with cyclic progestagen therapy in postmenopausal women. *Lancet* 1997; 349: 458-461.

Binstock R.H., The war on "anti-ageing medicine". *Gerontologist* 2003; 43:4-14.

Birkmayer, J.G.D., Coenzyme Nicotinamide Adenine Dinucleotide—New Therapeutic Approach for Improving Dementia of the Alzheimer Type. *Ann Clin and Lab Science* 26(1):1-9, 1996

Bloch M., Schmidt P.J., Danaceau M.A., *et al.*, Dehydroepiandrosterone treatment of midlife dysthymia. *Biol Psychiatry* 1999; 45:1533-41.

Bonnicksen A.L., Crafting a cloning policy: from Dolly to stem cells. Washington, DC: Georgetown University Press, 2002.

Boylan M.T., Crockard A.D., Duddy M.E., Armstrong M.A., McMillan S.A., Hawkins S.A., Interferon-beta 1a administration results in a transient increase of serum amyloid A protein and C-reactive protein: comparison with other markers of inflammation. *Immunology Letters* 2001; 75: 191-197.

Brekwoldt M., Keck C., Karck U., Benefits and risks of hormone replacement therapy (HRT). *J Steroid Biochem Mol Bio* 1995; 53(1-6): 205-8.

Brett K.M., Madans J.H., Use of post-menopausal hormone replacement therapy: estimates from a nationally representative cohort study. *Am J Epidemiology* 1997; 145(6): 536-45.

Brinton L.A., Schairer C., Postmenopausal hormone-replacement therapy: time for reappraisal? *N Engl J Med* 1997; 336(25): 1821-22.

Brod, S.A., Unregulated inflammation shortens human functional longevity. *Inflamm. Res.* 2000 Nov; 49(11): 561-70.

Brower V. (2003), A second chance for hormone replacement therapy. *EMBO Rep* 4: 1112-15.

Burger C.W., van Leeuwen F.E., Scheele F., Kenemans P., Hormone replacement therapy in women treated for gynaecological malignancy. *Maturitas* 1999; 32(2):69-76.

Burke B.E., *et al.*, Randomized, double-blind, placebo-controlled trial of coenzyme Q10 in isolated systolic hypertension. *South Med J* 2001, Nov., 94(11): 1112-17.

Bush T.L, Whiteman MK. Hormone replacement therapy and risk of breast cancer. Editorial. JAMA 1999; 281(22): 2140-41.

Butler R.N., Is there an "anti-ageing" medicine?, *Generations* 2001; 25:63-5.

Casson P.R., Andersen R.N., Herrod H.G., *et al.*, Oral dehydroepiandrosterone in physiologic doses modulates immune function in postmenopausal women. *Am J Obstet Gynecol* 1993; 169:1536-39.

Casson P.R., Buster J.E., DHEA replacement after menopause: HRT 200 or nostrum of the '90s? *Contemporary OB/GYN* 1997; Apr. 119-33.

Castellsague J., Perez Gutthann S., Garcia Rodriguez L.A., Recent epidemiological studies of the association between hormone replacement therapy and venous thromboembolism. A review. *Drug Safety* 1998; 18(2): 117-23.

Ceder, G., *et al.*, Effects of 2-Dimethylaminoethanol (DMAE) on the metabolism of choline in plasma. *Journal of Neurochemistry*. 30:1293-1296, 1978.

Charcot J.M. (1881), Clinical Lectures on the Diseases of Old Age. [Translation, Hunt LH.], New York, NY, USA: W. Wood and Co.

Charles, S.T., Reynolds, C.A., and Gatz, M. (2001), Age-related differences and change in positive and negative affect over 23 years. *Journal of Personality and Social Psychology*, 80, 136-51.

Chen I., Safe S., Bjeldanes L., "Indole-3-carbinol and diindolylmethane as aryl hydrocarbon (Ah) receptor agonists and antagonists in T47D human breast cancer cells", *Biochem Pharmacol.* 1996 Apr. 26; 51(8):1069-76.

Childs A., Jacobs C., Kaminski T., Halliwell, B. and C., Leeuwenburgh. Supplementation with vitamin C and N-acetyl-cysteine increases oxidative stress in humans after an acute muscle injury induced by eccentric exercise. *Free Radical Biology Med*, 2001; 13(6):745-53.

Cibelli J.B., Stice, S.L., Golueke, P.J., *et al.*, Cloned transgenic calves produced from nonquiescent fetal fibroblasts, *Science*, 280: 1256-58, 1998.

Colditz G., Rosner B., For the Nurses' Health Study Research Group. Use of estrogen plus progestin is associated with greater increase in breast cancer risk than estrogen alone. *Am J Epidemiol* 1998; 147(suppl):84S.

Collaborative Group on Hormonal Factors in Breast Cancer. Breast cancer and hormone replacement therapy. *Lancet* 1997; 350:1047-1059.

Colman A., and Kind, A., Therapeutic cloning: concepts and practicalities. *Trends Biotechnol.* 18: 192-196, 2000.

Cook CI, Iron accumulation in ageing: modulation by dietary restriction, *Mechanisms Ageing and Development* 102: 1-13, 1998.

Cornelius J.G., Tchernev, V., Kao, K.J., and Peck, A.B., In vitro-generation of islets in long-term cultures of pluripotent stem cells from adult mouse pancreas. *Horm. Metab.* Res. 29: 271-277, 1997.

Cozzens S.E., Autonomy and power in science. In: Cozzens S.E., Gieryn T.F., editors. Theories of science in society. Bloomington, In: Indiana University Press, 1990:164-84.

Craig W.J., Iron status of vegetarians. *Am J Clin Nut* 59:12335-75, 1994.

Crissey S.D., *et al.*, Effect of dietary iron on the accumulation of iron in the liver of European Starlings, Proceedings *Am Assoc Zoo Veterinarians,* 1993.

Cristofalo V.J., Adelman, R., editors. Focus on modern topics in the biology of ageing: annual review of gerontology and geriatrics, Vol. 21. New York: Springer Publishing Company, 2002.

Curtis C.L., Hughes C.E., Flannery C.R., *et al.*, n-3 fatty acids specifically modulate catabolic factors involved in articular cartilage degradation. *Journal of Biological Chemistry,* 2000; 275:721-24.

De Falco, F.A., *et al.,* Effect of the chronic treatment with L-acetylcarnitine in Down's syndrome. *Clin Ther.* 144:123-127, 1994.

de Grey A.D.N.J., Ames B.N., Andersen J.K., *et al.,* Time to talk SENS: critiquing the immutability of human ageing. *Ann NY Acad Sci* 2002; 959: 452-62.

de Grey ADNJ, Gerontologists and the media: the dangers of over-pessimism. *Biogerontology* 2000; 1:369.

DeRitter E., Physiologic availability of dehydro-L-ascorbic acid and palmitoyl-L-ascorbic acid, *Science,* 1951; 113:628-31.

Derman D.P., *et al.,* Importance of ascorbic acid in the absorption of iron from infant foods, *Scand J Haematol* 25: 193-201, 1980.

Devaraj, S., Jialal, I., Alpha tocopherol supplementation decreases serum C-reactive protein and monocyte interleukin-6 levels in normal volunteers and type 2 diabetic patients. *Free Radical Biology, Med.* 2000, Oct 15; 29(8): 790-92.

Dorgan J.F., Sowell A., Swanson C.A., Potischman N, Miller R. Schussler N, Stephenson HEJr. Relationships of serum carotenoids, retinol, a-tocopherol and selenium with breast cancer risk: results from a prospective study in Columbia, Missouri (United States).*Cancer Causes Control* 9:89-97, 1998.

Dr. Marianne J., Engelhart of the Erasmus Medical Center in Rotterdam, the Netherlands: Those with the highest intake of vitamin C and vitamin E from food appeared to be the least likely to develop Alzheimer's disease. *The Journal of the American Medical Association*. 6/26/03.

Ebadi M., Govitrapong P., Sharma S., Muralikrishnan D., Shavali S., Pellett L., Schafer R., Albano C., Eken J., Ubiquinone (coenzyme q10) and mitochondria in oxidative stress of parkinson's disease. *Biol Signals Recept* 2001 May-Aug; 10(3-4):224-53.

Erlinger T.P., *Arch INtern Med* 2001 Aug 13-27; 161(15):1903-8.

Fahy, G.M., Organ cryopreservation. In: Advances in Anti-Ageing Medicine, Vol. 1 (R.M. Klatz, Ed.), Mary Ann Liebert, New York, 1996, pp. 249-55.

Farnsworth W.E., Roles of estrogen and SHBG in prostate physiology. *The Prostate* 1996; 28:17-23.

Farr S.A., Poon H.F., Dogrukol-Ak D., Drake J., Banks W.A., Eyerman E., Butterfield D.A., Morley J.E., "The antioxidants alpha-lipoic acid and N-acetylcysteine reverse memory impairment and brain oxidative stress in aged SAMP8 mice", Geriatric Research Education and Clinical Center (GRECC), VA Medical Center (151/JC), 915 N. Grand Boulevard, St. Louis, MO 63109, USA.

Festa A., D'Agostino R., Howard G., *et al.*, Chronic subclinical inflammation as part of the insulin resistance syndrome. The insulin resistance atherosclerosis study (IRAS). *Circulation*, 2000; 102:42-47.

Fisman M., Mersky H., Helmes E., Double-blind trial of 2-dimethylaminoethanol in Alzheimer's disease. *Am J Psych* 1981; 138:970-72.

Gaby A.R., Research review. *Nutr Healing*, 1996; Jan. 7.

Gerster H., High-dose vitamin C: a risk for persons with high iron stores? *Int J Vitam Nutr Res* 69:67-82, 1999.

Gieryn T.F., Boundary-work and the demarcation of science from non-science: strains and interests in professional ideologies of scientists, *Am Socio Rev*, 1983; 48:781-95.

Giovannucci E., Ascherio A., Rimm E.B., Stampfer M.J., Colditz G.A., Willerr W.C., Intake of carotenoids and retinol in relation to risk of prostate cancer. *J Natl Cancer Inst*, 87:1767-1776, 1995.

Global Social Change Reports One report describes global trends in ageing.

Gokce N., Keaney J.F. Jr., Frei B., Holbrook M., Olesiak M., Zachariah B.J., Leeuwenburgh C., Heinecke J.W., Vita J.A., Long-term ascorbic acid administration reverses endothelial vasomotor dysfunction in patients with coronary artery disease. *Circulation,* Jun 29; 99(25):3234-40.

Gokce N., Keaney J.F., Jr., Frei B., *et al.,* Long-term ascorbic acid administration reverses endothelial vasomotor dysfunction in patients with coronary artery disease. *Circulation.* 1999; 99(25):3234-40.

Goldwasser P., Feldman J., Association of serum albumin and mortality risk. *J Clin Epid* 50:693-703; 14, 1997; Aust SD. Ferritin as a source of iron and protection from iron-induced toxicities. *Toxicol Lett* 82:941-4, 1995. Aisen P., Brown E.B., The iron-binding function of transferrin in iron metabolism. Sem Hematol 14:31-46, 1977.

Gosden R.G. (1996), Cheating Time: Science, Sex and Ageing, London, UK: Macmillan.

Gosselin S.J., Kramer L.W., Pathophysiology of excessive iron storage in mynah birds, *J Am Veterinary Med Assoc,* 183: 1238-40, 1983.

Grady D., Herrington D., Bittner V., Blumenthal R., Davidson M., Hlatky M., Hsia J., Hulley S., Herd A., Khan S., Newby L.K., Waters D., Vittinghoff E., Wenger N., Cardiovascular disease outcomes during 6.8 years of hormone therapy, *JAMA* 2002; 288:49-57.

Grady D., Wenger N.K., Herrington D., Khan S., Furberg C., Hunninhake D., Vittinghoff E., Hulley S., Post-menopausal hormone therapy increases risk for venous thromboembolic disease. The Heart and Estrogen/ progestin Replacement Study, *Ann Intern Med,* 2000; 132:689-696.

Graf E., *et al.,* Phytic acid—a natural antioxidant. *J Biol Chem* 262:11647-50, 1987; No authors listed] Phytic acid: new doors open for a chelator, *Lancet* 2(8560):664-6, 1987.

Gregory J.F., 3rd. Ascorbic acid bioavailability in foods and supplements. *Nutr Rev.,* 1993; 51(10):301-303.

Griffiths, E., Iron and Infection. New York: John Wiley and Sons; 1987, pp. 1-25.

Grodstein F., *et al.*, Postmenopausal hormone therapy and mortality, *New England J Med,* 336: 1769-75, 1997.

Gruman G.J. (2003), A History of Ideas About the Prolongation of Life. Berlin, Germany: Springer.

Gruman G.J., A history of ideas about the prolongation of life: the evolution of prolongevity hypotheses to 1800, *Trans Am Philos Soc,* 1966; 56(Pt 9):6.

Hackler C., Troubling implications of doubling the human lifespan. *Generations,* 2001-2002; 25:15-9.

Hallberg L., Rossander L., Effect of different drinks on the absorption of non-heme iron from composite meals. *Hum Nutr Appl Nutr,* 36:116-23, 1982.

Hansen B.C., *et al.*, Calorie restriction in nonhuman primates: mechanisms of reduced morbidity and mortality, *Toxicology Letters,* 52: 56-60, 1999.

Heinonen O.P., Albanes D., Virtamo J., Taylor P.R., Huttunen J.K., Hartman A.M., Haapakoski J., Malila N., Rautalahti M., Ripatti S., Maenpaa H., Teerenhovi L., Koss L., Virolainen M., Edwards B.K., Prostate cancer and supplementation with alpha-tocopherol and beta-carotene: incidence and mortality in a controlled trial. Department of Public Health, University of Helsinki, Finland. *Journal National Cancer Institute,* 1998, Mar 18; 90(6):440-6, 441-7.

Herbert J.R., Hurley T.G., Oldenski B.C., *et al.*, Nutritional and socioeconomic factors in relation to prostate cancer mortality: A cross-sectional study, *Journal of the National Cancer Institute,* Nov. 4, 1998; Vol. 90, No. 21, pp. 1637-47.

Hlatky M.A., Boothroyd D., Vittinghoff E., Sharp P., Whooley M.A., Heary and Estrogen/Progestin Replacement Study Research Group. Quality-of-life and depressive symptoms in postmenopausal women after receiving hormone therapy: results from the Heart and Estrogen/Progestin Replacement Study trial, *JAMA,* 2002; 287:591-596.

Horwitz, E.M., Prockop, D.J., Fitzpatrick, L.A., *et al.*, Transplantability and therapeutic effects of bone marrow-derived mesenchymal cells in children with osteogenesis imperfecta. *Nature Medicine,* 5: 309-13, 1999.

Hufeland C.W. (1798), Die Kunst das menschliche Leben zu verlängern. Jena, Germany: Akademische Buchhandlung.

Hulley S., Furberg C., Barrett-Connor E., Cauley J., Grady D., Haskell W., Knopp R., Lowery M., Satterfield S., Schrott H., Vittinghoff E., Hunninghake D., Noncardiovascular disease outcomes during 6.8 years of hormone therapy, *JAMA,* 2002; 288:58-66.

Hulley S., Grady D., Bush T., *et al.,* Randomized trial of estrogen plus progestin for secondary prevention of coronary heart disease in postmenopausal women. *JAMA,* 1998; 280(7):605-13.

International Position Paper on Women's Health and Menopause: A Compreshensive Approach. *Best Clinical Practices,* 2002; Chapter 13.

Izaks G.J., Westendorp R.G.J. (2003), Ill or just old? Towards a conceptual framework of the relation between ageing and disease, *BMC Geriatr,* 3: 7.

Jacques P.F., The potential preventive effects of vitamins for cataract and age-related macular degeneration, *Int J Vit Nutr Res,* 1999; 69:198-205.

Johnston C.S., Luo B., Comparison of the absorption and excretion of three commercially available sources of vitamin C. *J Am Diet Assoc.* 1994; 94(7):779-81.

Juengst E.T., Binstock R.H., Mehlman M.J., *et al.,* Antiaging research and the need for public dialogue. *Science* 2003; 299:1323.

Juengst E.T., Binstock R.H., Mehlman M.J., Post S.G. (2003), Antiaging research and the need for public dialogue. *Science,* 299: 1323.

Juengst E.T., Binstok R.H., Mehlman M.J., Post S.G. (2003), Antiaging research and the need for public dialogue. *Science,* 299: 1323 [PubMed].

Kakar F., Weiss N.S., Strite S.A., Noncontraceptive estrogen use and risk of gallstone disease in women, *Am J Public Health,* 1988; 78:564.

Kamal-Eldin A., Appelqvist L.A., The chemistry and antioxidant properties of tocopherols and tocotrienols. *Lipids,* 1996; 31:671-701 [review].

Kamat J.P., Devasagayam T.P.A., Tocotrienols from palm oil as potent inhibitors of lipid peroxidation and protein oxidation in rat brain mitochondria. *Neurosci Lett,* 1995; 195:179-82.

Kang J.S., Kim D.J., Ahn B., Nam K.T., Kim K.S., Choi M., Jang D.D., "Post-initiation treatment with Indole-3-carbinol did not suppress N-methyl-N-nitrosourea induced mammary carcinogenesis in rats", *Cancer Lett.* 2001, Aug. 28; 169(2):147-54.

Kass L., L'Chaim and its limits: why not immortality? First Things 2001; 113:17-24.

Keller C., Fullerton J., Mobley C., Supplemental and complementary alternatives to hormone replacement therapy, *Amer Acac Nurse Pract,* 1999; 11(5):187-98.

Khorram O., Vu L., Yen S.S., Activation of immune function by dehydroepiandrosterone (DHEA) in age-advanced men, *J Gerontol A Biol Sci Med Sci,* 1997; 52:M1-7.

Kim S.J., *et al.*, Effect of glutathione, catechin, and epicatechin on the survival of Drosophila melanogaster under paraquat treatment, *Biosci Biotechnol Biochem,* 61: 225-29, 1997.

Kreijkamp-Kaspers S., Kok L., Grobbee D.E., de Haan E.H., Aleman A., Lampe J.W., van der Schouw Y.T. (2004), Effect of soy protein containing isoflavones on cognitive function, bone mineral density, and plasma lipids in postmenopausal women: a randomized controlled trial. *JAMA,* 292: 65-74.

Krieg M., *et al.*, Effect of ageing on endogenous levels of 5-alpha-dihydrotestosterone, testosterone, estradiol and estrone in epithelium and stroma of normal and hyperplastic human prostate, *J. Clin. Endocrinol. Metab,* 1993; 77: 375-81

Labrie F., Belanger A., Simard J., *et al.,* DHEA and peripheral androgen and estrogen formation: Intracrinology. *Ann NY Acad Sci,* 1995; 774:16-28.

Lacey J.V., Mink P.J., Lubin J.H., Sherman M.E., Troisi R., Hartge P., Schatzkin A., Schairer C., Menopausal hormone replacement therapy and risk of ovarian cancer in a prospective study, *JAMA,* 2002.

Lane M.A., Ingram D.K., Roth G.S., The serious search for an anti-ageing pill. *Sci Am,* 2002; 287:36-41.

Langsjoen H., Langsjoen P., Langsjoen P., Willis R., Folkers K., Usefulness of coenzyme Q10 in clinical cardiology: a long-term study. *Mol Aspects Med* 1994; 15 Suppl: 165-75.

Langsjoen P.H., Langsjoen P.H., Folkers K., Isolated diastolic dysfunction of the myocardium and its response to CoQ10 treatment, *Clin Investig,* 1993; 71(8 Suppl): S140-4.

Lanza R.P., Arrow, K.J., Baltimore, D., *et al.,* (73 scientists, 67 of them Nobel laureates), Science over politics, Science 283: 1849-50, 1999; see also Editor's note on page 1850.

Lanza R.P., Cibelli, J.B., and West, M.D. Human therapeutic cloning, *Nature Medicine,* 5:975-977, 1999.

Lanza R.P., Cibelli, J.B., and West, M.D. Prospects for the use of nuclear transfer in human transplantation, *Nature Biotechnology,* 17: 1171-74, 1999.

Lanza R.P., Cibelli, J.B., Blackwell, C., *et al.,* Telomere restoration and extension of cell lifespan in animals cloned from senescent somatic cells, *Science,* April 28, 2000.

Lau C.S., Morley K.D., Belch J.J.F., Effects of fish oil supplementation on non-steroidal anti inflammatory drug requirement in patients with mild rheumatoid arthritis—a double-blind placebo controlled study, *British Journal of Rheumatology,* 1993; 32:982-89.

Lavsky-Shulan M., Wallace R.B., Kohout F.J., *et al.,* Prevalence and functional correlates of low back pain in the elderly: The Iowa 65+ rural health study. *Journal of American Geriatrics Society,* 1985; Vol. 33, pp. 23-8.

Licinio J., Wong, M.L., The role of inflammatory mediators in the biology of major depression: central nervous system cytokines modulate the biological substrate of depressive symptoms, regulate stress-responsive systems, and contribute to neurotoxicity and neuroprotection, *Mol. Psychiatry,* 1999 Jul; 4(4): 317-27.

Lindahl *et al.,* 2000 Oct. 19; 343(16): 1139-47. Packard *et al.,* 2000; 287:3223-37, Rader, 2000, 3261-63, *The New England Journal of Medicine,* 2000

Lindahl B., *et al.,* Markers of myocardial damage and inflammation in relation to long-term mortality in unstable coronary artery disease. FRISC Study Group. Fragmin during Instability in Coronary Artery Disease. *New England Journal of Medicine,* 2000, Oct. 19; 343(16): 1139-47.

Liverman C.T., Blazer D.G., eds. (2004), Testosterone and Ageing: Clinical Research Directions. Washington, DC, USA: The National Academy Press.

Lockett B.A., Ageing, politics, and research: setting the federal agenda for research on ageing. New York: Springer Publishing Company, 1983.

Lopes G.K., *et al.,* Polyphenol tannic acid inhibits hydroxyl radical formation from Fenton reaction by complexing ferrous ions, *Biochim Biophys Acta,* 1472: 142-52, 1999.

Lopez-Burillo S., Tan D.X., Mayo J.C., Sainz R.M., Manchester L.C., Reiter R.J.

Malejka-Giganti D.; Niehans G.A.; Reichert M.A.; *et al.,* "Post-initiation treatment of rats with indole-3-carbinol or beta-naphthoflavone does not suppress 7, 12-dimethylbenz [a]anthracene-induced mammary gland carcinogenesis." *Cancer Lett,* 2000, Nov. 28; 160 (2):209-18.

Manson J.E., Buring H.E., *et al.,* Relation between a diet with a high glycemic load and plasma concentrations of high-sensitivity C-reactive protein in middle-aged women, *American Journal of Clinical Nutrition,* 2002; 75:492-498.

Mantovani G., Maccio A., Madeddu C., Mura L., Gramignano G., Lusso M.R., Murgia V., Camboni P., Ferreli L., Mocci M., Massa E., "The impact of different antioxidant agents alone or in combination on reactive oxygen species, antioxidant enzymes and cytokines in a series of advanced cancer patients at different sites: correlation with disease progression", *Free Radic Res.* 2003 Feb., 37(2):213-23, Department of Medical Oncology, University of Cagliari, Cagliari, Italy.

Masoro E.J. and Austad S.N. (eds.), Handbook of the Biology of Ageing, Sixth Edition, Academic Press, San Diego, CA, USA, 2006, ISBN 0-12-088387-2

Masoro E.J., Austad SN, editors. *Handbook of the biology of ageing* (5th ed.). San Diego, CA: Academic Press, 2001.

Masoro E.J., editor, Caloric restriction's effects on ageing: opportunities for research on human implications, *J Gerontol Bio Sci,* 2001; 56A (Special Issue 1).

Massie H.R., *et al.*, Inhibition of iron absorption prolongs the life span of Drosophila, *Mechanisms Ageing Development,* 67: 227-37, 1993.

Massie H.R., *et al.*, Iron accumulation during development and ageing of Drosophila, *Mechanisms Ageing Development,* 29: 215-20, 1985.

Mather, M., and Carstensen, L.L. (2005). Ageing and motivated cognition: The positivity effect in attention and memory, *Trends in Cognitive Sciences,* 9, 496-502. PDF.

Mazzeo R.S., Cavanaugh P., *et al.*, Exercise and physical activity for older adults. *Medicine and Science in Sports and Exercise,* June 1998; Vol. 30, No. 6, pp. 992-8.

McPherson K. (2004), Where are we now with hormone replacement therapy? *BMJ,* 328: 357-58.

Melatonin, xanthurenic acid, resveratrol, EGCG, vitamin C and alpha-lipoic acid differentially reduce oxidative DNA damage induced by Fenton reagents: a study of their individual and synergistic actions, Department of Biochemistry, Molecular Biology and Physiology, School of Medicine, University of Valladolid, Valladolid, Spain, 2001

Meydani M., Vitamin E and prevention of heart disease in high-risk patients, Nutr Rev 2000; 58:278-81.1993, The New England Journal of Medicine published two epidemiologic studies which found that people who took vitamin E supplements had fewer deaths from heart disease.

Miller R.A., Extending life: scientific prospects and political obstacles, *Milbank,* Q 2002; 80:155-74.

Moini H., Packer L., Saris N.E., Antioxidant and pro-oxidant activities of alpha-lipoic acid and dihydrolipoic acid, *Toxicol Appl Pharmacol,* 2002, Jul., 182:84-90

Morales A.J., Nolan J.J., Nelson J.C., Yen S.S.C., Effects of replacement dose of DHEA in men and women of advancing age, *J Clin EndorcrionolMetab,* 1994; 78:1360.

Mosca L., Grundy S.M., Judelson D., King K., Limacher M., Oparil S., Pasternak R., Pearson T.A., Redberg R.F., Smith S.C., Winston M., Zinberg S., Guide to preventive cardiology for women, *Circulation*, 1999; 99:2480-84.

Murphree H.B., *et al.*, The stimulant effect of 2-diethylaminoethanol (DMAE) in human volunteer subjects. *Clinical Pharmacology and Therapeutics*, 1:303-310, 1960.

Nass R., Thorner M.O. (2004), Life extension versus improving quality of life, *Best Pract Res Clin Endocrinol Metab*, 18: 381-91.

National Institute on Ageing, Action plan for ageing research: strategic plan for fiscal years 2001-05, Washington, DC: U.S. Department of Health and Human Services, 2001.

Nichol H., *et al.*, Iron metabolism in insects, *Annual Review Entomology*, 47: 535-59, 2002.

Oates M.B., McGhan W.F., Smith M.D., Hormone replacement therapy: a review of the risk versus benefit—Part II, *Med Interface*, 1997; 10(1):108-14.

Oberle S., *et al.*, Aspirin increases ferritin synthesis in endothelial cells: a novel antioxidant pathway. *Circ Res* 82:1016-20, 1998.

Olshansky J.S., Hayflick L., Carnes B.A., The truth about human ageing, Retrieved June 12, 2002 from http://sciam.com.

Olshansky S.J., Hayflick L., Carnes B.A. (2002), Position statement on human ageing. *J Gerontol A Biol Sci Med Sci*, 57: B292-B97 [PubMed].

Olshansky S.J., Hayflick L., Carnes B.A., No truth to the fountain of youth, *Sci Am*, 2002; 286:92-5.

Olshansky S.J., Hayflick L., Carnes B.A., Position statement on human ageing. *J Gerontol Biol Sci*, 2002; 57A:B292-7.

O'Meara E.S., Rossing M.A., Daling J.R., Elmore J.G., Barlow W.E., Weiss N.S., Hormone replacement therapy after a diagnosis of breast cancer in relation to recurrence and mortality, *J Natl Cancer Inst*, 2001; 93:754-62.

Overvad K., Diamant B., Holm L., Holmer G., Mortensen S.A., Stender S., Coenzyme Q10 in health and disease. *Eur J Clin Nutr*, 1999 Oct., 53 (10):764-70

Padayatty S.J., Levine M., Reevaluation of ascorbate in cancer treatment: emerging evidence, open minds and serendipity, *Journal American College Nutrition,* 2000; 19(4):423-25.

Pennisi E., Breakthrough of the year, the lamb that roared, *Science* 278, 2038-39, 1997.

Perle S.M., Mutell D.B., Romanelli R., Age-related changes in skeletal muscle strength and modifications through exercise: A literature review. *Journal of Sports Chiropractic and Rehabilitation,* Sept. 1997; Vol. 11, No. 3, pp. 97-103.

Persson I., Weiderpass E., Bergvist L., *et al.,* Risks of breast and endometrial cancer after estrogen and estrogen-progestin replacement, *Cancer Causes Control,* 1999; 10(4):253-60.

Pettegrew J.W., *et al.,* Clinical and neurochemical effects of acetyl-L-carnitine in Alzheimer's disease, *Neurobiol Ageing,* 16:1-4, 1995.

Pfeiffer C., *et al.,* Stimulant effect of 2-Dimethyl-l-aminoethanol (DMAE): Possible precursor of brain acetylcholine, *Science,* 126:610-611, 1957.

Pike M.C., Peters R.K., Cozen W., *et al.,* Estrogen-progestin replacement therapy and endometrial cancer. *J Natl Cancer Inst,* 1997; 89:1110-16.

Pittenger M.F., Mackay, A.M., Beck, S.C., *et al.,* Multilineage potential of adult human mesenchymal stem cells, *Science,* 284: 143-47, 1999.

Pradhan A.D., Manson J.E., Rifai N., *et al.,* C-reactive protein, interleukin-6, and risk of developing type 2 diabetes mellitus, *JAMA,* 2001; 286:327-34.

Rai G., *et al.,* Double-blind, placebo controlled study of acetyl-L-carnitine in patients with Alzheimer's dementia. *Current Medical Research and Opinion,* 11(10):638-647, 1989.

Raloxifene approval ushers in new drug class for osteoporosis. Estrogen-receptor effects vary by tissue type, *Am J Health Syst Pharm,* 1998; 55(2):104.

Ramiya V.K., Maraist, M., Arfors, K.E., Schatz, D.A., Peck, A.B., and Cornelius, J.G., Reversal of insulin-dependent diabetes using islets generated in vitro from pancreatic stem cells, *Nature Medicine,* 6: 278-282, 2000.

Recer P., Improving with age, Associated Press, August 10, 2000.

Reid I.R., Pharmacological management of osteoporosis in postmenopausal women: a comparative review, *Drugs Ageing*, 1999; 15(5):349-63.

Reiter W.J., Pycha A., Schatzl G., *et al.*, Dehydroepiandrosterone in the treatment of erectile dysfunction: a prospective, double-blind randomized, placebo-controlled study, *Urology*, 1999; 53:590-5.

Rider J.A., *et al.*, Double-blind comparison of effects of aspirin and namoxyrate on pH of gastric secretions, fecal blood loss, serum iron and iron-binding capacity in normal volunteers, *Curr Ther Res*, 7:633-8, 1965.

Ridker P.M., Hennekens C.H., Buring J.E., *et al.*, C-reactive protein and other markers of inflammation in the prediction of cardiovascular disease in women. *New England Journal of Medicine*, 2000; 342:836-43.

Riman T., Dickman P.W., Nilsson S., Correria N., Nordlinder H., Magnusson C.M., Weiderpass E., Persson I., Hormone replacement therapy and the risk of invasive ovarian cancer in Swedish women. *J Natl Cancer Inst*, 2002; 94:497-504.

Rodriguez C., Patel A.V., Calle E.E., Jacob E.J., Thun M.J., Estrogen replacement therapy and ovarian cancer mortality in a large prospective study of US women, *JAMA*, 2001; 285:14.

Rosano G.M., Painina G., Cardiovascular pharmacology of hormone replacement therapy, *Drugs Ageing* 1999; 15(3):219-34.

Rosenberg S., Vandromme J., Ayata N.B., *et al.*, Osteoporosis Management, *Int J Fertil Womens Med*, 1999; 44(5):241-9.

Ross R.K., Paganini-Hill A., Wan P.C., *et al.*, Effective hormone replacement therapy on breast cancer risk: estrogen versus estrogen plus progestin, *J Natl Cancer Inst*, 2000; 92:328-32.

Roth G.S., *et al.*, Caloric restriction in primates and relevance to humans, Annals NY Academy, *Science*, 928: 305-15, 2001.

Rudman D., Feller A.G., Nagraj H.S., Gergans G.A., Lalitha P.Y., Goldberg A.F., Schlenker R.A., Cohn L., Rudman

I.W., Mattson D.E. (1990), Effects of human growth hormone in men over 60 years old, *N Engl J Med,* 323: 1-6.

Saag K.G., Cerhan J.R., *et al.,* Cigarette smokers and rheumatoid arthritis severity, *Annals of the Rheumatic Diseases,* 1997; Vol. 56, pp. 463-69.

Sano, M., *et al.,* Double-blind parallel design pilot study of acetyl levocarnitine in patients with Alzheimer's disease, *Arch Neurol,* 49:1137-41, 1992.

Schairer C., Gail M., Byrne C., Rosenberg P., Sturgeon S., Brinton L., Hoover R., Estrogen replacement therapy and breast cancer survival in a large screening study, *J Natl Cancer Inst,* 1999; 91:264-70.

Schairer C., Lubin J., Troisi R., *et al.,* Menopausal estrogen and estrogen-progestin replacement therapy and breast cancer risk. *JAMA,* 2000; 283(4):485-91.

Seed M., Sands R.H., McLaren M., Kirk G., Darko D., The effect of hormone replacement therapy and route of administration on selected cardiovascular risk factors in post-menopausal women, *Fam Pract,* 2000; 17:497-507.

Seifert M., Galid A., Kubista E. Estrogen replacement therapy in women with a history of breast cancer, *Maturitas,* 1999; 32(2):63-8.

Seltzer M., editor, The impact of increased life expectancy: beyond the gray horizon, New York: Springer Publishing Company, 1995.

Serum retinol levels and the risk of fracture. K. Michaëlsson, H. Lithell, B. Vessby, *et al., New Engl J Med,* 2003, Vol. 348, pp. 287-94

Shamblott, M.J., Axelman, J., Wang, S., *et al.,* Derivation of pluripotent stem cells from cultured human primordial germ cells, *Proc. Nat'l. Acad. Sci.,* USA 95: 13726-31, 1998.

Shiels P.G., Kind A.J., Campbell K.H., Waddington D., Wilmut I., Colman A., and Schnieke A.E., Analysis of telomere lengths in cloned sheep, *Nature,* 27: 316-17, 1999.

Shults C.W., Oakes D., Kieburtz K., Beal M.F., Haas R., Plumb S., Juncos J.L., Nutt J., Shoulson I., Carter J., Kompoliti K., Perlmutter J.S., Reich S., Stern M., Watts

R.L., Kurlan R., Molho E., Harrison M., Lew M., Parkinson Study Group. Effects of coenzyme Q10 in early Parkinson disease: evidence of slowing of the functional decline, *Arch Neurol,* 2002, Oct., 59(10):1541-50.

Simin Liu, M.D., Ph.D., found that women who ate large amounts of high-glycemic (or diabetes promoting) carbohydrates, including potatoes, breakfast cereals, white bread, muffins, and white rice, had very high CRP levels, *Harvard Medical Journal,* 2000, Oct. 19; 343(16): 1139-47.

Simon J.A., Hunninghake D.B., Agarwal S.K., Cauley J.A., Ireland C.C., Pickar J.H., Effect of estrogen plus progestin on risk for biliary tract surgery in postmenopausal women with coronary artery disease. The Heart and Estrogen/progestin Replacement Study, *Ann Intern Med,* 2001; 135:493-501.

Singh R.B., Niaz M.A., Genetic variation and nutrition in relation to coronary artery disease, *J Assoc Physicians India,* 1999 Dec., 47 (12):1185-90

Sitzer M., Markus H.S., Mendall M.A., Liehr R., Knorr U., Steinmetz H., C-reactive protein and carotid intimal medial thickness in a community population. *J. Cardiovasc Risk,* 2002 Apr., 9 (2): 97-103.

Smith D.E., Roberts J., Gage F.H., and Tuszynski M.H., Age-associated neuronal atrophy occurs in the primate brain and is reversible by growth factor gene therapy, *Proc. Nat'l. Acad. Sci.,* USA 96: 10893-98, 1999.

Sokol R.J., Butler-Simon N., Conner C., Heubi J.E., Sinatra F.R., Suchy F.J., Heyman M.B., Perrault J., Rothbaum R.J., Levy J., *et al.,* "Multicenter trial of d-alpha-tocopheryl polyethylene glycol 1000 succinate for treatment of vitamin E deficiency in children with chronic cholestasis", *Gastroenterology,* 1993, Jun., 104(6):1727-35.

Stice S.L., Cibelli J., Robl J., Golueke P., Ponce de Leon F.A., Jerry D.J., Cloning using donor nuclei from proliferating somatic cells, U.S. Patent 5,945,577, issued August 31, 1999.

Stice S.L., Robl J.M., Ponce de Leon F.A., *et al.*, Cloning: New breakthroughs leading to commercial opportunities, *Theriogenology*, 49:129-138, 1998.

Stomati M., Rubino S., Spinetti A., *et al.*, Endocrine, neuroendocrine and behavioral effects of oral dehydroepiandrosterone sulfate supplementation in postmenopausal women, *Gynecol Endocrinol*, 1999; 13:15-25.

Sturdee D.W., Current hormone replacement therapy: what are the shortcomings? Advances in delivery, *Int J Clin Pract*, 1999; 53(6):468-72.

Suarna C., Hood R.L., Dean R.T., Stocker R., Comparative antioxidant activity of tocotrienols and other natural lipid-soluble antioxidants in a homogeneous system, and in rat and human lipoproteins, *Biochim Biophys Acta* 1993; 1166:163-70.

Swerdloff R.S., Wang C. (2004), Androgens and the ageing male, Best Pract Res Clin Endocrinol Metab, 18: 349-62

Tarkan L. (2004), As a substitute for hormones, soy is ever more popular, but is it safe?, *New York Times*, 24 Aug, p. 5.

Tavani A., La Vecchia C., The adverse effects of hormone replacement therapy, *Drugs Ageing*, 1999; 14(5):347-57.

The Women's Health Initiative Study Group. Design of the Women's Health Initiative clinical trial and observational study, *Control Clin Trials*, 1998; 19(1):61-109.

Theriault A., Chao J.T., Wang Q., *et al.*, Tocotrienol: a review of its therapeutic potential. *Clin Biochem* 1999; 32:309-19 [review].

Thomson, J.A., Itskovitz-Eldor, J., Shapiro, S.S., *et al.*, Embryonic stem cell lines derived from human blastocysts, *Science* 282: 1145-1147, 1998.

Tjäderhane L., Lamas M., A high-sucrose diet decreases the mechanical strength of bones in growing rats. *The Journal of Nutrition*, Oct. 10, 1998; Vol. 128, No. 10, pp. 1807-10.

Tran M.T., Mitchell T.M., Kennedy D.T., Giles J.T., Role of coenzyme Q10 in chronic heart failure, angina, and hypertension, *Pharmacotherapy*, 2001 Jul., 21(7):797-806.

Turgeon J.L., McDonnell D.P., Martin K.A., Wise P.M. (2004), Hormone therapy: physiological complexity belies therapeutic simplicity, *Science* 304:1269-73.

United Nations (2001) World Population Ageing: 1950-2050, New York, NY, USA: United Nations.

University of Illinois at Chicago. Silver Fleece Awards target anti-ageing hype. Office of Public Affairs, News Release, February 12, 2002, *Retrieved,* June 21, 2002 from http://tigger.uic.edu/htbin/cgiwrap/bin/newsbureau.

US Agricultural Research Service, *USDA Bulletin,* Dec. 23, 1998.

Vance M.L. (2003), Can growth hormone prevent ageing? *N Engl J Med,* 348: 779-80

Vellar O.D., Studies on sweat losses of nutrients, *Scand J Clin Lab Invest,* 21:157-67, 1968.

Vitamin E., TPGS: One year Chronic Intubation Study in Dogs, National Cancer Institute, *Bethesda,* MD 20892, 1994, *IRDC Report,* 560-041.

Warren M.P., Halpert S. (2004) Hormone replacement therapy: controversies, pros and cons, *Best Pract Res Clin Endocrinol Metab* 18: 317-332

Watts G.F., *et al.,* Coenzyme Q(10) improves endothelial dysfunction of the brachial artery in Type II diabetes mellitus, *Diabetologia,* 2002 Mar., 45(3):420-6.

Weinberg E.D., Iron loading and disease surveillance, *Emerging Infectious Diseases* 5: May-June, 1999.

Weintraug L.R., Current uses of phlebotomy therapy, Hospital Practice, June 15, 1987; Ulvik R.J., Bloodletting as medical therapy for 2500 years, *Tidsskr Nor Laegeforen,* 119: 2487-89, 1999.

Weiss N.S., Rossing M.A., Oestrogen-replacement therapy and risk of ovarian cancer, *Lancet,* 2001; 358:438.

Westendorp R.G.J. (2004), Are we becoming less disposable? *EMBO Rep,* 5:2-6.

White K.P., Speechley M., Harth M., Ostbye T., The London fibromyalgia epidemiology study: the prevalence of fibromyalgia syndrome in London, Ontario. J Rheumatol, 1999; 26:1570-1576. Ferris SH, Sathananthan G, Gershon S, *et al.,* Senile dementia. Treatment with Deanol, *J Am Ger Soc,* 1977; 25:241-44.

Whitfield J.B., *et al.*, Efects of alcohol consumption on indices of iron stores and of iron stores on alcohol intake markers, *Alcohol Clin Exp Res*, 25: 1037-45, 2001.

Wilmut, I., Schnieke, A.E., McWhir, J., Kind, A.J., and Campbell, K.H.S., Viable offspring derived from fetal and adult mammalian cells, *Nature* 385: 810-13, 1997.

Wolf O.T., Neumann O., Hellhammer D.H., *et al.*, Effects of a two-week physiological dehydroepiandrosterone substitution on cognitive performance and well-being in healthy elderly women and men, *J Clin Endocrinol Metab*, 1997; 82:2263-7.

Wolkowitz O.M., Reus V.I., Keebler A., *et al.*, Double-blind treatment of major depression with dehydroepiandrosterone, *Am J Psychiatry*, 1999; 156:646-9.

Writing Group for the Women's Health Initiative, Risks and benefits of combined estrogen and progestin in healthy postmenopausal women: Principal results from the Women's Health Initiative randomized controlled trial. *JAMA EXPRESS*, 2002.

Zacks R.T., Hasher, L., and Li, K.Z.H. (2000). Human memory. In F.I.M. Craik and T.A. Salthouse (Eds.), The Handbook of Ageing and Cognition (pp. 293-357), *Mahwah*, NJ: Erlbaum.

Zawada W.M., Cibelli, J.B., Choi, P.K., *et al.*, Somatic cell cloned transgenic bovine neurons for transplantation in parkinsonian rats, *Nature Medicine*, 4: 569-74, 1998.

Zs-Nagy I., *et al.*, On the role of cross-linking of cellular proteins in ageing, *Mech Ageing Dev*, 14:245-251, 1980.

Passeri M., *et al.*, Acetyl-L-carnitine in the treatment of mildly demented elderly patients, *International Journal of Clinical Pharmacology Research*, 10(1-2):75-79, 1990.

Zubialde J.P., *et al.*, Estimated gains in life expectancy with use of postmenopausal estrogen therapy: a decision analysis, *Journal Family Practice*, 36: 271-80, 1993.

Zumoff B., Does postmenopausal estrogen administration increase the risk of breast cancer? Contributions of animal, biochemical, and clinical investigative studies to a resolution of the controversey, *Proc Soc Exp Biol Med*, 1998; 217: 30-37.

Zurier R.B., Rossetti R.G., Jacobson E.W., *et al.*, Gamma-linolenic acid treatment of rheumatoid arthritis. A randomized, placebo-controlled study. Arthritis and Rheumatism, 1996; 11:1808 1817. 66. Ebeling P., Koivisto VA. Physiological importance of dehydroepiandrosterone, *Lancet*, 1994; 343:1479-81.

Index